I have to congratulate Mark Nolting on his new book, *Africa's Top Wildlife Countries*. I very much enjoyed his first book, *African Safari*. Mark certainly is *The Expert*. *Africa's Top Wildlife Countries* has so much — the many maps and illustrations and photos. The chart, *What Wildlife Is Best Seen Where*, is really special. What a great reference for travel agents as well as for the traveling public . . . I highly recommend this wonderful new book to everyone, whether planning to go to Africa or not!

Keith Tucker
Chief American Representative
East African Wildlife Society

Africa's Top Wildlife Countries will help any safari goer — whether first-timer or old Africa hand — to have the trip of a lifetime!

Diana E. McMeekin
Vice President
African Wildlife Foundation

Africa's Top Wildlife Countries is the most comprehensive and up-to-date guide to the top wildlife countries in Africa. Highly recommended for anyone interested in a photographic safari to Africa and for the armchair traveler as well. An excellent reference for travel agents.

M. Ralph Rafik
APTA President

Mark Nolting's *Africa's Top Wildlife Countries* is nearly as vast as the continent he is describing. This richly detailed study of the African travel market spells out virtually everything a traveler needs to know about the land, the people, customs, wildlife and safaris. In short, don't break camp without it!

Ed Sullivan
Managing Editor
TravelAge East

Mark Nolting's new *Africa's Top Wildlife Countries* provides lots of information and hard-to-find details on travel to Africa in a practical, no-nonsense format. His comprehensive, detailed guidebook is lightly laced with personal experiences and insights. His long-time experience with travel to Africa shines through clearly.

Linda Bell, Editor
Tour & Travel News

AFRICA'S TOP
WILDLIFE COUNTRIES

BY

MARK W. NOLTING

GLOBAL TRAVEL PUBLISHERS, INC.

ISBN: 0-939895-02-1
First Printing
Previous edition: *AFRICAN SAFARI: The Complete Travel Guide to 10 Top Game Viewing Countries.* Copyright ©1987 by Mark W. Nolting. ISBN: 0-939895-00-5.
Cover by Ratzlaff & Associates
Illustrations by James B. King
Library of Congress Cataloging-in-Publication Data

Nolting, Mark, 1951
    Africa's top wildlife countries / by Mark W. Nolting.
        p.   cm.
    Rev. ed. of: African safari. 1987
    ISBN 0-939895-02-1 : $14.95
    1. Wildlife watching--Africa, Sub-Saharan--Guide-books.
    2. Safaris--Africa, Sub-Saharan--Guide-books.   3. National parks
    and reserves--Africa, Sub-Saharan--Guide-books.   4. Africa, Sub-
    Saharan--Description and travel--1981--Guide-books.
    I. Nolting, Mark, 1951-   African safari.   II. Title.
QL337.S78N65   1990
333.95'4'9067--dc20   90-3285
                                                                    CIP

Photos: Photos by Mark Nolting unless credited otherwise.

PUBLISHER'S NOTE

TO ALL THOSE WHO HAVE VENTURED TO AFRICA,

AND BY VISITING THE PARKS AND RESERVES,

HAVE CONTRIBUTED TO THEIR PRESERVATION

AND THE WILDLIFE WITHIN THEM.

OTHER BOOKS BY MARK NOLTING

TRAVEL JOURNAL AFRICA

Dear Reader:

As President of The Africa Adventure Company, I have had the pleasure of sending hundreds of people from all walks of life on game viewing (photographic) safaris to Africa.

Why do so many people wish to go to Africa? Some want "to get on the edge of things" and live "where the excitement is!"

More and more people want to take trips which are meaningful and fulfill a greater need of involvement than just doing what others do on vacation.

Some seek the wonderful wilderness of a still primitive African continent where wildlife in its natural and exciting environment still abounds.

In other words, Africa means getting back to basics and feeling the thrill that goes with doing something entirely different from the world in which we live. Such adventures enhance an individual's perspective, refresh and hone the instincts.

I've also talked to many people who decided to "do Africa before they got any older or the animals got any fewer!"

Population pressures in Africa are causing many parks to be reduced in size, resulting in even further declines in wildlife. African governments must be able to prove to their people that the parks provide more jobs, foreign exchange and other benefits than if the land were given to their people for farming, grazing or other uses.

Going on a photographic safari is a donation in itself towards saving endangered wildlife in Africa. This could be the most enjoyable and rewarding donation you will ever make!

Sincerely,

The Africa Adventure Company

Mark W. Nolting
President

P.S. For more information on The Africa Adventure Company, please see page 477.

First Union Bank Bldg./Suite 900
1620 S. Federal Hwy., Pompano Beach, FL 33062 USA
Tele: (305) 781-3933   FAX: (305) 781-0984

A REQUEST:

Please write and tell us about your trip to Africa, including the highlights of your vacation, opinions of accommodation, transportation, tour operator, etc., so we may best help future travelers through accurate updates of this guide and through The Africa Adventure Company. Write to Mark Nolting, c/o Global Travel Publishers, Inc., P.O. Box 2567, Pompano Beach, FL 33062.

ACKNOWLEDGMENTS

The completion and accuracy of this guide would not have been possible without the assistance of many people. Many thanks to all who have contributed to this project, including the following (my apologies to those contributors I have unintentionally omitted): George and Patty Page, Ruppert Starr, Beth Gettes, Jenny and Scott Gardiner; Mike Culhane, Dave Herbert, Julie deKock, Vicki Le Boutillier, Debbie Urquhart and Peggy Phillpott of Gametrackers International; Tim Farrell of Ker Downey Selby; Cindy Samarin of Desert & Delta Safaris; Sue Carver and Jack Kerr of Bonaventure Travel; Northern Air; Jon Panos and Mike Lorentz of Safariplan; Heide Allmendinger, Pat and Heather Carr-Hartley, Brian and Jan Graham, and Dave Sanders; Burundi National Office of Tourism and Counselor Budigi of the Embassy of Burundi; Ms. Mulili, David Waweru and Maggie Maranga of the Kenyan Tourist Office; Roger Sylvester of UST; Cynthia Moss, Conrad Hirsh, Mr. Bowman of Hotel Inter-Continental, and Semhi C.J.S.; The Lesotho Tourist Board and Tommy Ryan of the Lesotho Pony Trekking and Marketing Program; Roselyne Hauchler of the Mauritius Government Tourist Office; Jeremy Pask of the Mauritius Government Tourist Information Service; Maurice Bare of Rwanda Travel Service; Mr. Christopher Habimana of the Embassy of Rwanda; Claude Ramsey of the Digit Fund, and Ross Battersby; Namibia Directorate of Trade and Tourism; Maricia Steward of SATOUR; Melanie Millen and Barbara Ickinger of Sun International; Phillip Lategan of Afroventures;

Swaziland Government Tourist Office and Mr. Gumedze of the Swaziland High Commission; Kjell and Maria Bergh, Naomi Simonson and Marianne Cooper of Borton Travel; Maggie Travas of Serengeti Select; Margaret and Per Kullander and Jean Gibb of Gibb's Farm; Johnathon and Annette Simonson of Tarangire Safari Lodge; Serengeti Safari Lodges, and Rob Davison of the AWF; the Honorable S. T. K. Katemta-Apuli, Ugandan Ambassador to the U.S.A., and Mr. Sebulime of the Permanent Mission of Uganda to the U.N.; Mr. Ngimbi and Ms. Shakembo of the Embassy of Zaire; Vanessa and John Lukas; Mr. Edson Tembo and Soneka Kamuhuza of the Zambia National Tourist Board; Burton Shanzi of Zambia Airways; Tommy Correia of MRI; Norman Carr of Kapani; Robin Pope, David Thompson, Marcel Baumann, and Richard Bell; Mary Hatendi and the Zimbabwe Tourist Development Corporation; Ron Stringfellow and Ian Cochrane of Zimbabwe Sun Hotels; Brian Bowyer and Stewart Irving of UTC; Ted Nelson of Air Zimbabwe; Anne Moore of the Department of National Parks of Zimbabwe; Jeremy Brooke and Ray Stocker of Shearwater Adventures; Garth Thomson of Garth Thomson Safari Consultants; Alan Elliot, Hans Strydom, Edward Chindori-Chininga, Sue Ryan, John Stevens, Gavin Ford, and Ron White.

Special thanks to Mike Appelbaum for the use of his photographs and his valuable input on the chapter on Kenya, to Bill Kaske and Mike Terwilleger for their assistance with the maps, and to Alison Wright for her insights into Zimbabwe and assistance with Zambia and Tanzania.

CONTENTS

MAPS

CHARTS AND ILLUSTRATIONS

CALL OF
THE WILD

CALL OF THE WILD

Feature films like *Out of Africa*, *African Queen* and *Gorillas in the Mist* have kindled in the hearts of many people the flame of desire for travel to Africa.

A visit to Africa allows you to experience nature at its finest — almost devoid of human interference, living according to a natural rhythm of life that has remained basically unchanged since the beginning of time.

At our deepest roots, the African continent communicates with our souls. Travelers return home, not only with exciting stories and adventures to share with friends and family, but with a feeling of accomplishment, increased self-confidence and broader horizons from having ventured where few have gone. Here's the kind of adventure about which many dream but few experience.

Having visited Africa once, you too will want to return again to the peace, tranquility and adventure it has to offer. I invite you to explore with me the reasons for this never ceasing pull as we journey to some of the most fascinating places on earth.

The time to visit Africa is now. In spite of international efforts, poaching is still rampant. In addition, the continent is rapidly becoming westernized, making it more and more difficult to see the indigenous peoples living as they have for thousands of years. Go now, while Africa can still deliver all that is promised — and more!

Africa's Top Wildlife Countries highlights and compares wildlife reserves and other major attractions in the continent's best countries for game viewing.

AFRICA

Most people travel to Africa to see lion, elephant, rhino, and other wildlife unique to this fascinating continent in their natural surroundings. *Africa's Top Wildlife Countries* makes planning your adventure of a lifetime easy.

After an exhilarating day on a photographic safari many guests return to revel in the day's adventures over exquisite European cuisine in deluxe camps and lodges. In addition, this captivating guide presents many options for the special interest traveler.

From the easy-to-read **When's The Best Time To Go** chart, you can conveniently choose the specific reserves and country(ies) that are best to visit during your vacation period. From the **What Is Best Found Where** chart, you can easily locate the reserves which have an abundance of the animals which you wish to see most.

The **glossary** contains words commonly used on safari as well as words and phrases in French and Swahili. English is the major language in most of the countries covered in this guide, so language is in fact not a problem. The **Safari Pages** (a safari directory) provide a veritable gold mine of difficult-to-find information and sources on Africa.

This guide is designed to help you decide the best place to go in Africa to do what you want to do, when you want to do it, in a manner of travel that personally suits you best.

In this guide, *game viewing* and *wildlife viewing* are used interchangeably. *Game* traditionally refers to animals that are hunted for sport but is also the term generally used in the travel industry when referring to photographic safaris to wildlife areas. This guide is about observing and photographing wildlife — not hunting.

Africa's Top Wildlife Countries, along with *Travel Journal Africa*, is actually a travel kit, providing you with convenient access to everything you need to enjoy the vacation of a lifetime.

First, read this book. Then contact a travel agent who specializes in Africa, or call me, Mark Nolting, at The Africa Adventure Company (305/781-3993 or toll free 1-800-882-9453) for assistance in booking your safari. I would love to help make your dream safari come true!

Africa has such a tremendous variety of attractions that most everyone can find something fascinating to do. In addition to fabulous wildlife, Africa boasts having the world's larg-

SOUTH, EAST AND CENTRAL AFRICA

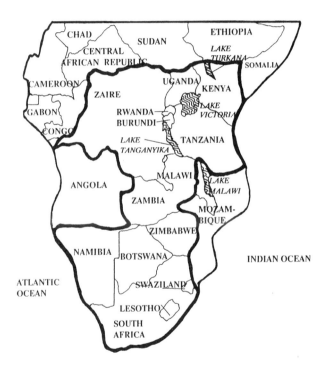

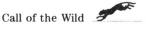

est waterfall by volume (Victoria Falls), the world's longest river (the Nile), the world's largest intact caldera or crater (Ngorongoro), and the world's highest mountain not part of a mountain range (Mt. Kilimanjaro). Africa is huge. It is the second largest continent on earth, covering over 20% of the world's land surface. More than three times the size of the United States, it is also larger than Europe, the United States and China combined. No wonder it has so much to offer!

THE SAFARI EXPERIENCE

"Alephaant, allephanntt," the Masai softly said as he escorted us to dinner that evening. Neither of us could understand him until he shined his flashlight on a tree-sized elephant browsing not 50 feet from where we stood. It was then I realized why we were requested to wait for the spear-wielding Masai assigned to our tent to escort us to dinner. The pathway to the dining tent was covered with giant pizza-sized footprints that were not there 45 minutes earlier. Carrying a spear in these parts is not a bad idea!

The dining tent was filled with people from the four corners of the earth, reveling in camaraderie and sumptuous cuisine by candlelight. An excellent selection of wines and desserts complimented the meal.

After dinner we sat around a roaring fire, sipping whiskey, and listening to bush lore from our entertaining host. Later we watched hippo grazing only a few feet from our tent. The night was alive with the sounds and scents of the Africa we had dreamed of — the untamed wilderness where man is but a temporary guest and not a controller of nature. Only then did we retire to our comfortable deluxe tent with private facilities to sleep that gentle sleep which comes with a sigh of contentment.

WHAT IS A SAFARI LIKE?

What happens on safari? What is a typical day like? Most safaris are centered around guests participating in two or three activities per day, such as game drives in mini-vans or four-wheel-drive vehicles. A game drive simply consists of having your guide drive you around a park or reserve in search of wildlife.

Most activities last two to four hours and are made when the wildlife is most active: early in the morning, often before breakfast, just after breakfast, in the late afternoon and at night (where allowed). Midday activities might include lazing around the swimming pool, reading or taking a nap. I must warn you that afternoon naps can become very habit forming, and, as far as I am concerned, are highly recommended.

Depending on the park or reserve, safari activities might include day game drives, night game drives, walks, boat safaris, canoeing, kayaking, white-water rafting, ballooning, mountain climbing, fishing — the options are almost endless. See **Types of Safaris** and the **Safari Activities Chart** which follow.

Wildlife reserves differ greatly in their rules and regulations. Three regulations that may affect your choice of parks to visit are the type of vehicles allowed and whether or not night safaris or walking safaris are permitted.

NIGHT GAME DRIVES

Night game drives open up a new world of adventure. Nocturnal animals, seldom if ever seen by day, are viewed with the aid of the vehicle's powerful search light. Bushbabies, night apes, leopard, and many other species can be seen.

In addition to the chart which follows, night game drives are allowed and often conducted outside of many reserves, including the Masai Mara (Kenya) and Hwange, Mana Pools and Matusadona National Parks (Zimbabwe).

SAFARI VEHICLES

Open vehicles usually have two rows of elevated seats behind the driver's seat. There are no side or rear windows or permanent roof, providing unobstructed views in all directions and a feeling of being part of the environment instead of on the outside looking in. This is my favorite type vehicle for viewing wildlife. When near lion the engine is usually kept running to allow quick getaways in case the predators approach too closely.

Game viewing by open vehicle. Photo: Ker Downey Selby.

Game viewing from a land cruiser with roof hatches in the Masai Mara, Kenya. Photo: Mike Appelbaum.

Game viewing from a pop-top mini van in East Africa.

Open vehicles are used in Botswana, Zambia, Zimbabwe and private reserves in South Africa.

In **vehicles with roof hatches or pop-top roofs**, riders stand up through the hatch for photographic opportunities. If the vehicle is full, riders usually must take turns using the hatches, making tours which guarantee window seats for every passenger (i.e., maximum of seven passengers in a nine-seat mini-van) all the more attractive. These vehicles are used in Kenya and Tanzania.

Wildlife viewing, and especially photography, are more difficult where **closed vehicles** are required. In Namibia and South Africa (except private reserves), closed vehicles are required.

DISPELLING MYTHS ABOUT TRAVEL ON THE DARK CONTINENT

Many prospective travelers to Africa seem to think that if they go on an African safari they may have to stay in mud or

grass huts or little pup tents and eat strange foods. Nothing could be farther from the truth! Almost all of the top parks and reserves covered in this guide have deluxe or first class (Class A or B by our grading system) lodges or camps (with private bathroom facilities) serving excellent food, specifically designed to cater to the discerning traveler's needs. Going on safari can be a very comfortable, fun-filled adventure!

Many prospective travelers to Africa have voiced their fear of being overwhelmed by mosquitoes and other insects, or the fear of encountering snakes on safari. I must admit that I shared, to a degree, this same apprehension before my first visit to sub-Sahara Africa.

However, I was pleasantly surprised to find that there was not one day in Africa where I experienced bugs nearly as badly as American parks I have visited in Florida. And in over three years of travel in Africa, I have only seen about five snakes — and I had to look for them!

The fact is, most safaris do not take place in the jungle, but on open savannah during the dry season. In any case, except for walking safaris, most all of your time in the bush will be spent in the safety of a vehicle or boat.

TYPES OF SAFARIS

Africa can be experienced in a myriad of exciting ways. What follows are several types of safaris. For additional information, refer to the country mentioned.

PHOTO SAFARIS

The term *photo safari*, in its broadest sense and as used in this guide, means any kind of safari *except* hunting safaris.

In its strictest sense, a photo safari is a safari escorted by a professional wildlife photographer, especially for the serious photographer. These safaris are mainly about learning wildlife photography and getting the best photos possible: These are recommended only for the serious shutter-bug.

Accommodations in deluxe fixed tented camps are roomy and comfortable.

Deluxe mobile tented camps offer privacy as well as excellent food and service.

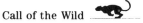

LODGE AND FIXED CAMP SAFARIS

Lodge safaris are simply safaris using lodges for accommodation. Some safaris mix lodges with fixed tented camps, or camps with chalets or bungalows, providing a greater range of experience for their guests.

CAMPING SAFARIS

Sitting by a campfire at night in the bush is an experience not to be missed. The night becomes very alive. Suddenly every noise means something. Was that a roar from the lion we spotted on this afternoon's game drive? Could it possibly walk right into camp and make a meal out of me? You then realize that your imagination is again running away with you while you are safe by the fire. To seek reassurance your eyes move upward. The Milky Way has never been more brilliant. Ah, this is the place to be!

DELUXE MOBILE TENTED CAMP SAFARIS

Deluxe mobile tented camp safaris, are, in my opinion, the best way to experience all that Africa has to offer. Each tent has a private shower and toilet tent. Food and service are excellent. Camp attendants take care of everything, including bringing hot water for your shower. Camp is usually set in remote areas of parks and reserves, providing a true *Out of Africa* experience. These safaris, however, are not cheap. For a party of four, the cost can exceed $500 per person per day.

MIDRANGE MOBILE TENTED CAMP SAFARIS

Comfortable (and less expensive) midrange mobile tented safaris are available in a number of countries. Like deluxe mobile tented safaris, camp staff take care of all the chores. The difference is that the tents are a bit smaller but are still large enough in which to stand. The service is very good, and guests from two or more tents may share toilet and shower (hot water) facilities. A combination of public and remote private campsites are often used.

BUDGET MOBILE TENTED CAMP SAFARIS

On budget mobile tented safaris, participants are most often required to help with camp chores. Park campsites with basic (if any) facilities are often used.

The advantage is price. Budget camping safaris are almost always less expensive than lodge safaris. However, like *Overland Safaris* (see below), these are recommended only for the hardiest of travelers. Most participants are under thirty years of age. Don't expect a hot shower every night; once every two or three days is more likely.

Campsites found in national parks and reserves are often very reasonably priced (except in Tanzania), but vary greatly in their quality of facilities.

Namibia, South Africa, and Zimbabwe have excellent campsites and recreational parks very similar to those in North America. Facilities (flush toilets, hot showers, etc.) in campsites in Burundi, Kenya, Tanzania, Rwanda, Uganda and Zaire are almost nonexistent.

Camping Tips

Never sleep out without some sort of shelter. Keep tent flaps closed at night. Animals will almost never try to enter a closed tent unless tempted by smell of food. Store meat or other food in your vehicle — not in your tent. While in your tent, if you hear lions around you that you wish would leave, shout, and they might go away.

Shake out your sleeping bag before entering it and your clothing and shoes before putting them on after a night in the bush. Beds and cots elevated off the ground in insect-proof tents seldom have insect intruders; however, this is still a good habit to get into.

If camping in the wild outside any official private or public campsite, always seek permission of the property owner in advance. In most cases they will be happy for you to stay. In many areas, it is best to hire a guard to help prevent theft.

WALKING SAFARIS

Walking safaris put one in closest touch with nature. Suddenly your five senses come alive — every sight, sound and

Following black rhino spoor (footprints) on foot until you find the source of the prints is quite an adventure.

smell becomes intensely meaningful. Could that flash of bronze in the dense brush ahead be a lion? I wonder how long ago these rhino tracks were made? Can that herd of elephant ahead see or smell us approaching?

Accompanied by an armed wildlife expert, walking safaris last anywhere from a few hours to several days. The bush can be examined up close and at a slower pace, allowing more attention to its fascinating detail than on a safari by vehicle.

Participants can often approach quite closely to game, depending on the direction of the wind and the cover available. This is experiencing the excitement and adventure of the bush at its best. Zambia and Zimbabwe are the top countries for walking safaris.

GORILLA SAFARIS

Gorilla trekking is one of the most exciting adventures one can have on the "dark continent" and is certainly one of the most exciting experiences of my life.

Elephant can often be approached closely on walking safaris.

Mountain gorillas may be seen in Volcano National Park (Rwanda), Kigezi Mountain Gorilla Reserve (Uganda,) Djomba Gorilla Sanctuary, and Rumangabo Station (Zaire). Volcano National Park and Djomba Gorilla Sanctuary are the best reserves to see mountain gorillas. Lowland gorillas have been habituated in Kahuzi-Biega National Park in Zaire.

Rwanda and Zaire have habituated several groups of gorillas to human presence; seeing gorillas here can almost be guaranteed on a daily basis. Gorillas in Uganda have yet to be habituated, and it often takes three days to find them.

Permits for gorilla trekking are limited and should be booked well in advance.

BALLOON SAFARIS

At 05:30 in the morning, we were awakened by steaming hot coffee and tea brought to our bedsides by our private

SAFARI ACTIVITIES

VEHICLES - NIGHT GAME DRIVES - WALKING SAFARIS - BOAT SAFARIS - CANOE SAFARIS

COUNTRY	MAJOR PARK OR RESERVE	TYPE OPEN	VEHICLE ALLOWED HATCHES	CLOSED	NIGHT DRIVES	WALKING SAFARIS	BOAT SAFARIS	CANOE SAFARIS
Botswana	Chobe	X					X	
	Moremi	X				*1	X	X
	Okavango Delta	X			X	X	X	X
	Savuti	X						
Kenya	Masai Mara		X		*1	*1		
	Mount Kenya		X			X		
	Other Parks		X					
Namibia	Etosha			X				
Rwanda	Akagera		X				X	
	Volcano		X			X		
South Africa	Kalahari - Gemsbok			X				
	Kruger			X		X		
	Private Reserves	X			X	X		
Tanzania	Selous, Rubondo Isl.		X			X	X	
	Arusha, Gombe St., Mahale		X			X		
	Other Parks		X					
Uganda	Murchison Falls		X				X	
	Queen Elizabeth N. P.		X				X	
	Kigezi Mt. Gorilla Res.		X			X		
	Others		X					
Zaire	Kahuzi - Biega		X			X		
	Rwindi (Virunga)		X					
	Djomba Gorilla Sanctuary		X			X		
	Ruwenzori Mountains		X			X		
Zambia	South Luangwa	X			X	X		
	Kafue	X			X	X	X	
Zimbabwe	Chizaria	X				X		
	Hwange	X			*1,*2	*1,*2		
	Mana Pools	X			*1	X	X	X
	Matusadona	X			*1	X	X	

*1. Activity is conducted on the outskirts of the park or reserve.
*2. Activity is conducted at Makalolo Camp within Hwange National Park.

Ballooning over the Masai Mara. Photo: Mike Appelbaum.

tentkeeper. Soon we were off at 06:00 for a short game drive to where the hot-air balloons were being filled. Moments later we lifted above the plains of the Masai Mara for the ride of a lifetime.

Silently viewing game from the perfect vantage point, we brushed the tops of giant acacias for close-up views of birds' nests and baboons. Most animals took little notice, but somehow the hippos knew we were there. Maybe it was our shadow or the occasional firing of the burners necessary to keep us aloft.

Our return to earth was an event in itself. One hour and 15 minutes after lift-off, our pilot made a perfect crash landing. By the way, all landings are crash landings, so just follow your pilot's instructions and join in the fun.

Minutes later a champagne breakfast appeared on the open savannah within clear view of herds of wildebeest, buffalo, and zebra. Our return to camp was another exciting game drive, only a little bumpier this time.

Hot-air balloon safaris are available in Kenya in the Masai Mara Game Reserve and at Taita Hills near Tsavo West National Park.

Ballooning over the Masai Mara.

Champagne breakfast after the balloon ride over the Masai Mara
(Kenya). The Siria (Esoit Oloololo) escarpment is in the background.

BOAT/CANOE/KAYAK SAFARIS

Wildlife viewing by boat, canoe or kayak from rivers or lakes often allows one to approach wildlife closer than by vehicle. Game viewing by **boat** is available in Chobe National Park and the Okavango Delta (Botswana), Kafue National Park (Zambia), Lake Kariba, along Matusadona National Park and the Zambezi River upstream from Victoria Falls (Zimbabwe). **Canoe safaris** from three to nine days are operated along the Zambezi River below Kariba Dam in Zimbabwe. Wildlife is best in the area along Mana Pools National Park. This is definitely one of my favorite adventures.

Three-day/two-night kayak safaris are operated on the Zambezi River in Zambezi National Park upstream from Victoria Falls, Zimbabwe.

WHITE-WATER RAFTING

For white-water enthusiasts and newcomers alike, the Zambezi River (Zambia/Zimbabwe) below Victoria Falls is one of the most challenging rivers in the world. Some rapids are *Class Five* — the highest class runable. Rafting safaris from one to seven days are available. No previous experience is required. Just hang on and have the time of your life!

BIRD WATCHING

If you are not a bird watcher now, there's a good chance you will be converted before the end of your safari. Bird watching in Africa is almost beyond belief. Some countries have recorded over 1000 different species and some parks over 500.

The best time of the year for bird watching is November-March in most areas covered in this guide. However, bird watching is very good year-round.

Keen birders planning to visit Southern Africa (Botswana, Lesotho, Namibia, South Africa, Swaziland, and Zimbabwe) will find *Newman's Birds of South Africa* by Kenneth Newman invaluable. *Birds of Eastern and Northern Africa* by C.W. Mackworth-Praed and C.H.B. Grant is excellent for eastern Africa.

MOUNTAIN CLIMBING

Africa has mountains to challenge the tenderfoot and the expert as well. Mt. Kilimanjaro (Tanzania), 19,340 feet in altitude, is the highest mountain in Africa, followed by Mt. Kenya (Kenya) at 17,058 feet. The Ruwenzoris, or *Mountains of the Moon* (Uganda/Zaire), is the highest mountain chain in Africa, rising to 16,794 feet. All of these mountains lie within a few degrees of the equator yet are snowcapped year-round. Hiking through fascinating and unique Afro-alpine vegetation found on all of these mountains gives one the feeling of being on another planet.

FISHING

Some of the finest **deep-sea fishing** in the world is found in the Indian Ocean off the coast of Kenya, off Pemba and Mafia Islands (Tanzania), and off the island country of Mauritius.

Freshwater fishing for Nile Perch (400+ pounds) and tiger fish (one of the best fighting fish in the world) is excellent in Lake Tanganyika (especially near Zambia), Lakes Turkana and Victoria (Kenya), and Lake Kariba (Zimbabwe). Trout fishing is very good in parks such as Nyanga (Zimbabwe) and the Aberdares (Kenya). Most freshwater fishing requires a license which can usually be obtained from your hotel, lodge or camp for a small fee.

OVERLAND SAFARIS

Overlanding generally refers to traveling mainly on land for several weeks, months, or even years, covering great distances. You can overland on your own or join one of many organized safaris with groups often ranging in size from 8-30. This rough-and-ready type of adventure is recommended only for the most rugged travelers.

Overlanding on a tour is similar to an extended budget camping safari (see **Budget Camping Safaris** above). Deviations from the intended route are sometimes necessary as some land borders that were open may be closed by the time you get there. When participating in an organized overland tour lasting several months, you should allow at least a week or two after the safari is scheduled to end, just in case prob-

Overland safaris often last several months and are only for the hardiest of adventurers.

lems delay your reaching your final destination.

Organized overland safaris usually require that participants "pitch in" and do the cooking, cleaning, pitching of their own tent, etc. On the other hand, the cost per day is low compared to full service safaris. Most participants are in their 20's and very few are over 35 years of age.

The adventure is the overland experience itself. Most of your time is spend "on the road." Compared to more standard safaris, relatively little time is spent in the game parks.

PRIVATE SAFARIS

For those who wish to avoid groups, a private safari is highly recommended for several reasons.

An itinerary can be specially designed according to the kind of experience *you* want, visiting the parks and reserves *you* wish to see most, and at the time of year that suits *you* best. You may spend your time doing what you wish to do rather than having to compromise with the group.

The key is to find an Africa travel expert who can match the kind of safari experience you are looking for with the best tailor-made itinerary for you.

What few people realize is that, in many cases, a private safari need not cost more than one with a large group.

In fact, I have sent many couples and small groups on private safaris for not much more (and sometimes less) than group departures with leading tour operators for the same (or superior) itinerary.

The key is knowing which tour company to contact. I have had quotes from tour operators that varied 75% for the exact same itinerary using the exact same hotels, camps and flights. Seventy-five percent? Amazing! That's why it's important to have an Africa travel specialist representing dozens of safari companies to make your booking — to save you money while acquiring the best safari for you.

SELF-DRIVE SAFARIS

One of the most adventurous ways of seeing the continent is to rent or buy a vehicle and hit the road — or dirt track, depending on your destination. A self-drive safari can be a real adventure. But you must be aware of what you are getting into.

One major disadvantage of a self-drive safari is that one misses the information and experience a driver/guide can provide. A good guide is also an excellent game spotter and knows when and where to look for the animals you wish to see most. He can communicate with other guides to find out where the wildlife has most recently been seen. This also leaves you free to concentrate on photography and game viewing instead of the road and eliminates the anxiety of perhaps getting lost.

Will a two-wheel-drive vehicle suit your purposes? If not, are you familiar with four-wheel-drive vehicles? Game viewing from a chauffeured vehicle is exciting, but driving up to your own herd of elephant or pride of lion is something else! This certainly isn't for everyone and is not recommended for the faint at heart or people without experience in the great outdoors.

The following story may give you an idea of the problems that could be encountered. One April we rented a Suzuki four-wheel-drive truck and drove around Kenya. We entered Tsavo West National Park near Taveta in the south and drove northward toward Kilaguni Lodge. Heavy rains caused flash floods, turning streams into torrential rivers. One "stream" we had to cross had water rushing over the bridge as well as

During the rainy season flash floods are common.

under it.

I walked out across the bridge to check the depth of the water, which rushed by so swiftly that it almost swept me off my feet. Deciding it was too dangerous, I studied the map for a different route. We drove to another crossing, only to find that there wasn't any bridge at all.

By then, darkness had fallen. So we had to drive very slowly to avoid hitting any animals. We returned to the previous bridge, only to find that the water had risen even more!

A decision had to be made. Our greatest fear was that the rushing water would hit the broad side of the vehicle, and we would be swept off the bridge and downstream, destroying the vehicle and leaving us as easy prey to any and all predators of the night.

Something told me that we could make it. I put the truck into first gear and drove slowly down the bank into the raging stream. When the headlights went under water, I almost had a heart attack — thinking for sure that all was lost. Somehow we kept going, and after what seemed like hours later (actually seconds), we drove up the opposite bank and celebrated our success.

My point is that game viewing on your own should not be taken lightly, and only people with extensive experience with four-wheel-drive vehicles should consider it.

Circumstances forced us to do several things which should not be done in the bush. Getting out of a vehicle unescorted by a game guard is dangerous, especially near streams, rivers and lakes where carnivores wait for prey, and hippos and crocs may be present. The number one rule is to never drive at night. Never! Broken-down vehicles and wild animals are often seen only after it is too late. And remember — in most African countries, driving is on the left! Self-drive safaris are relatively easy to do in countries with excellent roads as in South Africa. However, in the great majority of Africa, the roads are poor.

Carnet de Passage is required by most countries to take your own vehicle across borders without paying import duty or leaving a deposit with Customs; a *carnet* must be purchased before arrival.

Self-drive safaris widely differ in cost according to the type of vehicle, accommodation used, and country in which the safari takes place. Generally, they are more expensive than taking a package tour. Petrol (gasoline and diesel) are very expensive in Africa, often four times more expensive than in the U.S.A. and twice as expensive as in Europe. Depreciation is a major factor as roads are poor. In addition, most African countries have import duties on vehicles in excess of 100%.

In some cases two-wheel-drive vehicles are sufficient for game viewing, and the rates are lower than for four-wheel (4x4) vehicles. However, mini-buses or four-wheel vehicles are higher off the ground, and vehicles with open roofs are much better for game viewing than a car. In some countries such as Uganda and Tanzania, vehicles are available for rent only with a chauffeur. Be sure that gasoline or diesel is available in route, and carry extra if necessary.

Rentals in South Africa and Namibia are the least expensive of the top wildlife countries. For current rental rates, contact the agencies listed under "Auto/Vehicle Rentals" in the **Safari Pages** or contact an Africa travel specialist.

I suggest you get an International Driver's License from your automobile association, as it is required by most of the countries covered in this book. Contact the tourist offices, consulates, or embassies of the countries in which you wish to drive for any additional requirements.

OTHER SAFARIS

Additional options for the special interest traveler include anthropology, archeology, art, backpacking, camel safaris, horseback riding, SCUBA diving, and snorkeling.

WILDLIFE

HABITATS

Animals are most often found in and nearby the habitats in which they feed or hunt. These habitats fall roughly into four categories — savannah, desert, wetlands and forest.

Savannah is a very broad term referring to dry land which can be open grasslands, grasslands dotted with trees, or wooded areas. Grazers (grasseaters) and carnivores (meateaters) adept at hunting in savannah are most easily found here. Some browsers (leafeaters) also make the savannah their home.

Deserts have little or no standing water and very sparse vegetation. Many desert animals do not drink at all but derive water only from the plants they eat. Some savannah grazers and carnivores can be found in the desert.

African **forests** are thickly vegetated, often with grasses and shrubs growing to about ten feet in height, shorter trees 20-50 feet high, and a higher canopy reaching to 150 feet or more.

It is usually more difficult to spot animals in forests than in the other habitats. Many forest animals such as the elephant are more easily seen in open savannah areas adjacent to forests. Forest herbivores (planteaters) are browsers, preferring to feed on the leaves of plants and fruits usually found in forests. Carnivores have adapted to a style of hunting where they can closely approach their prey under cover.

Wetlands consist of lakes, rivers and swamps which often are part of a larger savannah or forest habitat. Many rivers wind through savannah regions, providing a habitat within a habitat. Wetlands are good places not only to see wetland species, but also other habitat species that come there to drink.

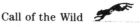

ANIMALS BY HABITAT

The animals listed below are classified according to the habitat where most of their time is spent. The animals are listed in order of size by weight.

SAVANNAH

Grazers:
white rhino
eland
zebra
waterbuck
roan antelope
sable antelope
gemsbok (oryx)
topi
hartebeest
wildebeest
tsessebe
warthog
reedbuck
Grant's gazelle
impala
springbok
Thomson's gazelle
gerenuk
klipspringer
steenbok

Browsers:
giraffe
black rhino
kudu
dikdik

Carnivores:
lion
hyena
cheetah
African wild dog
jackal
mongoose
bat-eared fox

FOREST

Browsers:
elephant
nyala
bongo
bushbuck
duiker

Primates:
gorilla
baboon
chimpanzee
colobus monkey
Sykes monkey

Carnivores:
leopard
serval
genet

WETLANDS

Grazers:
hippopotamus
buffalo
sitatunga

Carnivores:
crocodile
otter

DESERTS

see Savannah grazers and carnivores above

WILDLIFE AREAS BY HABITAT

Savannah Wildlife Areas

Botswana
Chobe
Savuti

Kenya
Amboseli
Masai Mara
Meru
Nairobi
Samburu
Tsavo

Namibia
Etosha

Rwanda
Akagera

South Africa
Kruger
Private Res.

Tanzania
Mikumi
Ngorongoro
Ruaha
Selous
Serengeti
Tarangire

Zaire
Virunga (Rwindi)

Zambia
Kafue
South Luangwa

Zimbabwe
Hwange
Motopos

Forest Wildlife Areas

Kenya
Aberdare
Mt. Elgon
Mt. Kenya

Rwanda
Volcano

Tanzania
Arusha
Gombe Stream
Mt. Kilimanjaro
Mahale

Zaire
Kahuzi-Biega
Virunga (other)

Wetland Wildlife Areas

Botswana
Moremi
Okavango Delta

Kenya
Lake Baringo
Lake Bogoria
Lake Naivasha
Lake Nakuru

Tanzania
Lake Manyara

Uganda
Murchison Falls
Ruwenzori

Zambia
Kafue
Lochnivar

Zimbabwe
Mana Pools
Matsudona

Desert Wildlife Areas

Namibia
Namib-Naukluft
Skeleton Coast

Botswana
Kalahari Desert

South Africa
Kalahari-Gemsbok

WHAT IS BEST SEEN WHERE?

COUNTRY	MAJOR PARK OR RESERVE	Lion	Leopard	Cheetah	Elephant	Black Rhino	White Rhino	Hippo	Buffalo	Eland	Greater Kudu	Sable Antelope	Gemsbok or Oryx
Botswana	Chobe	B	D	C	A+	/	F	B	B	D	B	B	D
	Moremi	B	D	C	A	/	F	A	B	F	C	B	/
	Okavango Delta	C	D	D	B	/	/	A+	B	F	D	C	/
	Savuti	A	C	C	A	/	F	/	B	D	C	B	/
Kenya	Amboseli	B	C	B	A	B	/	A	A	C	/	/	C
	Masai Mara	A	B	B	A	B	/	A	A	B	/	/	/
	Samburu	B	B¹	C	A	D	/	/	A	B	/	/	A
	Tsavo	B	D	C	A	D	/	B	A	C	/	/	C
Namibia	Etosha	B	C	B	A	C	/	/	/	B	B	D	A
S. Africa	Kruger	B	C	B	A	C	B	A	A	C	B	C	/
	Private Reserves	B	A²	B	A	C	A	A	A	C	B	C	/
Tanzania	Lake Manyara	B	D	D	A	D	/	A+	A	/	/	/	/
	Ngorongoro	A	C	B	A	A	/	A	A	C	/	/	B³
	Serengeti	A	B	A	B	D	/	B	A	C	/	/	B
	Tarangire	A	C	B	A+	D	/	B	B	C	F	/	A
Zambia	S. Luangwa	B	A²	F	A+	F	/	A	A	C	B	F	/
Zimbabwe	Hwange	B	C	C	A	C	B	/	A	C	B	A	D
	Mana Pools	B	C	/	A	F	/	A+	A	C	B	/	/
	Matusadona	B	C	/	A	B⁴	/	A	A+	/	B	F	/

A+ — Best reserves
A — Almost always seen (seen on almost all game drives)
B — Frequently seen (usually seen on every two-four game drives)
C — Occassionally seen (seen every one-two weeks).
D — Seldom seen (seen every two-four weeks)
F — Present but almost never seen
/ — Not seen in this reserve
[1] At lodges that bait for leopard
[2] On night game drives
[3] In Ngorongoro Conservation Area near Serengeti National Park
[4] Seen more often on walks than on game drives

The major parks and reserves listed above in the **Wildlife Areas by Habitat** chart are classified according to their most dominant habitat. Wildlife in the **Animals by Habitat** chart is classified by the most dominant habitat. Use the **What Wildlife is Best Seen Where** chart as a guide in finding the major parks and reserves that are most likely to have the animals you are most interested in seeing on safari.

Many of these wildlife areas are composed of more than one habitat, so consult the text of this book for in-depth descriptions. Keep in mind that savannah and forest animals visit wetland habitats to drink and that many forest animals are more easily seen on the open savannah.

A well-rounded safari includes visits to all three types of habitats and parks, giving the visitor an overall picture of wildlife and ecosystems.

WHEN'S THE BEST TIME TO GO?

The **When's the Best Time to Go?** chart shows at a glance when to go to best enjoy the countries, parks and reserves of your choice, and the best places to go in the month(s) in which your vacation is planned. In other words, how to be in the right place at the right time.

For example, your vacation is in February and your primary interest is game viewing on a photographic safari. Find the countries on the chart in which game viewing is "excellent," "good," or "fair" in February. Turn to the respective country chapters for additional information and choose the ones that intrigue you the most. Use this chart as a general guideline as conditions vary from year to year.

Timing can make a world of difference. For example, Hwange National Park in Zimbabwe is well-known for its population of over 25,000 elephants. I recently spent Christmas there (during the rainy season), and we didn't see one elephant. But during the dry season, they're everywhere.

In most cases the best game viewing, as exhibited on the chart, also corresponds to the dry season. Wildlife concentrates around water holes and rivers, and vegetation is less dense than in the wet season, making game easier to find. There are, however, exceptions. For instance, the Serengeti migration often begins at the height of the rains in Tanzania.

WHEN'S THE BEST TIME TO GO?

A — EXCELLENT   B — GOOD   C — FAIR   D — POOR   X — CLOSED

COUNTRY	PARK/RESERVE	JAN	FEB	MAR	APR	MAY	JUN	JUL	AUG	SEP	OCT	NOV	DEC
BOTSWANA	MOREMI AND OKAVANGO DELTA	D	D	C	C	B	B	A	A	A	A	B	C
	SAVUTI	C	C	B	A	B	B	A	A	A	B	C	C
	CHOBE	D	D	C	C	B	B	A	A	A	A	C	C
KENYA	AMBOSELI	A	A	A	C	C	B	A	A	A	A	B	B
	TSAVO	B	B	B	C	C	C	A	A	A	C	C	B
	MASAI MARA	A	A	A	B	C	B	A	A	A	B	B	B
	ABERDARE & MERU	A	A	B	C	C	B	A	A	A	B	C	A
	SAMBURU, BUFALLO SPRINGS & SHABA	A	A	A	B	B	B	A	A	A	B	B	A
NAMIBIA	ETOSHA	D	D	D	C	C	B	A	A	A	A	C	C
RWANDA	AKAGERA	D	D	D	D	C	B	A	A	A	B	C	C
SOUTH AFRICA	KRUGER AND PRIVATE RESERVE	D	D	D	D	C	B	A	A	A	B	C	C
TANZANIA	LAKE MANYARA	A	A	A	C	C	B	A	A	A	A	B	B
	NGORONGORO	A	A	A	B	B	A	A	A	A	A	B	A
	SERENGETI (SOUTHEASTERN)	A	A	A	A	A	B	C	C	C	C	B	A
	SERENGETI (NORTH & NORTHWEST)	C	C	C	C	C	B	A	A	A	A	B	C
	TARANGIRE	C	C	C	C	C	B	A	A	A	A	B	C
	SELOUS & RUAHA	D	D	D	D	D	C	A	A	A	A	C	D
ZAIRE	VIRUNGA (RWINDI)	A	A	B	D	D	B	A	A	A	B	C	B
ZAMBIA	SOUTH LUANGWA & KAFUE (NORTHERN PARTS)	X	X	X	X	X	B	A	A	A	A	X	X
	SOUTH LUANGWA & KAFUE (CENTRAL & SOUTHERN)	C	C	C	C	B	B	A	A	A	A	B	B
ZIMBABWE	HWANGE	D	D	D	C	C	B	A	A	A	B	B	C
	MATUSADONA	D	D	D	C	C	B	A	A	A	A	B	C
	MANA POOLS	D	D	D	D	C	B	A	A	A	A	C	D

COMMENTS:

During the rainy season the land is often luxuriously green, the air clear. People with dust allergies may wish to plan their visits soon after the rains are predicted to have started. Game is more difficult to find, but there may be fewer travelers in the parks and reserves. Most reserves in Africa are simply heaven for bird watchers. The best times for bird watching are often the opposite of the best times for big game viewing. Bird watching, however, is good year-round in many regions.

ACCOMMODATION

There is a great variety of styles and levels of comfort in accommodation available in the major cities and while on safari, ranging from basic huts to suites with private swimming pools. Options include hotels, lodges, small camps with chalets or bungalows, fixed tented camps and mobile tented safaris.

HOTELS

Many African cities such as Nairobi (Kenya), Harare (Zimbabwe), and Kigali (Rwanda) have four- and five-star (first class and deluxe) hotels comparable to anywhere in the world, with air-conditioning and private facilities, swimming pools and one or more excellent restaurants and bars.

LODGES

Lodges ranging from comfortable to deluxe (many have swimming pools) are located in or near most parks and reserves. Many lodges and camps are located in wildlife areas 3,000 feet or more above sea level, so air-conditioning is often not necessary.

CAMPS

There is often confusion over the term *camp*. A camp often refers to lodging in chalets, bungalows or tents in a remote location. Camps range from very basic to garishly plush. Deluxe camps often have better service and food, and most certainly a truer safari atmosphere, than large

Chalet accommodation at Sanyati Lodge, Matusadona National Park, Zimbabwe.

Fixed tented camp accommodation at Shindi Island Camp in the Okavango Delta, Botswana.

Elephants often visit Rochomechi Camp in Mana Pools National Park (Zimbabwe). Keep your distance — they are wild!

lodges and hotels.

Fixed tented camps are permanent camps that are not moved. Besides generally having better food and service than lodges, guests of deluxe fixed tented camps have more of a "safari experience." One is less isolated from the environment than if he were staying in a lodge. **Mobile tented camps** are discussed below under "Camping."

CHOOSING ACCOMMODATION

An important factor to consider when choosing accommodation or a tour is the size of the lodge or camp. In general, guests receive more personal attention at smaller camps and lodges than larger ones. Large properties tend to stick to a set schedule while smaller properties are often more willing to amend their schedules according to the preferences of their guests. Larger lodges and camps tend to have more amenities, such as swimming pools. Gregarious individuals may have a more enjoyable trip where there is a greater number of people to meet. A real plus is that larger properties tend to be less expensive, making tours using the larger properties more affordable.

Many larger properties (especially in Kenya) are surrounded by electrical fences, allowing guests to move about as they please without fear of bumping into elephant or other wildlife. Travelers (including myself) who enjoy having wildlife roaming about camp should seek properties that are not fenced; these properties are best for travelers who want to experience living in the bush.

Most properties in Kenya and Tanzania have 75-200 beds, whereas most camps in Botswana, Zambia, and Zimbabwe have 16 or less.

HOTEL CLASSIFICATIONS

Hotels are categorized as *Deluxe, First Class* and *Tourist Class*, while lodges and tented camps are classified as *Class A-F.*

Deluxe: An excellent hotel, rooms with private bath, air-conditioning, more than one restaurant serving very good food, swimming pool, bars, lounges, room service all the amenities of a four- or five-star international hotel.

First Class: A very comfortable hotel, rooms with private bath, air-conditioning, at least one restaurant and bar; most have a swimming pools.

Tourist Class: Comfortable hotel with simple rooms with private bath, many with a/c, restaurant, bar, and swimming pool.

LODGE AND TENTED CAMP CLASSIFICATIONS

CLASS A: Deluxe lodge or tented camp, excellent food and service, large nicely appointed rooms or tents with private bath, comfortable beds and tasteful decor; lodges may have air-conditioning.

Relaxing in camp. Photo: Ker Downey Selby.

CLASS A/B: An excellent lodge or tented camp; rooms in lodge with private facilities; bathroom facilities in camps may be ensuite or a short walk from the chalet or tent.

CLASS B: A very comfortable lodge or camp with very good food and service, many with swimming pools. Rooms in lodges have private baths; most tents, chalets or bungalows have private bathrooms.

Destruction of trees by elephant is a common sight in many parks and reserves.

CLASS B/C: Most often a "Class B" property that is somewhat inconsistent with the quality of accommodation, food and service.

CLASS C: A simple lodge with private bathroom or tented camp, chalet or bungalow with private or shared facilities, fair food and service, or a "Class B" structure with fair to poor food, service, or other problems such as water shortages (for bathing).

CLASS D: A basic lodge or tented camp. Lodges, chalets, bungalows and tents seldom have private bathrooms, or a "Class C" structure with poor food, service, or other problems such as water shortages (for bathing).

CLASS F: Very basic lodge or tented camp without private bathrooms, often self-service (no restaurant).

FOOD

Excellent European cuisine along with interesting local dishes are served in the top hotels, lodges, camps and restaurants. French cuisine is most likely European cuisine served in Rwanda, Zaire, and Burundi, while British cuisine predominates in the other countries covered in this guide. Restaurants serving cuisine from all over the world may be found in the larger cities in Africa.

Most international travelers are impressed with the quality of the food and drink served on their safari. However, there are a few countries that may not fall into this category. Uganda experiences shortages of various foods and beverages. Tanzania and Zambia occasionally experience shortages of imported items like Perier, imported beer, wine and soft drinks. However, the best hotels and camps in these countries serve excellent food.

If your travels take you to East Africa, try a few Swahili dishes, fresh seafood and Indian cuisine, especially along the coast. For tips on the best eating establishments in Kenya from the country's leading expert, pick up a copy of Kathy Eldon's *Eating Out Guide To Kenya.* Also look for Kathy's *Specialties of the House* featuring Kenya's tastiest recipes.

LANGUAGE

English is widely spoken in all these countries except Burundi, Rwanda, and Zaire, where French is the international language. Swahili is widely spoken in Kenya, Tanzania, Uganda, and parts of Rwanda and Zaire. To enhance your enjoyment of your safari, words and phrases in Swahili and French may be found on pages 440 to 443.

Travel Journal Africa (see **Catalog**) has illustrations of 75 animals with their names in English, Latin, French, and Swahili. Your guide will love it if you start naming the animals spotted in his native language!

PHOTOGRAPHY

ASA 64 and 100 are best during the day when there is plenty of light. ASA 200-ASA 400 is often needed in early mornings and late afternoons, especially when using telephoto or zoom lens. Use a flash or ASA 1000 or 1600 film at night. Bring extra camera and flash batteries and plenty of film as film and batteries are very expensive and difficult to obtain in Africa. At least thirty rolls of film should be brought (per couple) for a two-week safari.

For wildlife photography, 200mm zoom lens is the smallest that should be used; 300mm zoom is preferable. A 500mm or larger lens is necessary for bird photography. A wide-angle lens (28-35mm) is great for scenic shots.

I prefer a 35mm camera with automatic and manual settings. The Minolta 7000i has a fabulous automatic focusing feature which is invaluable when photographing moving animals. On my most recent safari, I took the 7000i body, 28-85mm and 100-300 zoom lens, and a 500mm mirror lens and was very satisfied with the results.

Consider bringing a small bean-bag or small tripod to help steady your camera when shooting from the roof of your vehicle. Monopods (one-legged support) are also useful, especially on walking safaris.

Vehicle vibrations can cause blurry photos, so ask your driver to turn off the engine for those special shots. Protect lens with UV filters. A polarizer helps cut glare and is especially effective when sky and water are in the photo. Store cameras and lens in plastic bags to protect them from dust and humidity, and clean them regularly with lens paper or lens brushes.

If you bring a camcorder or video recorder, be sure to bring at least one extra battery pack, a charging unit and converter (Africa uses 220-240 volts). Batteries can usually be recharged at your lodge or camp while the generator is running.

Do *not* take photographs of airports, bridges, railway stations, government buildings, telecommunication installations and offices, military and police installations and personnel. You may have your camera confiscated and waste a lot of time having to explain why you were taking the photos in the first place.

PRICES

Prices in Africa as well as in other parts of the world can change quickly according to variances in currency exchange rates and inflation. African currencies have been historically weak against the U.S. dollar, making Africa an especially attractive destination when the value of the dollar is down against the currencies of Europe, the Far East, and other destinations overseas.

The cost per day is most dependent on how comfortably you wish to travel (the level of accommodation), type of transportation used, whether you're on a private safari or on a tour, and the destinations involved. Deluxe accommodations and transportation are normally more expensive in countries off the beaten track than in the more popular tourism spots.

For example, deluxe (Class A) safari camps in Botswana are often more expensive than Class A lodges in Kenya. Camps in Botswana cater to smaller groups and are generally situated in more remote locations, and charter aircraft are often used to reach them.

Transportation is more costly in Zaire, for instance, than in The Republic of South Africa because in Zaire petrol is more expensive and poor roads give greater wear-and-tear on vehicles.

As in Europe and other parts of the world, general interest tours cost less than tours with more unique itineraries. Getting off the beaten track may be a little less comfortable and dip a bit more into the wallet, but many travelers find it well worthwhile. Personally I really enjoy traveling in areas where the residents seldom see people from the western world.

For current costs on package tours and tailor-made itineraries, contact an Africa travel specialist. See "Agencies Specializing in Africa" in **The Safari Pages.**

SAFARI TIPS

Read the **Safari Glossary** to become familiar with the terminology used in the bush. Once on safari, you will notice that when you ask people what animals they saw on their game drive, they might reply, "Elephant, lion, leopard and oryx," when in fact they saw several members of each species. This use of the singular form when one actually saw more than one of that species is common. However, one exception to this rule is saying *crocs* for *crocodile*. This form of "Safariese" will be used throughout this guide to help separate you from the amateur.

It is often better to sit quietly at a few water holes than to rush around in an attempt to visit as many locations as possible. Don't just look for large game; there is an abundance of reptiles, amphibians, smaller mammals, birds, and insects that are often fascinating to observe. Do not disturb the animals. Remember, we are guests in their world.

Put your valuables in a safety deposit box at your lodge or hotel. Do not call out to a person, signaling with an index finger. This is insulting to most Africans. Instead, use four fingers with your palm facing downward.

Wear colors that blend in with your surroundings (brown, tan, light green or khaki). Do not wear perfume or cologne while game viewing. Wildlife can detect unnatural smells for miles and unnatural colors for hundreds of yards, making close approaches difficult.

The very few tourists who get hurt on safari are almost always those travelers who ignore the laws of nature and most probably the advice and warnings of their guides. Common sense is the rule.

Stay in your vehicle when in the presence of dangerous animals. Do not wade or swim in rivers, lakes or streams unless you know for certain they are free of crocodiles, hippos, and bilharzia (a disease). Fast-moving areas of rivers are often safe, but are still risky. Also, do not walk along the banks of rivers near dawn, dusk or at night. Those that do so may inadvertently cut off a hippo's path to its water hole, and the hippo may charge. Hippos are responsible for more human deaths in Africa than any other game animal, most often from this type of occurrence.

Wear closed-toed shoes or boots at night and also during the day if venturing out into the bush. Bring a flashlight and always have it with you at night.

Don't venture out of camp without your guide, especially at night, dawn or dusk. However, if you do stray from camp, carry a large stick or pole. Lion in some areas still fear being speared by the local tribesmen.

Remember that wildlife is not confined to the parks and

reserves in many countries. On my first extensive expedition to Africa, I crossed the Sahara Desert and through Central Africa to Rwanda. After clearing customs at the Tanzanian border, I began to walk to the nearest village about 15 miles away. A customs agent stopped me, stating that two men had been devoured by lions a few days earlier on their way to that village and suggested that I might not wish to feed the wildlife in that manner. Discretion being the better part of valor, I took his advice and a few hours later rode with a family whose forefathers had immigrated to the region from the Middle Eastern country of Kuwait.

A few days later the vehicle on which I was riding ran out of diesel just as the sun was setting. The driver said that we might be there for days waiting for fuel and suggested that I walk with two Tanzanian passengers to the next village, about ten miles away.

This typical African night was so dark that I could not see the road beneath my feet. The two Tanzanians worked at a prison nearby and were in a great hurry to get there. When I asked why a prison had been built in such a remote area, one man replied, "Lions are heavily concentrated in this region. If a prisoner escapes, he usually doesn't get very far." Such words of comfort I could have done without!

Resist the temptation to jog in national parks, reserves or other areas where wildlife exists. To lion and other carnivores, we are just "meat on the hoof" — like any other animal — only much slower and less capable of defending ourselves.

A jogger was recently found cowering on the rooftop of a deserted building in Chobe National Park. He had come across a pack of African wild dogs which were feasting on an antelope killed only moments earlier and realized that they could have just as easily had him for breakfast instead. He was certainly glad to see the rescue team arrive.

Do as I suggest, not as I do, and, most importantly, enjoy the adventure!

WHAT TO WEAR — WHAT TO TAKE

Countries close to the equator (Burundi, Kenya, Rwanda, Tanzania, Uganda, and Zaire) have small differences in seasonal temperatures, with June-August being the coolest time

Waiting patiently for wildlife at water holes is often more productive than rushing around from spot to spot.

of the year; the main factor affecting temperature is altitude.

Countries in southern Africa (Lesotho, Namibia, South Africa, Swaziland, Zambia, and Zimbabwe) have more pronounced seasons, often cold (sometimes freezing) in winter (June-August) and hot in summer (October-February).

Casual clothing is usually worn by day. Dresses for ladies and coats and ties for men are only required in top restaurants in Kenya, South Africa, Zimbabwe, and at the Mount Kenya Safari Club (Kenya). In some restaurants, gentlemen's coats are available on request.

Bring at least one camera and lots of film, binoculars, sun block, electric converter and adapter, small extension cord, a copy of *Travel Journal Africa*, alarm clock, insect repellent, brown, khaki or light green cotton clothing including at least one pair of long pants and long-sleve shirt, wide-brimmed hat, rain gear, good walking shoes, flashlight and extra batteries, two pairs of sunglasses, two pairs of prescription glasses (for contact-lens wearers, too) and a copy of the prescription, prescription dugs with a letter from your doctor verifying your need, medical summary from your doctor if medical problems exist, Band-Aids, motion-sickness tablets, medicine for traveler's diarrhea, antimalarial prophylaxis, decongestant tablets, laxative, headache tablets, throat lozenges, antacid, and antibiotic ointment.

Everyone should have his own pair of binoculars. Compact, lightweight binoculars manufactured by Nikon and Minolta are available for under U.S. $100. I recommend 9 or 10 power (i.e., 9 x 25). Higher quality (and more expensive) binoculars are, of course, available.

Leave your dress watch at home and buy an inexpensive (under U.S. $50) waterproof watch with a light and alarm. Do not wear or bring any camouflage or dark green clothing; these colors are reserved for the military.

AFRICA'S TOP WILDLIFE COUNTRIES

BOTSWANA

BOTSWANA

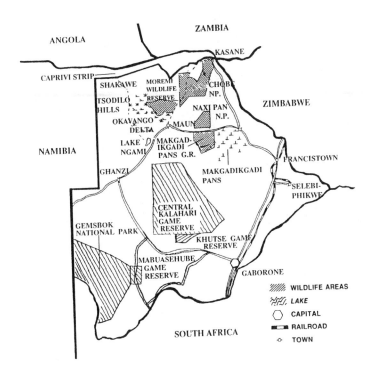

FACTS AT A GLANCE

AREA:	224,606 SQUARE MILES
APPROXIMATE SIZE:	TEXAS OR FRANCE
POPULATION:	1.2 MILLION (1990 EST.)
CAPITAL:	GABORONE (POP. EST. 70,000)
OFFICIAL LANGUAGES:	ENGLISH: SETSWANA IS THE NATIONAL LANGUAGE, ENGLISH IS WIDELY SPOKEN.

Sausage trees are easily recognized by the elongated shape of their fruit.

BOTSWANA

The best-selling book, *The Cry of the Kalahari*, and the hilarious feature film, *The God's Must Be Crazy*, have assisted Botswana in gaining international recognition as a top safari destination. More than four-fifths of the country is covered by the Kalahari sands, scrub savannah and grasslands. The land is basically flat with a mean elevation of 3280 feet. Over 85% of the population is concentrated near the better water resources in the eastern part of the country.

The Kalahari Desert is not a barren desert of rolling dunes as one might imagine. It has scattered grasslands, bush, shrub and tree savannah, dry river beds, and occasional rocky outcrops.

The "Pula" is Botswana's unit of currency, and also the Setswana word for rain, which is so critical to this country's wealth and survival. The rainy season is December-March, with the heaviest rains in January and February. Winter brings almost cloudless skies. January (summer) temperatures range from an average maximum of 92° F. to an average minimum of 64° F. July (winter) temperatures range from an average maximum of 72° F. to an average minimum of 42° F. Frost occasionally occurs in midwinter.

The San, Basarwa, or Bushmen were the first inhabitants of the area and may have come to southern Africa 30,000 years ago. Most of the estimated 60,000 Bushmen live in what is now Botswana and Namibia. Their language uses "clicking" sounds, distinguishing it from Bantu and most other languages in the world.

Traditionally Bushmen have been nomadic hunter-gatherers, but today only a few thousand live this kind of existence in the Kalahari. Men hunt with poisoned arrows and spears while women use sticks to dig up roots and gather other food for the group. Bushmen are unique in that they distribute wealth equally among the members of the group, share in the day-to-day aspects of life, and believe they are not superior to their environment and must live in harmony with it.

The Sotho-Tswana group of people comprise over half of the country's population and speak the Setswana language. The Batswana prefer to live in large, densely populated villages. Cattle are the most important sign of wealth and prestige. Ancestor worship was the chief form of religion until missionaries arrived in 1816 and converted large numbers of Batswana to Christianity.

Bechuanaland became a protectorate of the British Empire on September 30, 1885, and became the independent country of Botswana on September 30, 1966.

Today, very few of the people dress in their traditional costume except for special celebrations. However, for many Batswana, tribal customs are still important in day-to-day life. English is spoken by most of the people, and especially by the youth.

Botswana has a multi-party democracy and is one of the most economically successful and politically stable countries on the continent. Diamonds are Botswana's greatest foreign exchange earner, followed by cattle (there are three times as many cattle in Botswana as people), copper-nickel matte, and tourism.

WILDLIFE AND WILDLIFE AREAS

As far as wildlife is concerned, Botswana is one of Africa's best-kept secrets. National parks and reserves cover 17% of the country's area — one of the highest percentages of any country in the world.

Botswana's combination of very good game, uncrowded reserves, excellent small camps (most cater to 16 or less guests) with great food, and the use of open vehicles for game viewing is a combination difficult to beat anywhere on the continent.

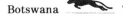

Chobe National Park and Moremi Wildlife Reserve rank as two of the best wildlife areas in Africa and fall easily within the top ten. The Okavango Delta is the largest inland delta in the world. This "water in the desert" phenomenon has created a unique and fascinating ecosystem well worth exploring.

The four main reserve areas most often visited by international tourists are all in Northern Botswana. These are the Okavango Delta, Moremi Wildlife Reserve, the Savuti (southwestern part of Chobe National Park) and the Serondela region in the northeastern part of Chobe National Park near Kasane. The latter three are Botswana's best reserves for seeing big game.

As these four regions are distinct in character, a well-rounded wildlife safari to Botswana should include two to three days in each region (if time allows).

Other northern attractions include Nxai Pan National Park and Makgadikgadi Pans Game Reserve. Reserves in the south are at times excellent but are seldom visited by international travelers.

Generally speaking, game viewing for the Okavango Delta, Chobe and Moremi is best in the dry winter season (June-October) and poorest December-February during the hot, rainy season. Game viewing in Nxai Pan is best in the wet summer season (November-April), and Makgadikgadi Pans is best January-April.

In the dry season, wildlife is concentrated near the swamps and along the rivers. After the first rains, much of the wildlife ventures far into the interior.

Most camps are serviced by small aircraft, allowing visitors to minimize time spent on bumpy roads between reserves and maximize time viewing wildlife and a variety of other activities the country has to offer.

Game viewing by air is usually quite fruitful. On one flight from the Savuti to the Okavango Delta, we spotted four large herds of elephant, among numerous other species. Most charter flights have weight limits of 22-30 pounds per person, so bring only what you need.

Calving season throughout the country is November-February during the rainy season. Fishing for tiger fish, bream, barbel and pike is very good.

The Wildlife Department runs the parks. Driving in the parks is not allowed at night. Camping is allowed at designated spots. Many private camps close January-February.

THE NORTH

MAUN

A dusty little town situated at the southeastern tip of the Okavango Delta, Maun is the safari center of the country's most important tourist region. Many travelers fly into Maun to join a safari. Others begin their safari at Victoria Falls (Zimbabwe) and end up in Maun.

The Duck Inn is a favorite meeting place in town. Within walking distance from the airport, this is a good place to have a drink or meal and meet the locals. The bar at Riley's Hotel is another good spot.

Maps of the Okavango Delta/Moremi Wildlife Reserve and Chobe National Park, books and souvenirs are available from shops a short walk from the airport.

ACCOMMODATION — FIRST CLASS: * Riley's Hotel is the best place to stay in Maun. The hotel has air-conditioned rooms with ensuite facilities, popular bar and restaurant. TOURIST CLASS: * Island Safari Lodge is located nine miles north of town on the western bank of the Thamalakane River and has brick and thatch bungalows with private facilities, campsites, swimming pool, bar and restaurant. * Sitatunga, a quiet fixed tented camp with camping sites, is nine miles southwest of Maun on the road to Lake Ngami. Available are a bar, prepared meals, and crocodile farm.

THE OKAVANGO DELTA

The Okavango, the largest inland delta in the world, covers over 4015 square miles and is in itself a unique and fascinating ecosystem. Instead of finding its way to the ocean as most rivers do, the Okavango River fans out into a vast system of thousands of waterways, separated by innumerable islands, to eventually disappear into the Kalahari sands.

The Okavango, an ornithologist's and botanist's dream come true, is beautifully presented in Peter Johnson and Anthony Bannister's book, *Okavango: Sea of Land, Land of Water* (Struik Publishers), and *Okavango: Jewel of the Kala-*

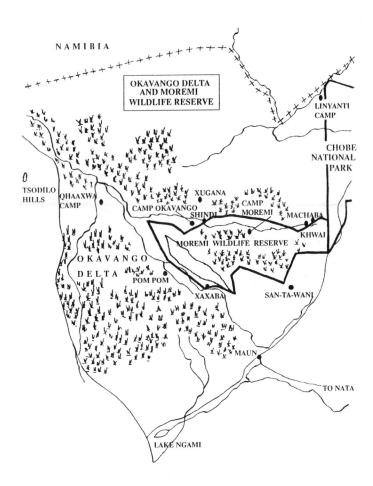

hari by Karen Ross (Macmillan Publishing Co.).

Game viewing for the larger land mammal species should not be your main reason for visiting the Okavango. Big game exists in the delta, but is less commonly seen than in Chobe. The main reason for visiting the Okavango should be to explore the wonder of this inland delta, to enjoy the primordial silence, the unusual flora, the birdlife, hippo, crocs, and excellent fishing.

However, this is not to say that large land mammals are not encountered in the delta. Large herds of buffalo and a variety of antelope are often seen; lion and other predators are occasionally encountered. Game viewing is actually quite good

Travel by mokoro in the Okavango Delta. Photo: Ker Downey Selby.

on Chief's Island and the outlying areas of the delta during the cooler months when the water is high.

Crocodiles are most heavily concentrated in the larger waterways and in the northern part of the delta where there is permanent deep water. However, crocs are found throughout the delta.

Mother nature must have smiled on this region, for the delta waters are highest during the dry season, since it takes six months for the rainy season flood waters to travel from their source in the Angolan highlands to the delta.

Most visitors reach the camps in the Okavango by small aircraft. Flying into the delta gives one a good overall perspective of the swamp and is an adventure in itself. Game can be easily spotted and photographed from the air.

A 150-mile-long buffalo fence has been constructed to keep cattle from the swamp: therefore, little game is found on the Maun (southern) side of the fence.

Calling the Okavango a "swamp" is a misnomer, since the waters are very clear. This is mainly due to the fact that there is only about a 200-foot drop in altitude over 150 miles from the top to the bottom of the delta. The water flows gradually and therefore carries very little sediment. Many people drink

directly from the delta waters. Apparently the desert sands filter out most of the impurities. Little bilharzia exists in the area.

An excellent way to experience the Okavango is by mokoro (dugout canoe). Traveling by mokoro allows you to become a part of the environment. Sitting inches from the waterline, thoughts of angry hippos or hungry crocodiles overturning your boat cross your mind, but soon pass away with assurances from your guide and the peacefulness of this pristine environment.

Patterns of gold are created from the reflection of papyrus on the still waters of the narrow channels at early morning and late afternoon. You sometimes pass through channels that often appear to be narrower than the boat itself. Silence is broken only by the ngashi (boatman's pole) penetrating and leaving the water, by the cries of countless birds, and the movement of mostly unseen game along the delta's banks. Tiny white bell frogs chime to some unknown melody. Sunsets with rosy-pink clouds reflected in the waters are too beautiful for words. Life slows to a regenerative pace. This relaxed form of adventure and exploration is difficult to match anywhere in the world.

On one occasion, I tried poling our canoe across a small lagoon. My guide was right. It's definitely not as easy as it looks!

Guided excursions, using mekoro (plural for mokoro), canoes or small motor boats, range in length from a few hours to a full day and can be arranged through your camp. Canoes are larger and therefore a little more comfortable; mekoro harmonize better with the natural surroundings. Motor boats allow you to visit more distant attractions and must be used where the water is too deep to pole a mokoro or canoe and for fishing.

Special mokoro expeditions up to a week or more can be arranged, where you "bush camp" (no facilities) on sand banks in the delta and sleep in small tents or under mosquito nets. This kind of safari is recommended for only the hardiest of traveler!

After an adventurous day in the delta, a sundowner cruise is especially welcome. On numerous occasions our guide waved a fish in the air and called to a fish eagle perched high in a tree over a half mile away, then tossed the fish into the water about 30 feet from the boat. Like magic, the eagle dived down

Fish eagle in action. Photo: Maryann Watson.

at full speed and plucked the fish from the water. You must be fast with a camera to catch that on film!

The Okavango has possibly the highest concentration of fish eagles in the world. Other bird species we spotted on a recent visit included the coppery-tailed coucal, purple heron, striped kingfisher, Mayer's parrot, black-collared barbet, yellow-fronted tinker barbet, hamerkop, red-billed woodhoopoe, saddle-billed stork, Dickenson's kestrel, little spotted eagle, grey lourie, swallow-tailed bee-eater, carmine bee-eater, slaty egret, little egret, reed cormorant, green-backed heron, goliath heron, blacksmith plover, pied kingfisher, yellow-billed kite, western banded snake eagle, African darter and African jacana.

Speeding along one afternoon in a small motorboat, we drove right by an eight-foot-long crocodile. We went back for a closer look and discovered it was fast asleep. We maneuvered the boat within five feet of it, and it still didn't wake up — and I'm glad it didn't!

On a canoe trip we spotted an elusive sitatunga running through the reeds. Later on a short walk, we saw impala and red lechwe.

The islands in the delta are thought to have been made over

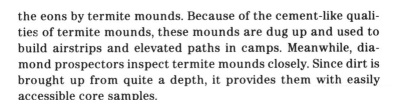

the eons by termite mounds. Because of the cement-like qualities of termite mounds, these mounds are dug up and used to build airstrips and elevated paths in camps. Meanwhile, diamond prospectors inspect termite mounds closely. Since dirt is brought up from quite a depth, it provides them with easily accessible core samples.

Fishing in the Okavango is best in the northwestern part of the delta. The Okavango River above the delta is too heavily fished. The best time of the year for catching tiger fish is October and November. For barbel, the best time is the end of September through October when the barbel are running (migrating). Overall, the best time for fishing is September through March.

In the extreme western part of the delta, near Qhaaxwa Camp, is a natural floating island which bounces you along as it gives way under your feet. The island, predominantly made of a thick layer of reeds and papyrus, is strong enough to support most humans. However, an extremely overweight woman, apparently with relatively small feet, fell through a week before my visit. Our guide proudly took us to the spot where history was made. The island was only about 15 inches (38 cm.) thick where she fell through. By the way, she was pulled out of the water unharmed and only a bit startled!

Activities in the Okavango include travel by mokoro or canoe, motor boat rides, fishing, walks and game drives. The activities offered by the camps vary according to their location in the delta. For instance, a camp located on a deep lagoon would offer motor boat rides, but not mokoro rides because the waters would be too deep for the pole used by your guide to push you. Where there is access by land, a four-wheel-drive vehicle is necessary.

If you wish to visit Tsodilo Hills to see the bushmen and rock paintings, consider making reservations in advance so you may fly there from your camp in the Okavango.

ACCOMMODATION — CLASS A: * *Xaxaba* has ten attractive reed and thatch chalets with private facilities and small swimming pool and is situated in the southcentral delta west of Chief's Island. The food is excellent. Mokoro rides, walks on nearby islands, fishing, excellent birdlife and sundowner cruises may be enjoyed. * *Qhaaxwa Camp* is a tented camp (16 beds) situated on the edge of a large lagoon under shady trees in the western part of the delta. Boat rides, walks, bird watching and fishing are offered. Excursions to the "Floating Island" and to local villages seldom visited by tourists can be arranged. * *Camp Okavango* is a 12-bed tented camp in the eastern delta. Emphasis is placed on a "luxury in the bush" experience. The tents are plushly decorated with open-roofed private facilities close by; silver candelabras accent the dinner tables, tea is served with silver service; and it enjoys one of the most well-stocked bars in the country. Activities include canoe safaris, boat safaris, excellent bird watching and walks. * *Shinde Island Camp* is a small camp a fun 30-45 minute boat ride from Xugana airstrip with seven tents (14 beds) with open-roofed shower and toilet facilities placed a few feet behind each tent. Activities include mokoro trips, boat rides, fishing, walks, day and night game drives. * *Pom Pom* has seven tents (14 beds) overlooking a lagoon in the central delta; activities include day and night game drives, walks, mokoro and boat rides.

CLASS A/B: * *Xugana Game Lodge*, situated under large shade tress on the banks of one of the Delta's largest lagoons in the northeastern Okavango, has eight double tents (16 beds) with separate shower and toilet facilities nearby. Xugana offers boat rides, game drives, walks, and a houseboat (the *African Skimmer*) for rent. Fishing is excellent.

MOREMI WILDLIFE RESERVE

Moremi is the most diversified of all the parks in terms of wildlife and scenery, and many people feel it is the most beautiful. Located in the northeastern part of the Okavango Delta, Moremi contains over 1160 square miles of permanent swamps, islands, flood plains, forests and dry land.

In the flood plains reedbuck, common waterbuck, lechwe, tsessebe, ostrich, sable and roan antelope, crocodile, hippo and otter can be found. In the riparian forest you may spot elephant, greater kudu, Southern giraffe, impala, buffalo, Burchell's zebra, along with such predators as lion, leopard, wild dog, ratel (honey badger), spotted hyena, and very rarely, rhino.

Black-backed and side-striped jackals are often seen in the riparian forest as well as in the flood plain. Seldom seen species include pangolin, bat-eared fox, porcupine and hedgehog.

Moremi Wildlife Reserve is a haven for birdlife and large mammals as well.

On a morning game drive, we saw two herds of sable antelope, elephant, greater kudu, tsessebe, impala and Burchell's zebra. On another game drive we spotted seven lion, cheetah, bat-eared fox, and several species of antelope.

One afternoon we spotted four young tsessebe standing alone under a tree. We approached within about 50 feet of them, but they still held their ground. Shortly afterwards, a herd of adult tsessebe came within about 100 feet of us and stopped. The two groups began communicating, using clicking sounds. A female ran from the adult herd to the juveniles, then ran off into the bush with what we guessed was her calf. A second female did the same thing, followed by two other females which took away the last two juveniles. It was a charming sight of mothers evidently collecting their children.

Elephant and buffalo are the only large animals that migrate. After the rains have begun, they move northward to the area between Moremi and the Kwando-Linyanti River

A lone hippo chasing a herd of elephant out of "its" water hole in the Moremi Wildlife Reserve.

systems. Other wildlife may move to the periphery of, or just outside, the reserve.

In the bush it is not always the larger animal, but more often the more aggressive one that gets his way. While on a game drive in Moremi, we experienced a perfect example of this. A lone hippopotamus chased an entire herd of over 20 elephant out of its water hole. Astounding!

Moremi is an ornithologist's delight. Fish eagles, kingfishers and bee-eaters abound. Other bird species include parrots, shrikes, egrets, jacanas, pelicans, hornbills, herons, saddle-billed storks, yellow-billed oxpeckers, wattled cranes, reed cormorant, spur-winged goose, long-tailed shrike and flocks of thousands of red-billed quelea which fly together in a sphere like a great spotted flying ball.

Moremi is open year-round; however, some areas may be temporarily closed due to heavy rains or floods. Four-wheel-drive vehicles are necessary. The South Gate is about 62 miles north of Maun.

ACCOMMODATION - CLASS A: * *Khwai River Lodge* borders Moremi's northern gate and has comfortable brick and thatch

Having tea and coffee at Khwai River Lodge before going on a morning game drive.

bandas with ensuite facilities for a maximum of 26 guests, and large swimming pool. Game drives are provided. * *Camp Moremi* is a twelve-bed deluxe tented camp just north of Moremi in a beautiful part of the park with an elevated bar and dining room overlooking Xakanaxa Lagoon. Private facilities are a short walk behind each tent. The camp offers game drives. Clients are sometimes transferred to Camp Okavango by boat. * *Machaba Camp* has seven large tents (14 beds) with ensuite facilities and is located a few miles from Khwai River Lodge. Bar and dining room are under canvas. The camp offers day and night game drives, fishing and walks. * *San-Ta-Wani Safari Lodge*, near Moremi's south gate, has brick and thatched chalets with private facilities in nearby bandas and caters to a maximum of 16 guests. Night and day game drives and walks are offered.

CAMPING: * SOUTH GATE CAMPSITE is located just outside the South Gate and has toilet facilities only. * *Third Bridge* is Moremi's most popular campsite and can be very crowded in peak season. This camp has long-drop toilets only. Water is available from the river. Beware of lions. * *Xaxanaka* has no

The Savuti is one of the best places in Africa to see lion.

facilities. * *North Gate* campsite is situated just inside the reserve and has shower and toilet facilities, and water.

SAVUTI

The Savuti is an arid region located in the southern part of Chobe National Park. The landscape ranges from sandveld to mopane forest, acacia savannah, marshlands (usually dry) to rocky outcrops. The Savuti Channel dried up about ten years ago, causing game to thin out until a few years ago when the area finally received some decent rains. The Savuti Swamps are dry except when there are heavy rains, which is quite uncommon.

Game viewing opportunities here are excellent. Savuti, like the northern part of Chobe National Park, is also known for its elephant. The area also contains large populations of zebra, buffalo, eland, kudu, roan, sable, waterbuck, tsessebe, wildebeest, impala, and many other members of the family of ungulates (hoofed mammals).

The predator population is correspondingly tremendous. The Savuti is famous for its lions, which occasionally are seen

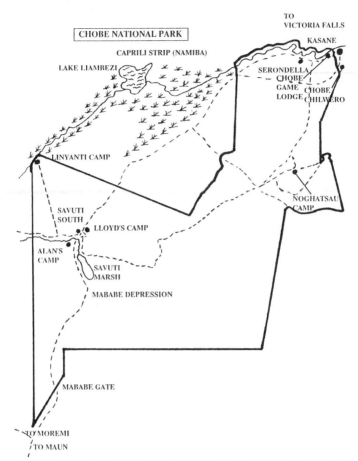

wearing radio-tracking collars. Within a two-month period prior to my recent visit, lions had killed 19 giraffe in the area.

On one recent game drive, we parked within 15 feet of a pride of nine lion and turned off the engine. I was sitting next to the driver in the open land cruiser. A very large male and a large female lion walked by within five feet of us. They both stood taller than I was sitting, and they could have easily dragged me out of the vehicle had they wanted. I simply held my breath and reminded myself that I was quite safe inside the vehicle.

Other predators include leopard, cheetah, wild dog, spotted hyena, black-backed jackal and bat-eared fox. Hyena have tremendous crushing power with their jaws; they have been known to chew hinges off of refrigerators in camps in the Savuti in order to get at the food inside.

On another game drive we spotted impala, five greater kudu, warthog, elephant, two black-backed jackal, steenbok, about 50 tsessebe, a herd of blue wildebeest, *twelve* bat-eared fox, tawny eagles, yellow-billed hornbills and kori bustards. We followed vultures to a warthog kill where we found only the head remaining and a large male lion in the bush nearby.

Sometimes during the dry season 70 to 90 elephant gather at the water hole (a borehole) at once. They are usually lone males gathering together; females tend to stick close to permanent water.

Game viewing is excellent July-September/October and good in June and November. Burchell's zebra migrate from the Mababe Depression, which is south of the Savuti Marsh, northward to the Linyanti Swamps in December and January, and return to the Mababe Depression around March. Therefore, game viewing in the Savuti, unlike Moremi or Northern Chobe, is also good March-May.

A few bushmen paintings may be seen not far from the camps listed below. Four-wheel-drive vehicles are necessary for the Savuti.

ACCOMMODATION — *Allan's Camp, Savuti South* and *Lloyd's Camp* are all within a few miles of each other, and all about 110 miles from Maun. Driving from Maun takes about seven hours while flying takes about 40 minutes.

CLASS A: * *Allan's Camp* has eight comfortable chalets (doubles) with toilets and showers ensuite. Game drives are offered.

CLASS A/B: * *Savuti South* is a 16-bed tented camp with large tents, and bathroom and toilet facilities in an ablution block nearby. Guests should not leave their tents after "lights out" (usually 10:30 p.m.) because lion and hyena pass through the camp almost every night. Bed pans are provided in each tent in case nature calls in the wee hours of the night. Game drives are offered.

CLASS B: * *Lloyd's Camp* is a tented camp with eight tents (16 beds) set on the banks of the dry Savuti Channel. The camp offers game drives.

CAMPING: A *National Parks Campsite* is located near the camps mentioned above. Toilet and shower facilities are not always operational.

Game viewing by boat on the Chobe River can be excellent, especially in the dry season.

CHOBE NATIONAL PARK

Famous for its large herds of elephant, Chobe National Park covers about 4200 square miles. The park is situated only about 50 miles from Victoria Falls in Zimbabwe with the Chobe River forming its northern and northwestern boundaries. Across the river is Namibia's Caprivi Strip. Birdlife is prolific, especially in the riverine areas.

The four main regions of the park are Serondela in the northeast near Kasane, the Corridor around Ngwezumba and Nogatsaa, the Linyanti Swamps in the northwest, and the Savuti (discussed above) in the west.

The Serondela region is famous for its huge elephant and buffalo populations numbering in the thousands. The elephant are the most vocal and active I've encountered on the continent, constantly trumpeting, making mock charges, and sometimes sparring with each other. Great entertainment!

Game viewing by boat along the Chobe River can be spectacular, especially July-October in the dry season. Often large herds of elephant and a variety of other wildlife come down to the river to drink. By boat you can get within very

Sundowner cruise on the Chobe River with Chobe Game Lodge in the background. Photo: Sun International.

close range of these animals. Large monitor lizards are commonly seen.

Along the Chobe River between the Chobe Game Lodge and the village of Kasane, you are likely to see numerous hippo, red lechwe, common waterbuck, warthog, and guinea fowl. Driving from the lodge towards Serondela Camp you can usually see giraffe, impala, zebra, and occasionally kudu and Chobe bushbuck. On one game drive we spotted white rhino (very rarely seen), red lechwe, warthog, lion, hamerkop, lilac-breasted roller, grey lourie, white-necked and white-backed vultures, among others.

The hot and dry Corridor (Ngwezumba to Nogatsaa) is the only area in the country where oribi is found. Gemsbok, eland, ostrich and steenbok are sometimes seen. Prevalent species include giraffe, elephant, roan and sable antelope.

The Linyanti Swamps, situated north of the Savuti, are predominately papyrus marsh and are home to many crocodiles, hippo, sitatunga, and lechwe, along with some elephant and buffalo.

The Serondela or northern region is accessible by two-wheel-drive vehicles, while four-wheel-drive vehicles are necessary for the rest of the park.

ACCOMMODATION — NORTHERN CHOBE — CLASS A: * *Chobe Chilwero Camp* has eight comfortable wooden chalets (doubles) with ensuite facilities situated on an escarpment overlooking Chobe National Park. One of the best views in Botswana is from the upstairs lounge. The food is excellent. Game drives are made by vehicle and by boat. * *Chobe Game Lodge* is a beautifully decorated Moorish-style lodge with 100 beds, set on the banks of the Chobe River within the park eight miles from Kasane. The lodge has a large swimming pool and beautifully kept spacious grounds. All rooms have private facilities, and four luxury suites have private swimming pools. Sundowner cruises and game drives are offered.

ACCOMMODATION — LINYANTI REGION — CLASS A/B: * *Linyanti Camp*, situated on a shaded riverbank in the Linyanti Swamps, has eight large tents (doubles); each two tents share a nearby ablution block. In addition to game drives, Linyanti offers game viewing from its double-decker barge and fishing.

CLASSES B AND C: See "Kasane" below.

CAMPING: The public campsites at Serondela, Linyanti, Savuti and Nogatsaa have toilets and showers while the campsite at Tjinga only has a water tank. Serondela is often very crowded; it is accessible by two-wheel-drive vehicles and is close to Kasane.

KASANE

Kasane is a small town a few miles northeast of Chobe National Park about a one-and-a-half-hour drive from Victoria Falls (Zimbabwe). Many tourists are driven here from Victoria Falls to begin their Botswana safari. Kasane Enterprises has a small shop of quality souvenirs.

ACCOMMODATION — CLASS B: * *Kubu Lodge* is a very comfortable lodge with wood and thatch chalets, private facilities, swimming pool and spacious lawns and is only a ten-minute drive from the Chobe National Park gate. Game drives are arranged on request.

CLASS C: * *Chobe Safari Lodge* has rooms and rondavels with private facilities, swimming pool, and boats for hire.

CAMPING: Sites available at *Chobe Safari Lodge*.

Southern giraffe near Moremi Wildlife Reserve.
Photo: Ker Downey Selby.

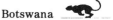

NXAI PAN NATIONAL PARK

Nxai Pan National Park, well known for its huge giraffe population, covers 810 square miles and is located 22 miles north of the Maun-Nata road in Northern Botswana. Nxai Pan is a fossil lake bed about 15 square miles in size; it is covered with grass during the rains. The landscape is dotted with trees. Kgama-Kgama Pan is second to Nxai Pan in size.

In addition to Southern giraffe, wildlife includes gemsbok, eland, greater kudu, blue wildebeest, red hartebeest, springbok, steenbok, brown and spotted hyena, cheetah, and other predators. During the rains, elephant and buffalo may also be seen. After the rains have fallen, game viewing can be excellent (i.e., December-April). Birdlife is excellent during the rains.

This park is seldom visited by international travelers as there are no permanent fully catered camps. A four-wheel-drive vehicle is necessary.

CAMPING: There are two campsites, one of which has an ablution block. Water is usually available at both sites. Some travelers prefer to camp at *Baines Baobabs* (no facilities), situated between the park and the Maun-Nata road, instead of camping in the park. Visitors must be totally self-sufficient.

Baines Baobabs were immortalized by the famous painter Thomas Baines in 1862. His painting, entitled "The Sleeping Five," is of the five baobabs, one of which is growing on its side. Seldom are baobab trees found growing so closely together. Baines Baobabs were later painted by Prince Charles.

MAKGADIKGADI PANS GAME RESERVE

Makgadikgadi Pans Game Reserve includes a portion of the 4600-square-mile Makgadikgadi Pans, which are the size of Portugal. The pans are nearly devoid of human habitation and give one a true feeling of isolation.

Once one of the largest prehistoric lakes, the Makgadikgadi Pans are salt plains covered with grasslands and isolated "land islands" of vegetation, baobab and palm trees.

The park itself covers about 1500 square miles and is located south of the Maun-Nata road in Northern Botswana, just south of Nxai Pan National Park. Large herds of blue wildebeest, zebra, springbok, gemsbok and thousands of

flamingos can usually be seen December-March. A four-wheel-drive vehicle is highly recommended.
ACCOMMODATION: There are no camping or other facilities, and travelers must be totally self-sufficient.

TSODILO HILLS

Over 2700 Bushmen paintings are scattered through the rocky outcrops of Tsodilo Hills, one of the last places in Botswana where Bushmen can be readily found. The largest of the four hills rises 1000 feet above the surrounding plain. Archaeological evidence indicates that these hills may have been inhabited as long as 30,000 years ago.

Located west of the Okavango Delta, Tsodilo Hills is accessible by a flight from Maun or from safari camps in Northern Botswana, or a very long and rough day's ride from Maun by four-wheel-drive vehicle. There are no facilities, so travelers must be totally self-sufficient. Please do not drink anything in the presence of Bushmen — water is scarce.
ACCOMMODATION: None.

CENTRAL KALAHARI GAME RESERVE

The Kalahari has an abundance of wildebeest, hartebeest, springbok, gemsbok, ostrich, eland and giraffe. Bushmen are very difficult to find in the Kalahari, so seeing them should be considered a bonus.

The Central Kalahari Game Reserve, which covers a portion of the Kalahari Desert, is closed to the public.

KHUTSE GAME RESERVE

The Khutse Game Reserve shares its northern boundary with the Central Kalahari Game Reserve and is the closest reserve to Gaborone. Khutse covers 950 square miles of gently rolling savannah and pans (over 50), and is best known for its birdlife.

Lion, leopard, cheetah, and antelope adapted to an arid environment are present. However, wildlife is seasonal, depending on the rains. If there has been little rain, then game is usually scarce.

Khutse is 136 miles (a five-hour drive) from Gaborone via

Cheetah with cubs. Photo: Mike Appelbaum.

Molepolole. The route is not well sign-posted.
ACCOMMODATION: None.
CAMPING: There is one public campsite with toilets. Water is available at the gate.

THE SOUTH

GABORONE

Gaborone, phonetically pronounced "Habarony," is the capital of Botswana. In the center of town is the main shopping and commercial center — the Mall. Besides some shopping, there is little of interest for the international traveler except for possibly the National Museum.

ACCOMMODATION — FIRST CLASS: * The *Gaborone Sun* is located on the outskirts of the city. This 158 room air-conditioned hotel has a swimming pool, tennis and squash courts, casino, resident band and cabaret. * The *President Hotel* is a very comfortable and attractive air-conditioned hotel centrally located in the Mall.

MABUASEHUBE GAME RESERVE

Mabuasehube is an extremely remote reserve located in southwestern Botswana. Mabuasehube shares its western border with Gemsbok National Park. The park has six large pans and sand dunes over 100 feet high. The best time to visit is during the rainy season October-April when an abundance of eland, hartebeest, gemsbok, wildebeest, springbok, lion and other predators are present. Mabuasehube is 330 miles from Gaborone. A four-wheel-drive vehicle is needed, and the drive takes at least 11 hours. ACCOMMODATION: None. CAMPING: No facilities. Water may be available at the Game Scouts Camp.

GEMSBOK NATIONAL PARK

Entry is only possible from the Republic of South Africa. See "Kalahari Gemsbok National Park" in the chapter on South Africa for details.

BURUNDI

BURUNDI

Burundi is one of the poorest and most densely populated countries in Africa. Presently Burundi is visited more by international tourists in transit than as a destination in itself. However, there are some attractions that warrant a short visit, especially for the prolific birdlife, chimpanzees and other primates.

Burundi is a hilly country with altitudes ranging from 2600-9000 feet. The weather in Bujumbura and along the shores of Lake Tanganyika is warm and humid with average temperatures ranging from 74° - 86° F. ; frost sometimes occurs at night in the highlands. Dry seasons are June-September and December-January; the principle rainy season is February-May.

The three major ethnic groups in the country are the Hutu, Tutsi and Twa (pygmy). Hutus are primarily farmers and comprise more than half the population; their Bantu-speaking ancestors came to Burundi over 800 years ago. The Tutsi are a pastoral tribe and comprise less than a quarter of the population; they came to the region a few hundred years after the Hutus. The pygmy (Twa) were the original inhabitants who presently comprise less than 2% of the population.

For centuries, the region what is now Burundi had a feudal social structure headed by a king. Although Europeans explored the region as early as 1858, Burundi did not come under European administration until it became part of German West Africa in the 1890's.

In 1916, Belgian troops occupied the country and the League of Nations mandated it to Belgium as part of the Territory of Ruanda-Urundi in 1923. Ruanda-Urundi became a UN Trust Territory under the administration of Belgium after World War II, and in 1962 became the independent country of Burundi.

French and Kirundi are the official languages, and Swahili is also spoken. At the top hotels, restaurants and shops some English-speaking staff are usually available to assist travelers; otherwise, very little English is spoken in the country. Most of the people are Catholic.

There are only two cities in the country — Bujumbura and Gitega. Over 90% of the population are subsistence farmers. Burundi's major exports include coffee, tea, cotton and food crops, with coffee providing 80%-90% of the country's foreign exchange earnings.

WILDLIFE AND WILDLIFE AREAS

The National Institute for the Conservation of Nature (INCN) has recently created several parks and nature reserves. Most of the parks and reserves lack access roads, camping sites and other facilities. Hunting is forbidden throughout the country.

Burundi's premier wildlife attraction is chimpanzees, along with crested mangabeys and red colobus monkeys. Other wildlife includes buffalo, several species of antelope, hyena, serval, wild cats, monkeys, baboons, a wide variety of birdlife and over 400 species of fish in Lake Tanganyika, more than most any other body of water in the world. Hippo and crocs are present in Lake Tanganyika, the Rusizi and Ruvubu Rivers.

The combination of varying altitude and water create a wide range of micro-climates giving rise to a great variety of flora.

RESERVE GEREE DE LA RUSIZI
(RUSIZI NATURE RESERVE)

Rusizi Nature Reserve is the smallest of the national parks; it is located less than ten miles northwest of Bujumbura. The park has hippo, crocs, and a variety of birdlife.

A lioness and her cub.

PARC NATIONAL DE LA KIBIRA
(KIBIRA NATIONAL PARK)

Kibira National Park and the Kibira Forest are the best areas in Burundi to look for chimpanzees, red colobus and crested mangabeys. This 155-square-mile park is situated 30 miles or more to the north and northeast of Bujumbura, and has a network of over 100 miles of tracks (poor roads).

PARC NATIONAL DE LA RUVUBU
(RUVUBU NATIONAL PARK)

Ruvubu National Park covers a strip of land from one to six miles wide along both sides of the Ruvubu River in eastern Burundi. Wildlife in the Ruvubu basin and Parc National de la Ruvubu includes hippo, crocs, buffalo, leopard, antelope, monkeys and some lion. The closest road access to the park is 140 miles from Bujumbura. The park has about 60 miles of tracks. Accommodation is available in a newly erected camp.

RESERVE NATURELLE GEREE DU LAC RWIHINDA (LAKE RWIHINDA NATURE RESERVE)

The Lake Rwihinda Nature Reserve and the other lakes in the northern part of the country, approximately 120 miles from Bujumbura, are called the "Lakes of the Birds" and include Lakes Cohoha, Rweru, Kanzigiri and Gacamirinda; they are a bird watcher's paradise. These lakes can be explored by barge or canoe.

BUJUMBURA

Founded in 1896 by the Germans, Bujumbura is the capital city, major port and commercial center of Burundi. The city has excellent French and Greek restaurants. A fun restaurant and bar on Lake Tanganyika is Cercle Nautique which also offers sailing, boating, and fishing, and has an abundance of hippos for entertainment. There is a public beach called Kakaga near Club du Lac Tanganyika.

The ethnological **Musée Vivant** has a traditional Burundian village and daily traditional drum shows. The **Parc du Reptiles** is next door. The **Musée du Géologie du Burundi** has a good fossil collection.

ACCOMMODATION - DELUXE: * *Novhotel* has 114 air-conditioned rooms with private facilities, swimming pool, video and tennis courts. * *Méridien Source du Nil* has 117 air-conditioned rooms with private facilities, swimming pool and all the usual amenities of Méridien hotels.

FIRST CLASS: * *Club du Lac Tanganyika*, situated a few miles from the center of town on Lake Tanganyika, has a swimming pool and air-conditioned rooms with private facilities.

TOURIST CLASS: * *Hotel Burundi-Palace* has 29 rooms with private facilities.

INLAND

The people outside Bujumbura seldom see tourists. Try to visit a village on market day to get a feeling of daily life in Burundi.

En route to Gitega, one passes **Muramvya**, the ancient city of the king and royal capital, and an active market at **Bugarama**.

The saddle-billed stork stands more than five feet high.

Gitega, the former colonial capital, is situated on the central plateau in the middle of the country, and is the second largest city. Sights include the National Museum, fine arts school, and beer market.

The artistic center of **Giheta**, seven miles from Gitega, sells wood carvings, leather goods, baskets and ceramics. The southernmost possible source of the Nile is four miles from **Rutovu** and about 60 miles from Gitega.

Martial eagle. Photo: Mike Appelbaum.

KENYA

KENYA

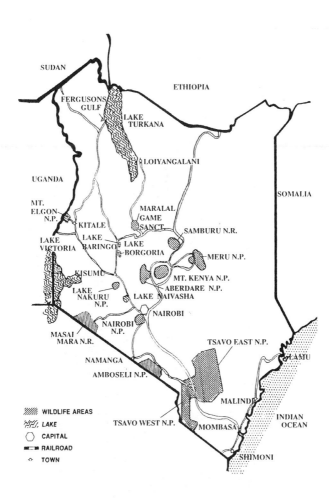

FACTS AT A GLANCE

AREA:	224,960 SQUARE MILES
APPROXIMATE SIZE:	TEXAS OR FRANCE
POPULATION:	22 MILLION (1990 EST.)
CAPITAL:	NAIROBI (POP. EST. 1.5 MILLION)
LANGUAGES:	OFFICIAL: KISWAHILI AND ENGLISH

Mother and child in a remote Samburu village.
Photo: Mike Appelbaum.

KENYA

The word safari is Swahili for "travel." and Kenya is where it all began. Great historical figures like Theodore Roosevelt and Ernest Hemingway immortalized this country. Kenya is now the most popular of the safari countries, with over 800,000 visitors per year. Visitors to Kenya can enjoy game viewing, bird watching, hot-air ballooning, mountaineering, SCUBA diving, freshwater and deep-sea fishing, and numerous other activities.

Kenya is well-known for the magnificent Serengeti migration (shared with Tanzania) of more than one million wildebeest and zebra, and for the colorful Masai, Samburu and other tribes that contribute so much to making this a top safari destination.

Kenya has one of the most diversely majestic landscapes on the continent. The Great Rift Valley, with the steep walled valley floor dropping as much as 2000-3000 feet from the surrounding countryside, is more breathtakingly dramatic here than anywhere else in Africa.

The eastern and northern regions of the country are arid. Most of the population and economic production is in the south which is characterized by a plateau ranging in altitude from 3,000-10,000 feet sloping down to Lake Victoria in the west and a coastal strip to the east.

The country has the highest population growth rate in the world (4.1%), with women having an average of eight children in their lifetimes. Over half the country is Christian, about 25% indigenous beliefs, and 6% Muslim concentrated along the coast. The Masai are found mainly to the west and south of

Samburu Morani. Photo: Mike Appelbaum.

A Masai herding cattle.

Nairobi, the Kikuyu in the highlands around Nairobi, and the Samburu in the North.

Bantu and Nilotic peoples moved into the area before Arab traders arrived on the Kenyan coast by the first century A.D. The Swahili language was created out of a mixture of Bantu and Arabic and became the universal trading language. The Portuguese arrived in 1498 and took command of the coast, followed by the Omani in the 1600's and the British in the late 19th century. Kenya gained its independence within the Commonwealth from Britain on December 12, 1963. Key foreign exchange earners are tourism, coffee and tea.

WILDLIFE AND WILDLIFE AREAS

Kenya is one of the best countries on the continent for game viewing. Its only drawback is that it is too popular. Many of the well-known parks are very crowded, so don't expect to be out there in the more popular parks on your own.

Unfortunately, several vehicles are commonly seen surrounding a few lion, or even a sole rhino, cheetah or leopard. However, on the positive side, safaris are generally less expensive here than in Tanzania, Botswana or Zimbabwe.

Richard Leakey, Director of National Parks and Wildlife, has instituted many positive changes which are reducing poaching and limiting the building of new lodges and camps in reserves.

The Masai Mara is the best park in Kenya for game viewing, and should, if all possible, be included in one's itinerary unless you will be touring the Serengeti National Park in Tanzania at the times of the year when wildlife is more concentrated in the Serengeti National Park.

In general, game viewing is best during the dry seasons January-March and July-October. Game is easiest to spot in the Masai Mara, Amboseli and Nairobi National Parks, which have great wide-open plains. Samburu National Park is also excellent for game viewing.

The country is an ornithologist's paradise with over 1000 species of birds recorded within its borders. Greater and lesser flamingos migrate along the Rift Valley and prefer the alkaline lakes of Magadi, Elmenteita, Nakuru, Bogoria or Turkana. Lakes Naivasha and Baringo are freshwater lakes. Bird watching is good year-round and excellent in the rainy season.

Flying safaris are available to many of the parks and reserves. Camel safaris are operated in the north where guests walk down dry river beds or ride these "ships of the desert."

THE SOUTH

NAIROBI

Nairobi is situated at about 6000 feet altitude and means "place of cool waters" in the Masai language. The availability of international-class accommodations and most western goods and services make living and visiting here an enjoyable adventure.

The **National Museum** of Nairobi features the Leakey family's paleoanthropological discoveries, botanical drawings of Joy Adamson, and taxidermy displays of wild animals that are good to study to help you identify the live game while on safari. Across from the museum is the **Snake Park**, exhibiting over 200 species of the well-loved reptilian family. The **Municipal Market** in the center of town on Market Street sells produce and curios (be sure to bargain). The **Railroad Museum** will be of interest to railroad enthusiasts. The **Nairobi Race Course** has horse racing on Sunday afternoons and is highly recommended as a place for people watching and meeting a diverse cross section of Nairobians.

One of the more popular dining and disco spots is the Carnivore, famous for its beef and game meat. The Horseman, located in the suburb of Karen, is also excellent. The Tamarind is known for excellent seafood. The Thorn Tree Cafe is a renowned meeting place for travelers on safari who leave messages on a bulletin board; it is a key center of communication for people on the move and the best spot in town for people watching. Other excellent restaurants include Alan Bobbies Bistro and the Red Bull.

Other attractions include the **Bomas of Kenya** which features daily performances of ethnic dances and 16 varying styles of Kenyan homesteads. At the **Giraffe Manor** guests can feed the Rothschild's giraffes from an elevated platform and learn more about them. The **Karen Blixen Museum** is interesting to visit.

ACCOMMODATION — LUXURY: * *Norfolk Hotel*, a landmark

Nairobi skyline. Photo: Kenya Tourist Office.

in Nairobi, has traditional safari atmosphere, swimming pool, the fabulous Ibis Grill, and an open-air bar especially popular on Friday nights. All rooms are air-conditioned with ensuite facilities. * *Nairobi Safari Club* is an air-conditioned, all-suite hotel (144 rooms) with private facilities, health club and swimming pool. * *Hilton International* is centrally located and has 329 air-conditioned rooms with facilities ensuite and swimming pool. * *Nairobi Serena Hotel*, located a ten-minute walk from town, has 200 air-conditioned rooms with private facilities and swimming pool. * *Inter-Continental Hotel*, near the center of town, has a swimming pool, 440 air-conditioned rooms with private facilities and casino.

FIRST CLASS: * *New Stanley Hotel*, located in the center of town, has 240 air-conditioned rooms with private facilities.

TOURIST CLASS: * *Boulevard Hotel*, located on the edge of town, has 70 rooms with private facilities and swimming pool.

* *Six Eighty Hotel* is located in the center of town and has 340 rooms with private facilities.

NAIROBI NATIONAL PARK

Nairobi National Park is only eight miles south of Nairobi and sporadically has an abundance of game (depending on the weather) including black rhino (on our first visit we saw three), lion, cheetah, hippo and a variety of antelope — a bit of everything but elephant.

There is something very strange about being in the midst of wild game and still within sight of a city's skyline. Altitudes range from 4950-5850 feet above sea level.

The Animal Orphanage (a small zoo) near the main park entrance cares for hurt, sick or stray animals. The side of the park facing Nairobi is fenced. A four-wheel-drive vehicle is recommended in the rainy season.

ACCOMMODATION — See "Nairobi."

CAMPING: Camping is not allowed in the park.

AMBOSELI NATIONAL PARK

The real attraction of this park is the spectacular backdrop of Mt. Kilimanjaro. Also, rhino are fairly easy to locate here, and this may be the best park in Kenya to see elephant. *Elephant Memories*, a fascinating book by Cynthia Moss, is based primarily on her research in Amboseli.

This 146-square-mile park is probably the most crowded in the country, and a large portion of it has been turned into a dust bowl. However, elephant, lion and giraffe are easily found, and watching and photographing them as they pass in front of majestic Mt. Kilimanjaro is one of the most treasured sights on the continent. The mountain seems so close; actually it is more than 30 miles from the park.

Amboseli National Park is surrounded by a game reserve;

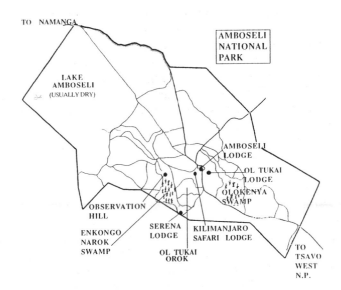

TO NAMANGA

AMBOSELI NATIONAL PARK

LAKE AMBOSELI
(USUALLY DRY)

AMBOSELI LODGE

OL TUKAI LODGE

OLOKENYA SWAMP

OBSERVATION HILL

ENKONGO NAROK SWAMP

SERENA LODGE

KILIMANJARO SAFARI LODGE

OL TUKAI OROK

TO TSAVO WEST N.P.

the park and reserve together cover 1235 square miles and average about 3900 feet in altitude.

From Nairobi travel south across the Athi Plains inhabited by the Masai. One enters the park on a badly corrugated road from Namanga and passes Lake Amboseli (a salt pan), bone dry except in the rainy seasons, eastward across sparsely vegetated chalk flats to Ol Tukai. Mirages are common under the midday sun.

Approaching the center of the park, the barren landscape turns refreshingly green from springs and swamps fed by underground runoff from the overshadowing Mt. Kilimanjaro. These swamps provide water for nearby grasslands and acacia woodlands, attracting an abundance of game and waterfowl, which give life to an otherwise parched land.

Large herds of elephant and buffalo are often seen around the swamps, especially at **Enkongo Narok Swamp** where it is easy to obtain photos of animals (especially elephant) in the foreground and Mt. Kilimanjaro in the background. Early morning is best before Kilimanjaro is covered in clouds; the clouds may partially clear in late afternoon.

Observation Hill is a good location for spotting lion and to get an overview of the park. One has a pretty good chance of spotting lion, cheetah, giraffe, and impala. Wild dog, aardwolf, oryx and gerenuk are less likely to be seen. Over 420 species of birds have been recorded. Game viewing is best January-March (also best views of Kilimanjaro) and July-October.

In order to limit destruction to the environment, driving off the roads is forbidden, and heavy fines are being levied against those who break the rules. Please do not ask your driver to leave the road for a closer look at wildlife. The park is about 140 miles from Nairobi.

ACCOMMODATION — *Amboseli Lodge, Kilimanjaro Safari Lodge* and park headquarters are located at Ol Tukai in the center of the park.

CLASS A/B: * *Amboseli Serena Lodge,* located in the south of the park, is a modern lodge with 96 rooms with private facilities and swimming pool.

CLASS B: * *Amboseli Lodge* has 60 rooms with facilities ensuite and swimming pool. * *Kilimanjaro Safari Lodge* has rooms with ensuite facilities and swimming pool.

CLASS D: * *Ol Tukai Lodge* has self-service bandas.

CAMPING: Campsites are located outside the park on Masai land four miles past Observation Hill. No facilities except long-drop (pit) toilets. Bring your own water.

TSAVO WEST NATIONAL PARK

Halfway between Nairobi and Mombasa lies West and East Tsavo National Parks, which together total 8,231 square miles. Large herds of over 100 elephant, with a total of over 15,000 in Tsavo West and East combined, over 60 species of mammals and 400 species of birds have been recorded. Also present are lion, caracal, giraffe, zebra, and a variety of antelope.

During the rainy season, however, wildlife is greatly scattered. During a two-day visit one April, we saw only three elephant.

Tsavo West is predominately extensive semiarid plains broken by occasional granite outcrops. Lava fields are located near Kilaguni Lodge. Altitudes range from 1000 feet to nearly 6000 feet in the Ngulia Mountains in the northern region of the park.

Mzima Springs, located just south of Kilaguni Lodge, is the park's premier attraction. From an underwater viewing platform, visitors may be lucky enough to watch hippo swim about the clear waters with grace and ease. Crocs and numerous

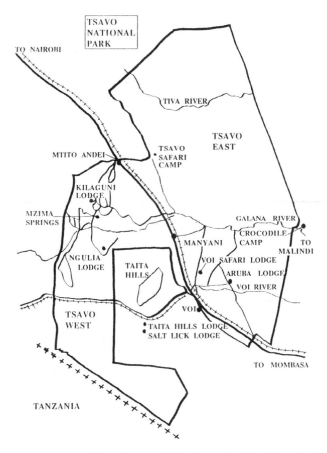

species of fish can also be seen. The best viewing is early in the morning. Kilaguni Lodge is about 180 miles from Nairobi.

ACCOMMODATION — CLASS B: * *Kilaguni Lodge* has 50 rooms with facilities ensuite and swimming pool. * *Ngulia Lodge* has 52 rooms with ensuite facilities and swimming pool. CLASS D: * *Nguila Safari Camp* is located near Ngulia Lodge and has self-service bandas. * *Kitani Lodge* is located near Mzima Springs and has self-service bandas. * *Jipe Public Campsite*, located on Lake Jipe, has self-service bandas.

CAMPING: Campsites are available at Kitani, Kamboyo and Kangechwa, and at the following park gates: Mtito Andei, Ziwani, Chyulu (Kilaguni), Kasigau and Tsavo. Jipe and Chyulu have showers and toilets; the other campsites have basic (if any) facilities.

Due to poaching, "big tuskers" like this one are rare.
Photo: Mike Appelbaum.

ACCOMMODATION NEAR TSAVO NATIONAL PARK — CLASS A: * Taita Hills Lodge and Salt Lick Lodge are situated between the southern extensions of Tsavo East and West Parks, about 240 miles from Nairobi. * *Salt Lick Lodge*, built on stilts to enhance viewing of wildlife visiting the salt lick, has 64 rooms with facilities ensuite and swimming pool. * *Taita Hills Lodge* has 62 rooms with ensuite facilities and swimming pool.

TSAVO EAST NATIONAL PARK

Tsavo East is mostly arid bush dotted with rocky outcrops traversed by seasonal rivers lined with riverine forest. Tsavo East is generally hotter, dryer, and lies at a lower altitude (about 1000 feet) than its western counterpart. The 3000 square miles south of the Galana River is the main region open to the public.

East Tsavo's only permanent water hole is at Aruba Dam, and the drive from Voi makes for a good game run. Just north of the dam is an isolated hill, Mudanda Rock, another good spot for game. The scenic drive along the Galana River often produces sightings of hippos and crocs.

Tsavo East receives fewer visitors than Tsavo West; wildlife is generally more heavily concentrated in Tsavo West. Voi is about 210 miles from Nairobi.

ACCOMMODATION — CLASS C: * *Voi Safari Lodge*, in the hills above the town of Voi, has 52 rooms with facilities ensuite, swimming pool and photographic hide. * *Tsavo Safari Camp*, located 15 miles from Mtito Andei gate on the Athi River, has tents with facilities ensuite. * *Crocodile Tented Camp* has a swimming pool and is located on the Galana River two miles east of Sala Gate on the park's eastern boundary.

CLASS D: * *Aruba Lodge* is a self-service lodge located at Aruba Dam.

CAMPING: Campsites are available at Voi, Sala and Buchuma gates, and at Aruba Lodge. There are little or no facilities.

MASAI MARA NATIONAL RESERVE

This is the finest reserve in Kenya. All the big game is here: elephant, lion, leopard, cheetah and buffalo are prevalent, along with over 20 black rhino. Other commonly sighted species include zebra, wildebeest, Thomson's gazelle, eland,

Cheetah and cub in the Masai Mara. Photo: Mike Appelbaum.

and Masai giraffe. This is the only place in Kenya where topi are common.

Masai Mara National Reserve, a northern extension of the Serengeti Plains (Tanzania), is located southwest of Nairobi and covers 590 square miles of open plains, acacia woodlands, and riverine forest along the banks on the Mara and Talek Rivers, which are home for many hippos, crocs and water fowl.

One of the best places to look for game (including African wild dog) is in the **Mara Triangle** in the western part of the reserve, bounded by the Siria (Esoit Oloololo) Escarpment

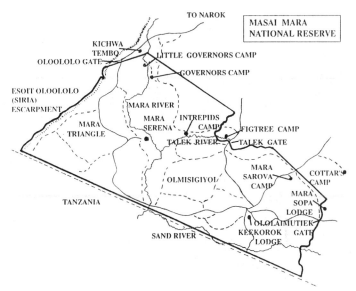

rising 1000 feet above the plains on the west, the Tanzanian border to the south and the Mara River to the east. A multitude of savannah animals can be found on these open grasslands. Lion are distributed throughout the park. Cheetah are most often seen on the short grass plains. Rhino are most highly concentrated in the Olmisigiyoi Region in the center of the park, in the northwest and extreme east parts of the park; there are no rhino in the Mara Triangle.

The best time to visit is during the Serengeti migration from approximately mid/late-July to mid-September when great herds of wildebeest (1.4 million) and zebra (400,000) reside in the area before returning to Tanzania. At this time prides of 40 or more lion may be seen. From the Serengeti of Tanzania, the migration moves to Lake Victoria, then north across the Mara River into Kenya in search of grass, usually returning to Tanzania in October.

Over a period of three days during my most recent visit, we saw wild dog, five rhino, lion, spotted hyena, a herd of 40 elephant and several smaller herds, buffalo, Masai giraffe, black-backed jackal, wildebeest, zebra, topi, and ostrich, among other species.

In the Mara Triangle and the northwestern part of the park, four-wheel-drive vehicles are recommended. There are two

The guy on the left looks like he could use a little help.
Photo: Mike Appelbaum.

flights a day from Nairobi servicing the park. Keekorok Lodge is located about 170 miles and the Mara Serena about 210 miles from Nairobi.

Fishing safaris by private air charter to **Rusinga Island** on Lake Victoria are available from all the camps (book in advance).

Elephant crossing the Mara River. Photo: Mike Appelbaum.

ACCOMMODATION: All lodges and camps listed below either conduct hot-air balloon safaris or will take you to where one is being offered. Many guests fly into the Mara (highly recommended) and are taken game viewing in four-wheel-drive vehicles. Most camps and lodges are a five-to-six-hour drive from Nairobi.

ACCOMMODATION IN THE RESERVE — CLASS A: * *Mara Intrepids Club* is situated on the Talek River and has 22 deluxe tents (44 beds) with ensuite facilities and swimming pool. Groups of two to four tents share a private mess tent with bar and refrigerator. * *Little Governor's Camp*, located in the northwest part of the park on the Mara River, has 17 tents with facilities ensuite. Guests reach the camp from Governor's (Main) Camp by crossing the Mara River. * *Governor's Camp*, located a few miles from Little Governor's Camp on the Mara River, has 36 tents with ensuite facilities, excellent food and service. CLASS A/B: * *Mara Sopa Lodge*, located on the eastern border of the park high on a ridge overlooking the Mara near Ololaimutiek Gate, has 66 rooms with facilities ensuite, swimming pool and excellent food. * *Mara Serena Lodge*, located in the central western part of the park, has 78 rooms with private facilities and swimming pool.

CLASS B: * *Keekorok Lodge* is an old-style lodge with 91 rooms and 12 tents with private facilities and swimming pool. CLASS C: * *Sarova Mara Camp* has 100 tents with private facilities and swimming pool.

ACCOMMODATION ON THE PERIPHERY OF THE RESERVE — CLASS A/B: * *Kichwa Tembo Camp* has 45 tents with private facilities and swimming pool. * *Mara Safari Club*, located on the Mara River, has 40 luxury tents with ensuite facilities and swimming pool. CLASS B: * *Cottar's Masai Mara Camp* has tents with facilities ensuite. Walks and night game drives are offered. CLASS B/C: * *Fig Tree Camp*, located on the Talek River, has chalets and tents (100 beds total) with facilities ensuite and swimming pool. Walks, night game drives are offered. CAMPING: Sites are located outside the park along the Talek River.

THE WEST

MT. ELGON NATIONAL PARK

Seldom visited, this 65-square-mile park is a huge, extinct volcano shared with Uganda, and at 14,178 feet is the second highest mountain in Kenya. Mt. Elgon also has the giant Afro-alpine flora found on Mts. Kenya and Kilimanjaro.

The forests are often so thick that a full-grown elephant could be standing 20 feet from the road and not be seen. Buffalo, waterbuck, and bushbuck are more likely to be spotted.

Kitum and Makingeny Caves are unique in having a good portion of their size created by elephants. Small herds enter the caves near dusk to spend several hours in complete darkness mining salts with their tusks. Thousands of bats keep the elephants company. Makingeny is the largest, but Kitum is more frequently visited by elephants. During our visit elephant droppings were everywhere, foreshadowing the real possibility of their sources being inside.

To explore the caves be sure to bring two or more strong flashlights. Access to the park is difficult in the rainy season, when four-wheel-drive vehicles are recommended. There are no huts on the mountain; campers must bring their own tents. The park is 255 miles from Nairobi.

ACCOMMODATION — CLASS C: * *Mount Elgon Lodge*, situ-

ated less than a mile before the park entrance, has 17 rooms with private facilities.
CAMPING: Several campsites are available in the park.

KISUMU

Kisumu, located on the shores of **Lake Victoria** about 215 miles from Nairobi, is the third largest city in Kenya with a population of over 125,000.
ACCOMMODATION — TOURIST CLASS: * *Sunset Hotel* has 50 air-conditioned rooms with private facilities and swimming pool.

THE MOUNT KENYA CIRCUIT

ABERDARE NATIONAL PARK

This 230-square-mile park of luxuriant forest includes much of the Aberdare (renamed Nyandarua) Range of mountains. Guests of two tree hotels, Treetops and the Ark, are entertained by a variety of wildlife visiting their water holes and salt licks.

The park can be divided into two sections by altitude. A high plateau of undulating moorlands with tussock grasses and giant heather lies between Ol Doinyo Lasatima (13,120 ft.) and Kinangop (12,816 ft.). This region affords excellent views of Mt. Kenya and the Rift Valley. Black rhino, lion, hyena, buffalo, elephant, eland, reedbuck, suni, black serval cat, bush pig and, very rarely, the nocturnal bongo can be seen.

On the eastern slopes below lies the forested hills and valleys of the Salient, home to rhino, leopard, forest elephant, buffalo, waterbuck, bushbuck, giant forest hog, and black and white colobus monkey.

Night temperatures range from cool to freezing as most of the park lies above 9800 feet. A four-wheel-drive vehicle is recommended for travel within the park. The Ark and Treetops are about 110 miles from Nairobi.
ACCOMMODATION — CLASS B/C: * The *Ark*, a "tree hotel" overlooking a water hole, has rooms without facilities, suites with private facilities (102 beds total), glass-enclosed main viewing lounge, and outside verandas on each level, floodlit for

Treetops Lodge in Aberdare National Park.
Photo: Kenya Tourist Office.

all-night game viewing, and ground-level photo hide. The area near the Ark is a rhino reserve. Game drives into the Salient are offered. Guests usually have lunch at the Aberdare Country Club before being transferred to the Ark and are transferred back to the Aberdare Country Club by 9:00 the following morning. Children under seven are usually not allowed.

CLASS C: * *Treetops*, the first of the "tree hotels" (on stilts), is older and more rustic than the Ark. Guests usually have a buffet lunch at the Outspan Hotel before being transferred to Treetops and are transferred back to the Outspan by 9:00 the following morning. Children under 12 are not allowed.

CAMPING: Only by special permission from the warden. Beware of lions.

MOUNT KENYA NATIONAL PARK

Kenya's highest mountain and the second highest on the continent, Mount Kenya lies just below the equator, yet has

Nocturnal visit of rhino to The Ark. Photo: Mike Appelbaum.

several permanent glaciers.

Mount Kenya's two highest peaks, **Batian** (17,058 ft./ 5199 m.) and **Nelion** (17,023 ft./5188 m.), are accessible by about 25 routes and should be attempted only by experienced rock climbers. **Point Lenana** (16,355 ft./4985 m.) is a non-technical climb accessible to hikers in good condition and is best climbed in the dry seasons. January-February is the best time to go when views are the clearest and temperatures are warmer on top; July-October is also dry but colder. Vegetation changes are similar to those described for the Ruwenzori Mountains (see Zaire) and Mt. Kilimanjaro (see Tanzania).

Rock climbing routes on the south side of the mountain are in best condition from late December to mid-March, while routes on the north side are best climbed from late June to mid-October. Ice routes are best attempted during the same periods but on opposite sides of the mountain. Howell Hut (17,023 ft./5188 m.), located on the summit of Nelion, sleeps two.

Although rarely seen, climbers should be on the lookout for buffalo and forest elephant. Other wildlife that may be encountered includes leopard, duiker, bushbuck, giant forest hog, Sykes' monkeys, and colobus monkeys.

Our getting to Mt. Kenya proved almost as difficult as the

The ground-level photo hide at The Ark. Photo: Mike Appelbaum.

climb itself. My partner and I loaded our backpacks on the handlebars of two motorcycles and began a pleasant drive from the town of Nakuru on a beautiful sunny day. Soon it began to rain and the back roads turned to mud so slick that my bike slipped right out from under me, and I crashed on the rock-strewn road.

The mud became too deep to ride, and we had to push the bikes for miles. We had planned to camp at the Met Station that evening to acclimatize, but darkness overcame us even before we reached the Naro Moru Lodge. As I limped into the lodge covered from head to toe with mud, I thought, What a way to begin a climbing expedition!

Because climbers can ascend to high altitudes very quickly, Mount Kenya claims more than half of the world's deaths from pulmonary edema. My climbing partner had symptoms of pulmonary edema after reaching Austrian Hut (15,715 ft.), and we had to abandon our attempt of Batian Peak and return to lower altitudes. Therefore, a slow, sensible approach is recommended.

The world's highest altitude SCUBA diving record was shattered at Two Tarn Lake (14,720 ft.), one of the more than 30 lakes on the mountain. The previous record of 12,500 feet was set at Lake Titicaca in Bolivia. In addition, climbers are occasionally seen ice skating on the Curling Pond below the Lewis Glacier.

Naro Moru Route

The climb to Point Lenana normally takes two or three days up and one or two down. The first night is often spent at Naro Moru Lodge, or better yet, at the Met — Meteorological Station — (10,000 ft./3050 m.) to assist altitude acclimatization. From Nairobi, drive 105 miles to Naro Moru, then ten miles on a dirt road to the park gate (7874 ft./2400 m.). You may be able to drive to the Met Station unless the road has been washed out by the rains. However, walking is better for acclimatizing to the altitude.

From the park gate, hike for about three and one half hours (six miles) through conifer, hardwood and bamboo forests to the *Met Station*. Beware of buffalo on route. The Met Station has self-service bandas with mattresses, cooking facilities, long-drop toilets and water. In order to help you acclimatize, consider hiking for about an hour up to tree line (10,500 ft./3200 m.) in the afternoon.

From the Met Station, hike through the muddy **Vertical Bog**, a series of muddy hills with patches of tussock grass. In order to keep your boots dry, you may wish to wear tennis shoes through the bog. Cross the Naro Moru River and continue to **Teleki Valley**, where Mt. Kenya's peaks finally come in clear view (if it is not cloudy). Since leaving the tree line, vegetation has changed to tussock grass and heather moorlands with everlasting flowers, giant groundsel, and giant lobelia sometimes exceeding 30 feet in height.

From the Met Station, it takes about six hours to reach *Mackinder's Camp* (13,780 ft./4200 m.), which has a brick lodge and campsites. *American Camp* (14,173 ft,/4320 m.), a camping spot one hour from Mackinder's Camp, is used by some campers who bring their own tents. Water is available from a nearby stream.

Austrian Hut (15,715 ft./4790 m.) is a three-to-four-hour hike from Mackinder's Hut. Another hour is usually required to gain the additional 640 feet (195 m.) in altitude needed to reach Point Lenana, only a half mile away.

Austrian Hut is bitterly cold at night and is most often used by technical rock climbers attempting Nelion or Batian peaks. Many climbers wishing to conquer Point Lenana begin from their camps in the Teleki Valley (Mackinder's, American) long before sunrise to reach Point Lenana shortly after sunrise and return to Teleki Valley for the night. The view from Point Lenana is the clearest and one of the most magnificent panoramas I've seen from any mountain — and well worth the effort!

Around the Peaks

From Mackinder's Camp, hike two to three hours to *Two Tarns Hut* (14,731 ft./4490 m.). Stop for the night or continue for another three or four hours over two passes exceeding 15,000 feet to *Kami Hut* (14,564 ft./4439 m.), located on the north side of the peaks. From Kami Hut, it is a five-to-six-hour hike up the north ridge of Point Lenana or directly to Austrian Hut. Return via the Naro Moru Route described above.

Chogoria Route

This is the most scenic route on the mountain. From the Chogoria Forest Station on the eastern side of Mt. Kenya, hike or drive ten miles to *Bairunyi Clearing* (8858 ft./2700 m.) and camp, or continue for another four miles (four-wheel-drive required) to *Chogoria Lodge* (9898 ft./3017 m.) and stay in their self-catering bandas.

Hike through hagenia forest to *Urumandi Hut* (10,050 ft./ 3063 m.) owned by the Mountain Club of Kenya. Room for camping is available nearby. *Minto's Hut* (14,075 ft./4290 m.) is about a six-hour hike from Chogoria Lodge. Space for tents is available nearby. *Two Campsites*, situated a mile beyond Minto's Hut, is another good place to camp.

Austrian Hut is a four-hour hike from Minto's Hut. Some climbers descend using the Naro Moru Route.

Sirimon Route

Ten miles past Nanyuki on the Nanyuki-Timau Road, turn right on a dirt road and drive six miles to the park gate. Sirimon is the least used and most strenuous of the three major routes on Mt. Kenya.

Mt. Kenya Safari Club.

The northern side of the mountain, being much drier than the western side (Naro Moru Route), has no bamboo or hagenia zone. Acacia grasslands cover much of the northern slopes; zebra and a variety of antelope are likely to be seen.

Although the track continues up to the moorlands to about 13,000 feet (3960 m.), it is better to make your first camp around 8000-9000 feet in order to acclimatize. There is another campsite at 10,990 ft. (3350 m.), five miles from the park gate. About a mile further is *Judmeier Camp* (operated by Bantu Lodge). *Liki North Hut* (13,090 ft./3990 m.) is about a four-hour hike from Judmeier. Another four-hour hike brings you to *Shipton's Cave Campsite* (13,450 ft./4100 m.). *Shipton's Camp* (operated by Bantu Lodge) is a little further up the mountain. Austrian Hut is a five-hour hike from Shipton's Cave.

Lone climbers are usually not allowed to enter the park. The Mountain Club of Kenya (Wilson Airport, P.O. Box 45741, Nairobi; tel: 501747) has meetings at the MCK Clubhouse every Tuesday night around 7:30 p.m.; this is a good place to look for partners.

Huts and camping sites may be booked at Naro Moru River Lodge. Guides and porters may also be booked at the lodge or at the park gate. Tour operators can handle all details.

Little equipment is available in Kenya, so bring whatever you need. For climbing tips and equipment checklist, see

"Mt. Kilimanjaro" in the chapter on Tanzania. ACCOMMODATION NEAR THE PARK — CLASS A: * *The Mount Kenya Safari Club*, located on the slopes of Mt. Kenya outside the national park near Nanyuki about 140 miles from Nairobi, was built by actor William Holden and is the most famous lodge in all of East Africa. The spacious gardens are frequented by many species of exotic birds. Facilities include swimming pool, nine-hole golf course, very comfortable rooms, suites and luxury cottages with fireplaces (264 beds total). The Animal Orphanage contains a number of rare species such as zebra duiker and bongo. Game drives are not conducted here.

CLASS B: * *Mountain Lodge*, about 110 miles north of Nairobi, is a "tree hotel" set in a forest outside the park boundary overlooking a water hole and salt lick, similar to Treetops and the Ark. All 42 double rooms have private facilities and face the water hole.

CLASS C, D & F: * *Naro Moru River Lodge*, located below the entrance to the park, has chalets with private facilities, rustic self-service cabins and a bunkhouse. Climbers often stay here before and after their attempts at Mt. Kenya's peaks. Trout fishing here is very good.

CAMPING: * Camping is allowed at the Naro Moru Lodge and at sites in the park.

OL PEJETA RANCH

This 110,000-acre private game reserve of savannah and riverine forest has a variety of wildlife, including rhino, reticulated giraffe, buffalo, zebra, oryx, kongoni, and Thomson's gazelle. As this is private property, night drives may be conducted. Camels are also available for riding. A four-wheel-drive vehicle may be necessary to reach the camp from the main road during the rains.

ACCOMMODATION — CLASS A: * *Sweetwaters Tented Camp* has 25 huge tents with private facilities facing a water hole, and swimming pool. The camp is located 150 miles north of Nairobi.

MERU NATIONAL PARK

Meru is best known for where Elsa, the lioness of Joy Adamson's *Born Free*, was rehabilitated to the wild. This 300-square-

mile park is located east of Mt. Kenya, 230 miles from Nairobi (via Nyeri). The swamps are host to most of Meru's 5,000 buffalo, sometimes seen in herds of more than 200, and a number of elephant. Oryx, eland, reticulated giraffe, and Grevy's zebra are plentiful on the plains where lion are also most likely to be seen. Lesser kudu, gerenuk, and cheetah can be found along with hippo and crocs within the Tana River. Leopard are also prevalent, and over 300 species of birds have been recorded.
ACCOMMODATION — CLASS C: * *Meru Mulika Lodge* has 66 chalets with private facilities and swimming pool.
CAMPING: Sites are available at Murera Gate and Park Headquarters.

UP THE RIFT VALLEY

LAKE NAIVASHA

Lake Naivasha, about an hour's drive (55 miles) northwest of Nairobi, is a freshwater lake prolific in birdlife and a favorite spot for picnics and water sports for Nairobi residents.
Take a boat ride to **Crescent Island** and walk around this game and bird sanctuary, which is host to zebra, giraffe, several antelope species, and a few camels.
ACCOMMODATION — CLASS B: * *Lake Naivasha Hotel* is a beautifully landscaped hotel with 48 rooms with private facilities, swimming pool and golf course. A special Sunday afternoon tea is served.
CLASS C: * *Safariland Lodge* has 56 rooms with ensuite facilities and swimming pool. Horseback riding is available.
CAMPING: Campsites are available at The Safariland Lodge and Fisherman's Camp.

NAKURU NATIONAL PARK

Nakuru National Park encompasses the alkaline lake of the same name and is frequently visited by hundreds of thousands (sometimes more than a million) of greater and lesser flamingos — more than 400 bird species in all. Located 100 miles northwest of Nairobi on a fair road, the park covers 78 square miles — most of which is the lake itself.

Other wildlife includes leopard, Rothschild's giraffe (introduced), waterbuck, reedbuck, hippo, baboon, pelican, and cormorant. Rhino were introduced to the park and are closely guarded in a fenced area.

ACCOMMODATION — CLASS C: * *Sarova Lion Hill Lodge* is located in the park and has bandas with ensuite facilities and swimming pool.

CAMPING: Camping sites with running water are available in the park.

NYAHURURU FALLS (THOMPSON'S FALLS)

Thompson's Falls, located at 7800 feet altitude about 115 miles above the Rift Valley between Nanyuki and Nakuru, is a refreshing place to relax.

ACCOMMODATION — CLASS C: * *Thompson's Falls Lodge* is a rustic country hotel; rooms have private facilities.

LAKE BOGORIA NATIONAL RESERVE

The Lake Bogoria National Reserve, located north of Nakuru, has numerous hot springs and geysers along the lake shore. Thousands of flamingos frequent this alkaline lake, as do greater kudu on the steep slopes of the lake's eastern and southern shores.

CAMPING: Three campsites, Acacia, Riverside and Fig Tree, are situated at the south end of the lake.

LAKE BARINGO

Lake Baringo, a freshwater lake located 20 miles north of Lake Bogoria, is a haven for a colorful and mixed variety of birdlife (over 400 species recorded) and a sporting center for water skiing, fishing and boating.

The early morning boat ride along the lake shore is one of the finest bird watching excursions I've experienced. Hippo, crocodile, fishermen and villages along the shore may also be seen.

ACCOMMODATION — CLASS B: * *Island Camp* is a very peaceful tented camp located in the center of Lake Baringo on Ol Kokwa Island. All tents have private facilities. Take a walk and you may see a few waterbuck and meet the Njemps tribes-

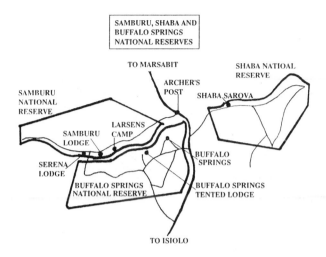

SAMBURU, SHABA AND
BUFFALO SPRINGS
NATIONAL RESERVES

people who also inhabit the island. Boat safaris and water sports (beware of hippo and crocs) are available. * *Lake Baringo Lodge* has rooms (100 beds) with ensuite facilities and swimming pool. Boat and fishing trips are offered.

CLASS F: * *Betty Robert's Campsite*, situated on the lake shore, has bandas.

CAMPING: * *Betty Robert's Campsite.*

THE NORTH

SAMBURU NATIONAL RESERVE

This relatively small (40-square-mile), but excellent park of scrub desert, thornbush, riverine forest, and swamps along the Ewaso Ngiro River is situated north of Mt. Kenya.

Elephant and lion are plentiful as are Beisa oryx, Somali ostrich, reticulated giraffe, gerenuk, Grevy's zebra, and other species adapted to an arid environment.

The park is located about 220 miles north of Nairobi.

ACCOMMODATION — CLASS A: * *Larsen's Tented Camp*, situated on the banks of the Ewaso Ngiro River, has 13 double and four huge suite tents, all with facilities ensuite (34 beds total).

Grevy's zebra.

Beisa oryx.

The gerenuk, or "giraffe antelope." Photo: Mike Appelbaum.

CLASS B: * *Samburu Serena Lodge*, also situated on the banks of the Ewaso Ngiro River, has 52 rooms with facilities ensuite and swimming pool. The lodge baits for croc and leopard. * *Samburu Lodge*, located on the banks of the Ewaso Ngiro River, has rooms, cottages and tents (75 units) with private facilities and swimming pool. The lodge baits for croc and leopard.

CAMPING: Campsites are located along the Ewaso Ngiro River between the West Gate and Samburu Lodge. Most sites have long-drop toilets only.

Somali ostrich. Photo: Mike Appelbaum.

BUFFALO SPRINGS NATIONAL RESERVE

Buffalo Springs is located south of the Ewaso Ngiro River, which serves as its northern border with Samburu National Park. The unusual doum palm, the only palm tree species whose trunk divides into branches, grows to over 60 feet in height in this arid park. Wildlife seen here is similar to what is seen in Samburu National Park.

On a two-hour game drive during our most recent visit, we encountered oryx, gerenuk, Grant's gazelle, waterbuck, and two large herds of elephant. Baboon are often found drinking at the springs.

CLASS C: * *Buffalo Springs Tented Camp* has tents and bandas (76 beds) with private facilities, and swimming pool. The camp baits for crocodile.

CAMPING: Campsites have no facilities.

Shaba National Reserve.

SHABA NATIONAL RESERVE

The turnoff to the entrance to Shaba National Reserve is located east of Samburu National Reserve, two miles south of Archer's Post. The Ewaso Ngiro River forms the reserve's northwestern border and flows through the western part of the reserve.

The park is characterized by rocky hills and scattered thornbush. Volcanic rock is present in many areas. Mt. Shaba, a 5300-foot-high volcanic cone after which the park was named, lies to the south of the park.

A marsh in the center of the park is a good spot to look for game. During my most recent visit to this rugged, rocky park, we spotted oryx, gerenuk, common waterbuck, Thomson's and Grant's gazelle, dikdik, and ostrich.

Wildlife is less abundant and cannot be approached as closely as in the Samburu and Buffalo Springs National Reserves. However, there is much less traffic in this reserve.

ACCOMMODATION — CLASS A: * *Shaba Sarova Lodge*, situated on the Ewaso Ngiro River. This resort-style lodge has rooms with facilities ensuite and a huge swimming pool.

CAMPING: Ask at the gate.

MARALAL NATIONAL SANCTUARY

Maralal National Sanctuary, located northwest of Samburu and 95 miles north of Nyahururu (205 miles from Nairobi) near the town of Maralal, has zebra, buffalo, eland, impala and hyena which come to drink at the water hole adjacent to the Maralal Safari Lodge. Leopard are baited and can often be seen just before sunset from the blind near the lodge. We fortunately saw two of these fascinating creatures during our visit.

ACCOMMODATION — CLASS B: * *Maralal Safari Lodge* has 24 cabins with fireplaces, private facilities and swimming pool.

CLASS F & CAMPING: * *Yare Safaris Hostel and Campsite*, located two miles south of Maralal, has bandas, dormitories and campsites.

LAKE TURKANA

Called the Jade Sea because of its deep green color, Lake Turkana is a huge inland sea surrounded by semidesert near the Ethiopian border, three days of hard driving over rough terrain from Nairobi.

Formerly named Lake Rudolf, this huge lake is over 175 miles long and 10 to 30 miles wide, set in a lunar-like landscape of lava rocks, dried up river beds and scattered oases.

The brown Omo River flows from the Ethiopian highlands into the northern part of the lake where the water is fairly fresh, but becomes increasingly saline further south due to intense evaporation. The presence of puffer fish imply that the lake was at one time connected to the Mediterranean Sea by the River Nile.

One of the continent's largest populations of crocodiles is found here. Because the bitter alkaline waters render their skins useless for commercial trade, crocodiles are not hunted and grow to abnormally large sizes. Although the water is very tempting in such a hot, dry climate, swim only at your own risk!

Fishing is a major attraction. Nile perch, the world's largest freshwater fish, can exceed 400 pounds. Tiger fish, however, put up a more exciting fight. The El Molo tribe, the smallest tribe in Kenya (about 500 members), can be found near Loyangalani.

Central Island National Park, a two-square-mile island containing three volcanic cones, is the most highly concentrated breeding ground of crocodiles in Africa. Half-day excursions are available from Lake Turkana Lodge. Excursions to **South Island National Park**, also volcanic and full of crocodiles, are available from the Oasis Lodge.

Easiest access to the park is by small aircraft. Four-wheel-drive vehicles are necessary. Loyangalani is about 415 miles and Ferguson's Gulf about 500 miles north of Nairobi.

ACCOMMODATION — CLASS C: * *Lake Turkana Lodge*, situated on the western shore of the lake on Ferguson's Gulf, has thatched roof, double bandas with private facilities, and swimming pool. Fishing boats and equipment are available for hire. * *Oasis Lodge*, located on the southeastern shore of the lake at Loyangalani, has rooms with facilities ensuite, two swimming pools, fishing boats and equipment for hire.

CLASS D: * *El Molo Lodge* has bandas.

CAMPING: At El Molo Lodge, Sunset Strip Campsite and El Molo Bay.

THE COAST

MOMBASA

Mombasa is the second largest city in Kenya with a population of over 600,000. This island 307 miles from Nairobi on a paved road, is a blend of the Middle East, Asia and Africa.

The **Old Harbor** is a haven for dhows carrying goods for trade between Arabia and the Indian subcontinent and Africa, especially December-April. **Kilindini** ("place of deep water") is the modern harbor and largest port on the east coast of Africa.

Built by the Portuguese in 1593, **Fort Jesus** now serves as a museum. The **Old Town** is Muslim and Indian in flavor with winding, narrow streets and alleys too narrow for cars, tall 19th century buildings with handcarved doors and overhanging balconies, and small shops. Old Town and Fort Jesus are best seen on foot.

Mombasa is the best place in Kenya for excellent Swahili food. The Tamarind Restaurant, located just north of Mombasa, and the Nomad Restaurant, located in Diani Beach, serve

The Kenyan coast has beautiful white sand beaches that are especially popular with Europeans in winter.

excellent seafood.

The city of Mombasa has no beaches so most international visitors stay on the beautiful white sand beaches to the south or north of the island. Nyali Beach, Mombasa Beach, Kenyatta Beach and Shanzu Beach lie just to the north of Mombasa, while Diani Beach lies about 20 miles to the south.

Most beach hotels on the coast offer a variety of water sports for their guests, including sailing, wind surfing, water skiing, SCUBA diving and snorkeling on beautiful coral reefs. ACCOMMODATION IN MOMBASA — TOURIST CLASS: * *Castle Hotel*, located on Mombasa Island, has 59 rooms with facilities ensuite. ACCOMMODATION JUST NORTH OF MOMBASA — DELUXE: * *Hotel Inter-Continental*, located eight miles north of Mombasa, is a five-star hotel with 192 air-conditioned rooms with facilities ensuite, swimming pool, health club, squash and tennis. * *Nyali Beach Hotel* has 235 air-conditioned rooms with ensuite facilities and minibars, disco, nightclub and swimming pool. * *Serena Beach Hotel* has air-conditioned rooms with

facilities ensuite, swimming pool and tennis.
FIRST CLASS: * *White Sands Hotel* has 170 air-conditioned rooms with private facilities, swimming pool and tennis.
ACCOMMODATION JUST SOUTH OF MOMBASA ON DIANI BEACH — DELUXE: * *Diani Reef Hotel* has 149 air-conditioned rooms with facilities ensuite, swimming pool, dive school, and tennis courts.
FIRST CLASS: * *Jadini Beach Hotel* has air-conditioned rooms with private facilities and swimming pool.
CAMPING: Campsites available at *Twiga Lodge* (Tiwi Beach) and *Dan's Trench* (Diani Beach).

SOUTH OF MOMBASA

KISITE MPUNGUTI MARINE RESERVE

Kisite Mpunguti Marine Reserve is situated near the small fishing village of **Shimoni** ("place of the caves") where slaves were held before shipment, near the Tanzanian border far from the mainstream of tourism. Delightful boat excursions to **Wasini Island**, an ancient Arab settlement across a channel from Shimoni, and snorkeling excursions are available.

The **Pemba Channel**, just off Shimoni, is one of the world's finest marlin fishing grounds. The nearest diving equipment rentals are in Diani Beach.

ACCOMMODATION — TOURIST CLASS: * *Shimoni Reef Fishing Lodge* and the *Pemba Channel Fishing Club* have rooms with private facilities.

NORTH OF MOMBASA

MALINDI-WATAMU MARINE NATIONAL RESERVE

Malindi-Watamu Marine National Reserve encompasses the area south of Malindi to south of Watamu, from 100 feet to three nautical miles offshore, and has very good diving and snorkeling.

ACCOMMODATION IN WATAMU — FIRST CLASS * *Hemingway's* has rooms with private facilities, swimming pool, and charter boats for deep-sea fishing and diving.

Lamu town.

MALINDI

Malindi, located 75 miles north of Mombasa (two hours by car), has numerous beach hotels, nightclubs and shops. The International Bill Fishing competition is held here every January.

The waters are occasionally muddied by the Galana (Sabaki) River, which flows into the Indian Ocean just north of Malindi.

TOURIST CLASS: * *Driftwood Beach Club* has rooms with private facilities and swimming pool.

CAMPING: * *Silversands Campsite* is one mile north of town.

LAMU

Swahili culture has changed little in the past few hundred years on the island of Lamu. The only motorized vehicle on the island is owned by a government official, but plenty of donkey carts provide substitutes. Narrow, winding streets and a maze of alleyways add to the timeless atmosphere. Many travelers have compared Lamu to a mini-Katmandu.

The **Lamu Museum** has exhibits of Swahili craftwork. Of the more than 30 mosques on Lamu, only a few are open to visitors. The best beaches are at **Shela**, a 45-minute walk

Lamu.

or short boat ride from the town of Lamu to the Peponi Beach Hotel. **Matondoni** is a fishing village where dhows, fishing nets and traps are made. Numerous attractions also lie on nearby islands. The best way to reach the island is to fly; day and overnight excursions from Mombasa and Malindi are available. The road from Malindi is very rough and may be impassable in the rainy season.

ACCOMMODATION — FIRST CLASS: * *Peponi Beach Hotel*, a pleasant beach resort, is located about one mile from the town of Lamu. All rooms have facilities ensuite.

TOURIST CLASS: * *Petley's Inn* has been a landmark since the 19th century with the only bar in town, rustic atmosphere, and rooms with private facilities and ceiling fans.

LUNATIC EXPRESS

Highly recommended is the overnight train between Nairobi and Mombasa for a real taste of old-time colonial Kenya. Dinner and breakfast are served with silver settings on this journey which passes Mt. Kilimanjaro in the night. There are daily departures from both Nairobi and Mombasa.

Dhow off the coast of Lamu.

LESOTHO

LESOTHO

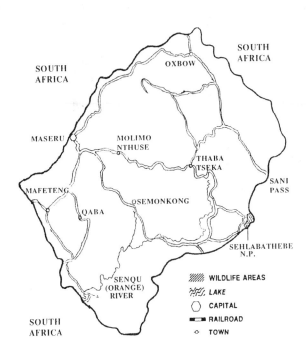

SOUTH
AFRICA

SOUTH
AFRICA

OXBOW

MASERU

MOLIMO
NTHUSE

THABA
TSEKA

SANI
PASS

MAFETENG

QABA

OSEMONKONG

SEHLABATHEBE
N.P.

SOUTH
AFRICA

SENQU
(ORANGE)
RIVER

///// WILDLIFE AREAS
≈≈≈ LAKE
◯ CAPITAL
▭ RAILROAD
◇ TOWN

FACTS AT A GLANCE

AREA:	11,700 SQUARE MILES
APPROXIMATE SIZE:	MARYLAND OR BELGIUM
POPULATION:	1.7 MILLION (1990 EST.)
CAPITAL:	MASERU (POP. EST. 110,000)
OFFICIAL LANGUAGES:	ENGLISH AND SESOTHO
	ENGLISH IS WIDELY SPOKEN.

Day pony treks are available from Molimo Nthuse to refreshing Qiloane Falls. Photo: Sun International.

LESOTHO

Lesotho is a rugged country with spectacular mountain scenery which can best be explored on pony treks, hiking and camping in the remote regions of the country. Called the "Kingdom in the Sky," Lesotho has the highest lowest altitude of any country in the world. The lowest point is 4530 feet above sea level, higher than the lowest point of any other country; most of the country lies above 6000 feet.

Lesotho is an "island" surrounded by the Republic of South Africa which makes it one of only three countries in the world (including the Vatican and the Republic of San Marino) surrounded entirely by one other country.

The country is called Lesotho (pronounced *Lesutu*), an individual is called Mosotho, and the people Basotho. Many men wear multi-colored traditional blankets to keep them warm in the cool and often freezing air; they also wear the traditional conical basket hats.

The Basotho are the only Africans to adapt to below-freezing temperatures that can drop to -8° F. Snow can fall in the mountains any time of the year and in the lowlands between March and September. Summer temperatures seldom rise over 90° F. The rainy season is during the summer with 85% of the annual rainfall (about 28 inches) occurring October-April, making many roads impassable.

The western part of the country is lowland with altitudes of 5000-6000 feet. The eastern three-quarters of the country is highland rising to 11,000 feet in the Drakensberg Mountain Range, bordering the Natal Province of South Africa.

Bushmen (Qhuaique) inhabited Basutoland (now Lesotho)

until the end of the 16th century. For the following 300 years, the area was inhabited by refugees from numerous tribal wars in the region; these refugees formed the Basotho tribal group.

Moshoeshoe I reigned from 1823-1870, and his kingdom was powerful enough to keep the warring Zulus at bay. Wars with South Africa from 1823-1868 resulted in the loss of much land, called the "Lost Territory". Lesotho asked to become a British Protectorate to gain assistance in halting the encroachment of its lands by the Orange Free State (South Africa). Lesotho was a British Protectorate for 96 years from 1868 until its independence on October 4, 1966.

Lesotho has the highest literacy rate in Africa. Its economy is based on agriculture and earnings from laborers working in mines in South Africa. Diamonds and tourism are also important foreign exchange earners.

The mountains of Lesotho are Southern Africa's most important watershed; the Highlands Water Project, a large project that involves selling water to South Africa, is underway and promises to provide Lesotho with much needed income.

The two best ways of seeing what this country has to offer is by pony trekking or a four-wheel-drive safari into its most remote regions.

WILDLIFE AND WILDLIFE AREAS

Sehlabathebe National Park, small by African standards, is Lesotho's premier wildlife reserve. The country is more often visited for its scenic beauty than wildlife, which should be considered a bonus.

PONY TREKKING

Lesotho is one of the best countries in the world for pony trekking. The Basotho pony is the chief means of transportation in the mountainous two-thirds of this country and the best way to explore this land of few roads. Bridle paths crisscross the pristine landscape from one village or family settlement to the next.

The Basotho pony is the best pony in the world for mountain travel and was highly prized during wartime. It can climb and descend steep, rocky paths with ease which other breeds of horses would not attempt. The riding style in

Pony trekking. Photo: Sun International.

Lesotho, as in most countries in Africa, is *English*.

BASOTHO PONY TREKKING
AND MARKETING PROGRAM

The Basotho Pony Trekking and Marketing Program is located at Molimo Nthuse, about an hour drive (34 miles) on a good tarred road from Maseru. Escorted day trips to the refreshing rock pools of **Qiloane Falls** and other rides of up to seven days in length are offered. The ponies are well trained and a pleasure to ride.

Pony treks are conducted year-round — in "swimsuit" weather in the summer as well as in cold, snowy weather in winter. Remember, the seasons are reversed from the northern hemisphere!

Accommodation on overnight treks is in Basotho huts (for a small charge) or camping (bring your own tent). Bring your

own food and drink, ice chest, cutlery and crockery, sleeping bag, insulated pad, warm clothing, rain gear, eating utensils, riding boots and pants. For reservations, contact the Basotho Pony Project, P.O. Box 1027, Maseru, Lesotho; tel: 050-314165.
ACCOMMODATION — CLASS C: * *The Molimo Nthuse Lodge* offers 16 rooms with veranda and private facilities in a beautiful mountain setting.

LESOTHO TOURIST BOARD PONY TREKKING

The Lesotho Tourist Board offers a variety of all-inclusive pony treks throughout the country September-April. One of the most interesting treks is a four-day ride from Qaba in southwestern Lesotho to Semonkong and Maletsunyane Falls — the highest single-drop waterfall in southern Africa.

The pony trek begins after examining some interesting Bushman rock paintings and rock pools near **Qaba**. Riding east, the dark-blue skies are broken by high mountains in the distance. Basotho, wrapped in their traditional blankets and traveling on foot and by pony, offer friendly greetings and warm smiles. Riding in a cool breeze on a moonlit night in these remote mountains calms the soul and brings peace and harmony to one's spirit.

The nights are spent in traditional huts usually owned by the headman of the village, providing a first-hand knowledge of how the people live. Hikes to view **Ribaneng Falls** and **Ketane Falls** (495 ft.) are made along the way.

The final destination is **Maletsunyane Falls**, a few miles and less than a half-hour ride from Semonkong. These impressive falls drop over 620 feet in a majestic setting.

Semonkong is a dusty little town resembling America's "Wild, Wild West" with a general store, hitching posts, stables and horses providing the main means of transportation. Scheduled flights on Air Lesotho back to Maseru are available.

Bring your own sleeping bag, insulated pad, warm clothing, rain gear, eating utensils, riding boots and pants.

For reservations, contact the Lesotho Tourist Board, P.O. Box 1378, Maseru, Lesotho; tel: 050-322896.
ACCOMMODATION — CLASS F: QABA: * *Fraser Holiday Lodge* is a small self-service lodge with 12 beds. SEMON-KONG: * *Fraser Lodge* is a small self-service lodge with twelve beds; rooms do not have private facilities.

CAMPING: Campsites available at Fraser Holiday Lodge (Qaba) and Fraser Lodge (Semonkong).

THE MOUNTAIN ROAD

This route cuts through the center of Lesotho from west to east through spectacular mountain scenery to "The Roof of Africa." From Maseru the road ascends over **Bushmen Pass** (Lekhalong la Baroa) to **Molimo Nthuse** ("God Help Me Pass") and the Basotho Pony Trekking Station (see above). Between December and March colorful scarlet and yellow red-hot pokers (flowers) may be seen in this area.

Continue to **Thaba Tseka** where the good road ends and four-wheel-drive is necessary to negotiate the tracks that pass small villages and isolated herd-boys. After **Sehonghong** the route descends into the **Orange (Senqu) River Canyon** dotted with unusual rock formations, then climbs over **Matebeng Pass** (9670 ft.) which had snow, sleet and ice cycles during my visit in April, and onward to Sehlabathebe National Park.

SEHLABATHEBE NATIONAL PARK

Sehlabathebe has the highest sandstone formations (including arches) in southern Africa. This park is situated on a high plateau with small lakes offering tremendous views of the Drakensberg Mountains and Natal. Sehlabathebe means "Plateau of the Shield" and has an average altitude of over 8000 feet. Three peaks, called "The Three Bushmen" (Baroa-ba-Bararo), dominate the skyline.

This small 26-square-mile fenced park has oribi, eland, reedbuck, wildebeest, baboons, and abundant birdlife, including the rare lammergeyer.

The best time to visit Sehlabathebe for game viewing, hiking and for some of the best freshwater fishing in southern Africa is November-March. Quickest access is by charter flight. Land access is by a 185-mile drive across Lesotho from Maseru or from South Africa via Qacha's Nek, Sani Pass, or a five-to-six hour hike of 15 miles from Bushman's Nek Lodge.

ACCOMMODATION — CLASS D: * *Sehlabathebe Park Lodge* is a self-service lodge with 18 double rooms. Book through Lesotho National Parks, Ministry of Agriculture, P.O. Box 24, Maseru.

CLASS F: Dormitory accommodation is available.
CAMPING: Campsites are available near the lodge.

MASERU

This is the capital and largest city, and is located in the western lowlands. Sights include the Cathedral and the Royal Lesotho Carpet Factory. The tourist office is next to the Victoria Hotel.

Some interesting day excursions from Maseru include **Thaba-Bosiu** (The Mountain at Night), the table mountain fortress 19 miles from Maseru where the Basotho fought off the Boers, and the **Ha Khotso** rock paintings, considered to be some of the finest in southern Africa, located 28 miles from Maseru off the mountain road.

ACCOMMODATION — DELUXE: * *The Lesotho Sun* is situated on a hill overlooking Maseru, with 238 rooms with ensuite facilities, swimming pool, tennis courts, health club and casino.

FIRST CLASS: * *Casino Hotel Maseru* has 172 rooms with ensuite facilities.

TOURIST CLASS: * *The Victoria Hotel* has 102 rooms — all with private facilities and most with air conditioning, swimming pool and disco.

MAURITIUS

MAURITIUS

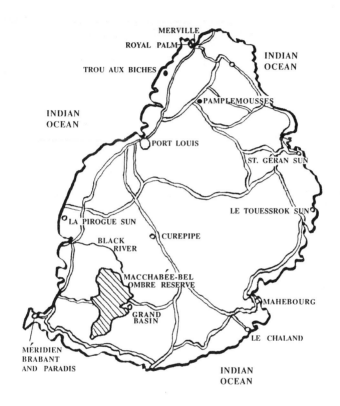

FACTS AT A GLANCE

AREA:	720 SQUARE MILES
APPROXIMATE SIZE:	RHODE ISLAND OR LUXEMBOURG
POPULATION:	1.1 MILLION (1990 EST.)
CAPITAL:	PORT LOUIS (POP. EST. 142,000)
LANGUAGES:	OFFICIAL: ENGLISH, FRENCH AND CREOLE PREDOMINATE.

Ile-Aux-Cerfs (Isle of Stags). Photo: Sun International.

MAURITIUS

If you have come part way around the world to visit Africa, you'll want to think about visiting Mauritius which lies east of the coast of Southern Africa. Mauritius is a favorite destination for jet-setters, celebrities and royalty from around the world, many of whom rate this as one of the best get-aways on earth. The combination of a cosmopolitan atmosphere, virgin-white beaches, crystal-clear waters, exquisite Creole, Indian, Chinese and European cuisine, chic hotels and service to match is difficult to beat.

This mountainous island paradise lies in the middle of the Indian Ocean in the tropics about 1200 miles east of Durban (South Africa), 1100 miles southeast of Mombasa (Kenya), 2900 miles southwest of Bombay (India) and 3700 miles west of Perth (Australia).

As you can see, incorporating a visit to this remote island with a tour on the African mainland or an around-the-world vacation should be seriously considered. The most appropriate and frequently heard phrase on this island is "No Problem in Paradise." Unlike many "paradises," the people here have maintained their genuine and refreshing friendliness in the face of tourism.

This 720-square-mile island has a central plateau with the south being more mountainous than the north. Much of the lush vegetation has been converted into sugar cane and banana fields.

The population of just over one million consists of Indians, Creoles, French and Chinese. Hindu, Muslim, Christian and Chinese festivals occur with uncanny frequency. English is the official language and French is widely spoken, while most of the people prefer to speak Creole.

The island is known for the awkward Dodo bird which, it is believed, lost its ability to fly because there were no predators from which it needed to escape. This evolutionary trait ironically contributed to its demise; the dodo was easily hunted to extinction during Dutch rule in the 1800's.

Creole cooking, emphasizing the use of curries, fresh seafood and tropical fruits, is often served. Mauritian beer and rum are popular.

Mauritius has a tropical oceanic climate. The best time to visit this island paradise for a beach holiday is from September to mid-December and April-June, when the days are sunny and temperatures warm. From mid-December to March is the cyclone season, bringing occasional tropical rains. June-August (winter) nights are cool and the temperatures along the coastline pleasant.

The average daily maximum temperature in January is 86° F. and in July is 75° F. Surf temperatures inside the reefs near shore are around 74° F. in winter and 81° F. in summer.

The first known discovery of Mauritius was by colonizers from Iran in 975 AD, but they chose not to settle. They moved on to what is now Mombasa and Pemba Island. Later in the 16th century, the Portuguese used the island as a staging post along their trade route to India.

The Dutch came in 1598 led by Wybrandt van Warwyck who named the island Mauritius after Prince Maurice of Nassau. However, the Dutch did not settle on the island until 1638. In 1710 they left the island to be replaced by the French in 1715; the French renamed it *Ile de France*. The island then became a "legal" haven for pirates who preyed on British cargo ships in time of war between Britain and France. In fact, this type of pirating was viewed by many as a respectable business.

After 95 years of French control and influence, the British took over in 1810. Slavery was abolished in 1835. As the emancipated slaves no longer wished to work on the sugar plantations, thousands of indentured Chinese and Indian workers were brought in to fill their places.

Mauritius became an independent member of the British Commonwealth in 1968. Mauritius has a parliamentary democracy, holding elections every five years.

Industrial products and sugar are the country's major

exports. Tea and tobacco are also exported.

WILDLIFE AND WILDLIFE AREAS

Mauritius' major wildlife attractions are found both on land and below the surface of the Indian Ocean.

BIRDLIFE

Mauritius has a number of endemic species of birds — birds which are found nowhere else in the world. Many ornithologists or keen birders wishing to add unique species to their lists will find the long journey to this island paradise well worthwhile.

The pic-pic is the only one of the nine known remaining endemic species on the island commonly seen. The pink pigeon is thought to be the rarest pigeon in the world. The Mauritius kestrel is one of the rarest birds in the world; only four were known to exist in 1974. The other endemic species include the fly catcher, parakeet, Mauritius fody, olive white-eye, the Merle, and the cuckoo shrike.

About 45 species in total are found on the island. *Birds of Mauritius*, a book by Claude Michel, is available on Mauritius.

MACCHABEE-BEL OMBRE RESERVE

There are a number of small nature reserves on Mauritius. The best for hiking and spotting the endemic bird species mentioned is the Macchabée-Bel Ombre Reserve, located on the southwest of the island. The reserve's upland and lowland forests provide a variety of habitats for birdlife.

SCUBA DIVING/SNORKELING

The 100-mile coastline of Mauritius is almost completely surrounded by coral reefs, making this an excellent destination for snorkeling and SCUBA diving. There are colorful coral reefs and over 50 wrecks harboring a great variety of sea life on which to dive.

The best conditions for SCUBA diving and sailing are October-March. Most of the larger beach hotels offer dive excursions, dive lessons, and rent equipment.

Spearfishing while diving with an aqualung is prohibited; spearfishing while snorkeling is allowed, but the catch cannot exceed ten fish per day.

BIG GAME FISHING

Big game fish, including blue marlin (plentiful), black marlin, yellow fin and skipjack tuna, jackfish, wahoo, barracuda, sea bass and many species of sharks can be caught. Fishing is excellent only a few miles off shore; the ocean drops to over 2300 feet in depth just one mile out!

The best fishing is from December-March and is sometimes good as late as May. An international fishing tournament is held every year in December.

The largest fleets of deep-sea fishing boats are based at the Centre de Pêche at Rivière Noire (Black River) and at the Organization de Pêche du Nord at Trou-aux-Biches. Boats can be hired through your hotel or travel agencies and should be booked well in advance during this season. Fishing in the lagoons during this same period is also very good.

PORT LOUIS

Port Louis is the chief harbor and capital city with a population of approximately 142,000. The city is partially surrounded by mountains and is multifaceted in character. Port Louis has a large market selling indigenous fruits and vegetables, pareos (colorful cloth wraps) and other clothing and souvenirs. Just off the main square along Place d'Armes are some 18th century buildings including the Government House and Municipal Theatre (18th century).

Chinatown is also worth a visit. The Chinese casino, L'Amicale de Port Louis, located on Royal Street, is popular. The season for horse racing at the Champ de Mars is from May to November.

CUREPIPE

Curepipe is a large town located on the central plateau and is a good place to cool off from the warm coast and to shop. The extinct volcano, Trou aux Cerfs, may be visited nearby.

PAMPLEMOUSSES

The world-renowned botanical gardens of Pamplemousses have dozens of bizarre plants and trees including the talipot palm — at 100 years of age, it blooms for the first time then dies. Giant water lilies imported from Brazil are also found here.

TERRES DE COULEURS

The land takes on the colors of the rainbow (on sunny days) at Terres de Couleurs (the colored earth), located in the southwest in the mountains near Chamarel.

GRAND BASSIN

Grand Bassin is a lake in an extinct volcano: it is the holy lake of the Hindus who celebrate the Maha Shivaratree, an exotic festival held yearly in February or March.

GORGES DE LA RIVIERE NOIRE

Gorges de la Rivière Noire (Black River Gorges) are gorges — located in the highest mountain chain on the island and offer splendid views of the countryside.

ACCOMMODATION — BEACH HOTELS

The beaches, water sports, fabulous holiday hotels and exquisite dining are by far the major attractions of the island.

Hotels are spread out, so visitors spend most of their time enjoying the many activities and sports their particular hotel has to offer. In many of the top hotels, most water and land sports, with the exception of SCUBA diving, horseback riding and big-game fishing, are free, including wind-surfing, water-skiing, sailing, snorkeling, volleyball, golf and tennis. Small sailboats are available at most resorts. Casinos are operated at the St. Géran Sun, La Piroque Sun, Méridien Brabant and Paradis and Trou aux Biches.

St. Géran Sun Hotel located on Pointe de Flacq.
Photo: Sun International.

If you wish to visit the island during the high season, December-February and July-August, I suggest you book your trip several months in advance. Demand for accommodation in the top hotels is high year-round.

DELUXE * *Royal Palm Hotel* is an elegant 84-room deluxe hotel located on Grand Bay on the northwest tip of the island. This is a good hotel for couples looking for a quiet hotel with nightly entertainment. * *St. Géran Sun* is a hotel resort of the highest standard with an international flair unmatched on the island. If you are going to see anyone famous while on this island, it will probably be here. Located on Pointe de Flacq on the east coast of the island, facilities include a casino, 9-hole golf course, sailing and SCUBA diving. All 177 rooms are air-conditioned with private facilities. * *Le Touessrok Sun Hotel* is a splendid holiday hotel, situated on the east coast south of the St. Géran at Trou d'Eau Douce. Facilities include two swimming pools, two superb restaurants, disco, shops, and beauty parlor. What truly sets this resort apart from the rest is the pristine Ile-aux-Cerfs (Isle of Stags). Guests have complimentary transfers by boat to this nearby island. Ile-aux-Cerfs has miles and miles of the most beautiful beaches you will ever see. The hotel has 162 air-conditioned rooms, each with private facilities, refrigerator and mini-bar. * *Méridien Paradis* is located in the southwest of the island on a lagoon at the foot of the dramatic Le Morne mountain. The hotel has air-conditioned rooms with facilities ensuite, swimming pool, casino, disco,

Le Touessrok Sun Hotel, located at Trou d'Eau Douce.
Photo: Sun International.

nightly entertainment, and a fleet of deep sea fishing boats.
FIRST CLASS * *La Piroque Sun* is located on a fine white
beach at Flic-en-Flac on the island's west coast. Thatched cottages are spread out from the main building with its distinctive
sail-like roof. There is a casino, and all 234 rooms are air-
conditioned with private facilities. * *Méridien Brabant* has
air-conditioned rooms with private facilities and is situated
next to Méridien Paradis. Guests of the Méridien Brabant may
use the facilities of Méridien Paradis.
TOURIST CLASS * The *Merville Beach Hotel* is a comfortable
hotel situated on Grand Bay near the northern tip of the
island, with 112-air-conditioned rooms with private facilities,
swimming pool, and the usual water sports. * *Beachcomber
Club Le Chaland* is conveniently located four miles from the
international airport on Blue Bay at the southeastern coast.
This 83-room bungalow hotel has a fine beach, all the usual
water sports, and tennis. All rooms are air-conditioned with
private facilities.

La Piroque Sun Hotel at Flic-en-Flac. Photo: Sun International.

NAMIBIA

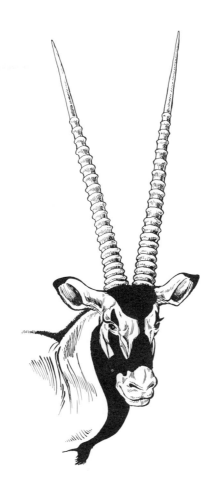

NAMIBIA

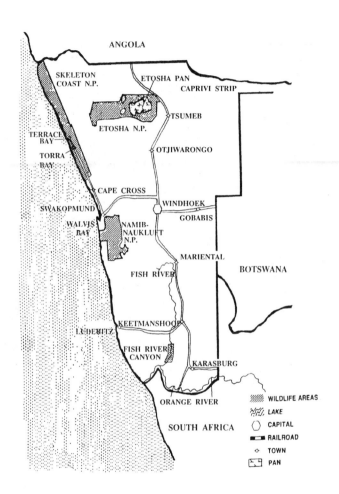

FACTS AT A GLANCE

AREA:	321,000 SQUARE MILES
APPROXIMATE SIZE:	TEXAS + OKLAHOMA OR ONE AND A HALF TIMES THE SIZE OF FRANCE
POPULATION:	1.3 MILLION (1990 EST.)
CAPITAL:	WINDHOEK (POP. EST. 100,000)
LANGUAGES:	OFFICIAL: AFRIKAANS, ENGLISH, GERMAN.

Namibia is a geologist's paradise. The Micha Schist is located inland from Skeleton Coast National Park. Photo: Amy Schoeman.

NAMIBIA

Namibia is one of the most sparsely populated countries in the world. It is famous for its stark beauty and is a geologist's and naturalist's paradise.

Namibia has a subtropical climate. Inland summer (October-April) days are warm to hot with cool nights. Summer is the rainy season, with most rainfall occurring in the north and northeast.

Namibia's population is 86% black, 7% white and 7% colored (of mixed descent). Most people live in the northern part of the country where there is more water. Herero women, colorfully dressed in red and black, continue to wear conservative, impractical and extremely hot attire fashioned for them by puritanical nineteenth century missionaries who wished to cover the savage breast.

In 1884 much of the coast became German South West Africa until 1915 when South Africa took control during World War I. The Union of South Africa received a mandate by the League of Nations over the region in 1920; the United Nations retracted the mandate in 1966 and renamed the country Namibia. The country became independent on March 21, 1990.

Namibia is the world's largest producer of diamonds, and has the world's largest uranium mine. Tsumeb is the only known mine which has produced over 200 different minerals.

WILDLIFE AND WILDLIFE AREAS

Etosha National Park is Namibia's premier reserve for wildlife and is one of the best reserves in Africa. Skeleton Coast and

Namib-Naukluft National Parks have small concentrations of wildlife in fascinating desert environments with spectacular scenery.

Winter (May-September) is the best time to visit the game parks and the central and northern regions when days are warm with clear skies and nights are cold. The rules for Namibia's national parks are the same as for South African national parks. Only closed vehicles are allowed in the wildlife reserves. The parks are well-organized and the facilities clean. For information and reservations contact the Directorate of Nature Conservation (Private Bag 13267, Windhoek 9000; tel: 061-36975; tx: 0908-3180).

THE NORTH

WINDHOEK

Windhoek is the capital, administrative, commercial and educational center of Namibia, situated in the center of the country at 5600 feet above sea level.

Sights include the three Windhoek castles (Schwerinsburg, Sanderburg and Heinitzburg) built between 1913-1918 and the State Museum at the Alte Feste (Old Fort).

ACCOMMODATION — FIRST CLASS * *Hotel Safari*, located two miles out of town, has 200 air-conditioned luxury rooms with ensuite facilities, swimming pool and free transport to and from Windhoek. * *Kalahari Sands* has 180 air-conditioned rooms with private facilities, disco, swimming pool, and fitness center.

TOURIST CLASS * *Continental Hotel* has 70 air-conditioned rooms, most with ensuite facilities, a popular nightclub and disco.

CAMPING: * *Daan Viljoen Game Park*, 17 miles from Windhoek, has campsites available.

ETOSHA NATIONAL PARK

Etosha is Namibia's foremost attraction and one of Africa's greatest parks, covering 8600 square miles in the northern part of the country. Etosha lies 3300-4900 feet above sea level.

The park is mainly mixed scrub, mopane savannah and dry woodland surrounding the huge Etosha Pan. The pan is a

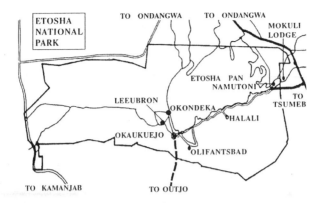

silvery-white shallow depression, dry except during the rainy season. Mirages and dust-devils play across what was once a lake fed by a river that long ago changed course. Along the edge of the pan are springs that attract wildlife during the dry winter season.

The eastern areas of the park experience the most rainfall and have denser bush than the northwestern region which is mainly open grasslands. About 40 water holes spread out along 500 miles of roads provide many vantage points from which to watch game.

Etosha is famous for its huge elephant population which is most visible August-September in the center of the park. When the rains begin in October-November, elephants migrate north to Angola and west to Kaokoland and begin returning in March. Large populations of zebra, blue wildebeest, springbok and gemsbok (oryx) migrate westward from the Namutoni area in October-November to the west and northwest of Okaukuejo Camp where they stay until around March-May. From June-August they migrate eastward again past Okaukuejo and Halali Camps to the Namutoni plains where there is water year-round. The park is totally fenced although this does not always stop the elephants from going where they please.

Lion are commonly seen, and zebra are often sighted way out on the barren pan where lions have no cover from which to launch an attack. Black-faced impala and Damara dikdik are two distinctive species of this area. Rhino prefer the western regions.

The Etosha Pan.

During my most recent visit, we spotted black rhino, elephant, lion, red hartebeest, greater kudu, giraffe, gemsbok, zebra, blue wildebeest, springbok, black-faced impala, black-backed jackal, honey badger, warthog and mongoose. Other wildlife in the park includes brown hyena, spotted hyena, caracal, African wild cat, leopard, cheetah, aardwolf, silver fox, bat-eared fox, eland, roan and grey duiker.

Birdlife is prolific with over 325 species recorded, particularly on the Etosha Pan during the summer rainy season from mid-January to March. However, a diverse range of bird species can be seen year-round. Kites, pelicans, greater and lesser flamingos, and marabou storks migrate seasonally. Other species commonly sighted include kori bustards, guinea fowl, francolins, ostrich, turtle doves, lilac-breasted roller, Namaqua sandgrouse and crimson-breasted shrike (Namibia's emblem bird).

Roads run along the eastern, southern and western borders of the Etosha pan. The area around Namutoni Camp in the eastern part of the park receives more rain than other regions of the park. Eland, kudu and the Damara dikdik, Afri-

Zebra at one of many water holes in Etosha National Park.

ca's smallest antelope, are often seen in this area. A good spot to see elephants is at Olifantsbad, a water hole between Halali and Okaukuejo Camps.

At the floodlit water hole at Okaukuejo Camp, we witnessed a stand off between a black rhino and two elephants over control of the waterhole. A lioness also came for a drink. The flatulence of the elephants was almost deafening!

From Okaukuejo one can drive west along the southern edge of the pan to Okondeka and west to the Haunted Forest, a dense concentration of eerie-looking African moringa trees. I wouldn't want to walk through this forest at night! On the road from Okaukuejo to Leeubron, one passes under a social weaver's nest (bird's nest) the size of a car.

ACCOMMODATION — CLASS B: * *Mokuti Lodge*, located 500 yards from the Van Lindequist Gate (near Namutoni Camp), has 110 air-conditioned chalets with private facilities, swimming pool and air strip. Guided tours of the park are available. CLASS C/D: There are three National Park camps: Namutoni, Halali, and Okaukuejo. All three camps have lodge accommodations, caravan and camping sites, swimming pool, restaurant, store, petrol station and landing strip. The camps are fenced for the visitor's protection. In spite of this, jackal roam through the camps and will snatch food left unguarded, even meat right off the grill, but they are no danger to campers. Namutoni and Okaukuejo are open year-round while Halali is presently open from the second Friday in March to October 31. * *Namutoni Camp*, situated in the eastern part of the park seven miles from the Van Lindequist Gate, features a very attractive fortress built in 1903 and converted to hotel rooms, many of which have private facilities. * *Halali Camp*, the most modern of the camps, lies halfway between Namutoni and Okaukuejo Camps at the foot of a dolomite hill. Some rooms have private facilities. * *Okaukuejo Camp* lies to the west of the other camps, 11 miles from the Anderson Gate entrance. Okaukuejo has a floodlit water hole. All rooms have private facilities.

THE COAST

The freezing Benguela Current of the Atlantic flows from Antarctica northward along the Namibian coastline and meets the hot, dry air of the Namib Desert, forming a thick fog bank which often penetrates inland up to 60 miles. The best time to visit the coast for sunbathing, fishing, and surfing is from December-February; June-July is cold and rainy.

SKELETON COAST NATIONAL PARK

Skeletons of shipwrecks and whales dot the treacherous coast of this park which stretches along the seashore and covers over 2000 square miles of wind-shaped dunes, canyons and jagged peaks of the Namib.

Fog penetrates inland for over 20 miles almost every day and often lingers until the desert sun burns it off at 9:00-10:00 a.m. When the wind blows from the east, there is instant sunshine.

The park is divided into southern and northern sections. The southern section is more accessible and lies between the Ugab and Hoanib Rivers. Permits and reservations (paid in advance) must be made with the Directorate of Nature Conservation for stays at either Torra Bay or Terrace Bay.

The northern part of the park has been designated as a

Dune strata in Skeleton Coast National Park. Photo: Amy Schoeman.

wilderness area and can only be visited with fly-in safaris run by Louw Schoeman. Louw and his wife Amy know this region better than anyone. Amy is the author of *Skeleton Coast* (Macmillan Publishers), a superb pictorial and factual representation of this fascinating region.

From Windhoek guests are flown to Swakopmund, then northward some 370 miles to Louw's fully-catered tented camp between Rocky Point and Cape Frio. Daily excursions from camp are made to explore the area.

A walk down the "**roaring dunes**" will give you the surprise

Louw Schoeman's Camp on the Khumib River (Dry) in the Skeleton Coast National Park. Photo: Amy Schoeman.

of your life. Suddenly everyone is looking up to spot the B-52 bomber that must be overhead. Apparently the sand is just the right diameter and consistency to create a loud noise when millions of its granules slide down the steep dune. Incredible!

Driving through Hoarusib Canyon, one witnesses striking contrasts of dark-green grasses against verdite canyon walls and near-vertical white dunes. Elephant and lion spoor (prints) are numerous. Small fish dart about in shallow ponds as lizards make their way along the rocky walls. One then passes a fairy tale land of castles and other dynamic water-sculptured figures of sand created over eons by this stream. A rising moon, though, places a soft loving spell over this merciless landscape. From February to April, many colorful desert flowers are in bloom.

Large game is not as evident as in Etosha National Park. Many small, but just as fascinating, creatures have uniquely adapted to this environment and help make this one of the most interesting deserts in the world. Larger wildlife includes black rhino, desert elephant, lion, leopard, and baboon. Brown hyena are plentiful but rarely seen. Black-backed jackal, springbok and gemsbok are often sighted.

Lion living along the coast have become especially adapted to living off seals, fish and birds. Lion spore are often seen in or around camp.

The east wind brings detrite (small bits of plant matter) providing much needed compost for plants and food for lizards and beetles. The west wind brings moisture on which most life depends in this desert, which is almost completely devoid of water.

ACCOMMODATION — CLASS C: * *Louw Schoeman's Camp* is a small tented camp in the northern part of the park. Access is by private charter flight from Windhoek.

CLASS D: * *Terrace Bay* is open year-round and offers full board and lodging in basic bungalows with private facilities. There is a landing strip for light aircraft.

CAMPING * *Torra Bay* has tents, campsites and caravan sites, and is open only over the holidays from December 1 through January 31.

SWAKOPMUND

The resort town of Swakopmund, located on the coast and surrounded by the Namib Desert, has many fine examples of German colonial architecture.

ACCOMMODATION — TOURIST CLASS: * The *Hansa Hotel* is an attractive hotel with 34 rooms with private facilities. * The *Strand Hotel* is located on the beach front and has 42 rooms with private facilities.

CAPE CROSS SEAL RESERVE

Cape Cross Seal Reserve, home of over 200,000 seals, is open daily during school and public holidays, December 16th till the end of February, and on weekends and Wednesdays. Safari companies can visit Cape Cross out of season.

THE SOUTH

NAMIB-NAUKLUFT NATIONAL PARK

The consolidation of the Namib Desert Park and the Naukluft Mountain Zebra Park and incorporation of other lands created the largest park in Namibia and one of the largest in the world, covering 8,900 square miles of desert savannah grasslands, gypsum and quartz plains, granite mountains, an estuarine lagoon, a canyon and huge drifting apricot-colored dunes.

The Kuiseb River runs through the center of the park from east to west and acts as a natural boundary separating the northern grayish-white gravel plains from the southern deserts.

Herds of mountain zebra, gemsbok, springbok and flocks of ostrich roam the region. The dunes are home to numerous unique creatures such as the translucent Palmato gecko, the shovel-nosed lizard and the golden mole.

The five main regions of the park are the Namib, Sandvis, Naukluft, Sesriem and Sossusvlei areas.

The **Namib** may well be the world's oldest desert. The Welwitschia flats region lies on a dirt road about 22 miles north of the Swakopmund-Windhoek road and is the best area to see the prehistoric *Welwitschia mirabilis* plants. Actually classified as trees, many welwitschia are thousands of years old and are perfect examples of adaptation to an extremely hostile environment. The water holes at Hotsas and Ganab are good locations to spot game; Ganab and Aruvlei are known for mountain zebra.

If you plan to deviate from the main road through the park, a permit is required and is obtainable weekdays only at the Nature Conservation office in Swakopmund or the Nature Conservation Reservation Office Windhoek.

The **Sandvis** area includes Sandwich Harbour, 26 miles south of Walvis Bay, and is accessible only by four-wheel-drive vehicles. Fresh water seeps from under the dunes into the salt-water lagoon, resulting in a unique environment. Bird watching is excellent September-March, and at times over half a million birds are present. Only day trips are allowed to the harbour and the area is closed on Sundays. Permits are required and may be obtained from Department of Nature

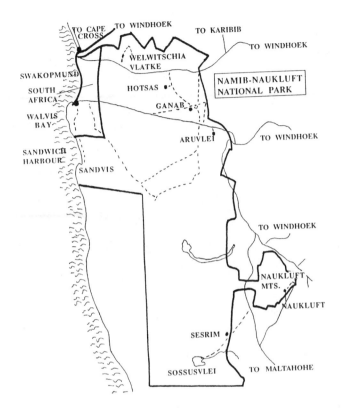

Conservation or from Service Stations in Walvis Bay.

The **Naukluft** region is an important watershed character-ized by dolomitic mountains over 6300 feet in height with massive picturesque rock formations and thickly foliated river beds. Large numbers of mountain zebra, along with springbok, kudu, klipspringer, rock rabbits, baboons and black eagles, are frequently sighted. Also present are cheetah and leopard.

There are several hiking trails from which to choose. One of the more interesting trails is the Naukluft Trail, 10 1/2 miles in length, requiring six to seven hours of hiking.

Sesriem Canyon is about 0.6 mile long and is as narrow as 6 feet wide with walls about 100 feet high. When the river is high, one can swim upstream where the canyon takes on a cave or tunnel-like appearance. The canyon is only a few minutes drive from Sesriem Camp.

Sossusvlei is located in the extreme southern part of the park and has the highest sand dunes in the world, exceeding

Many *Welwitschia mirabilis* trees common in Namib-Naukluft National Park, are more than 2,000 years old.
Photo: Amy Schoeman.

1000 feet. The base of the second highest sand dune in the world is about a 15-minute walk from the closest point to which you can drive. A four-wheel-drive vehicle may be needed for the last two miles before reaching this point.

The hike along the knife-edge rim to the top is strenuous, requiring 1-1 1/2 hours of taking two steps up and sliding one step down. The view from the top into other valleys and of the mountains beyond is marvelous. Even up here, colorful beetles, ants, and other desert critters roam about.

My travels almost ended here when my guide and I dune-

The sand dune, the second highest in the world (about 1,000 ft.), is located at Sossusvlei.

boarded, or slid down this monster of a dune on thin, flat boards. About 900 feet down the side of the dune, traveling at full speed, the front of my board caught on a large clump of grass, and I flipped six times before coming to a skidding stop. My camera and compass were smashed and metal canteen crushed, but it was still a highlight of my trip — though not on my recommended list of things to do.

Driving back to camp from Sossusvlei, a gemsbok ran full speed beside our vehicle for several minutes, proving the strength and resiliency of these majestic animals.

Plan on leaving camp at Sesriem about 5:00 a.m. to see a spectacular sunrise on these magnificent and colorful dunes. At Sossusvlei, camping is not allowed and there is no accommodation.

CAMPING: Campsites with ablution facilities are available in the Namib, Naukluft and Sesriem regions of the park. *Namib Campsites* have no firewood or water. *Naukluft Campsites* have water, firewood and ablution facilities. *Sesriem Campsite* has two ablution blocks with hot and cold water; firewood and fuel are available.

FISH RIVER CANYON

Second in size only to the Grand Canyon, Fish River Canyon is 100 miles in length, up to 17 miles in width, and up to 1800 feet deep. The Fish River cuts its way through the canyon to the Orange River, which empties into the Atlantic Ocean.

The vegetation and wildlife are very interesting. Many red aloes make the area appear like one imagines the planet Mars. Baboons, mountain zebra, rock rabbits, ground squirrels and klipspringer are often seen, while kudu and leopard remain elusive. The river water is cold and deep enough in areas to swim.

There is a well-marked path into the canyon in the north of the park where the four-day hike begins. For those hiking into the canyon for the day, allow 45-60 minutes down, and 1-1/2 hours back up.

The main hiking trail is 53 miles in length and is open May-August. The going is tough since much of the walking is on the sandy, rock-strewn floor. No facilities exist en route, so this hike is not for the tenderfoot. Water is readily available from the many pools that join to become a river during the rainy summers. Hot sulphur springs are located about halfway through the hike.

A maximum group of 40 people is allowed per day. Permits must be obtained in advance from the Department of Nature Conservation. A medical certificate of fitness is also required.

ACCOMMODATION — CLASS C: * *Ai-Ais Hot Springs*, located at the southern end of the canyon at the end of the hiking trail, has rooms with private facilities, refrigerators and hot plates, large thermally heated swimming pool and mineral baths. Ai-Ais is open from the second Friday in March until the 31st of October.

CAMPING: *Campsites at Ai-Ais* have cold showers. Basic camping facilities (no water or supplies) are located in the north of the park where the four-day hike begins.

RWANDA

193

RWANDA

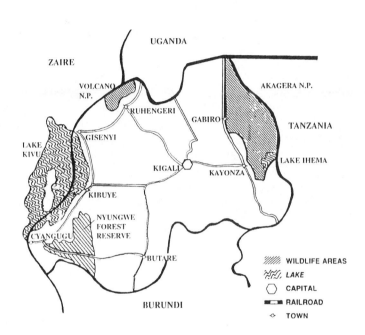

FACTS AT A GLANCE

AREA:	10,169 SQUARE MILES
APPROXIMATE SIZE:	MARYLAND OR BELGIUM
POPULATION:	7 MILLION (1990 EST.)
CAPITAL:	KIGALI (POP. EST. 270,000)
OFFICIAL LANGUAGES:	KINYARWANDA AND FRENCH

Rwanda is appropriately called "The country of a thousand hills."

RWANDA

Mountain gorillas are by far Rwanda's major international attraction. After the release of the feature film *Gorillas In The Mist* about Dian Fossey's pioneering work habituating the gorillas, gorilla trekking reached new heights. Travelers from all over the world venture to this remote country to experience these magnificent animals in their native environment. Watching these fascinating creatures on television is exciting enough but nothing in comparison to the thrill of visiting them first-hand.

Appropriately called, "The Country of a Thousand Hills," Rwanda is predominantly grassy uplands and hills, with altitudes above sea level varying from a low of 3960 feet to Mt. Karisimbi, the highest of a range of extinct volcanoes in the northwest which reach almost 14,800 feet. Lake Kivu forms part of the border with Zaire and is one of the most beautiful lakes in Africa.

Also called "The Country of Perpetual Spring," Rwanda's comfortable climate is temperate and mild with an average daytime temperature of 77° F. The main rainy season is from mid-February to mid-May, and the shorter one is from mid-October to mid-December.

Ninety-seven percent of the people live in self-contained compounds and work the adjacent land. Sixty percent of the population is Christian (80% of which are Catholic), though many people follow traditional African beliefs. About 90% of the population is Hutu (Bahutu), 9% Tutsi (Batusi) and 1% Twa (Batwa) pygmies.

The Tutsi dominated the Hutu farmers with a feudal system

analogous to that of medieval England. The system was based on cattle and was surpassed in Africa only by Ethiopia.

Because of its physical isolation and fearsome reputation, Rwanda was not affected by the slave and ivory trade from Zanzibar in the 1800's. The area peacefully became a German protectorate in 1899 and in 1916 was occupied by the Belgians.

Following World War One, Rwanda and Burundi were mandated by the League of Nations to Belgium as the territory of Ruanda-Urundi. Full independence for Rwanda and Burundi was achieved on July 1, 1962.

High population density is at the root of Rwanda's economic problems. Almost all arable land is under cultivation. Coffee is the country's major export. French and Kinyarwanda are widely spoken while Kiswahili is spoken in the major towns and regions close to the borders. English is spoken in the deluxe hotels and exclusive shops, but very little English is spoken in the countryside.

WILDLIFE AND WILDLIFE AREAS

Rwanda has two world-class national parks — Volcano National Park and Akagera National Park. In addition, the Nyungwe Forest Reserve has a number of species of primates and is rapidly gaining popularity.

Many tourists combine a trip to Rwanda with the parks of eastern Zaire, Kenya and/or Tanzania. The Tourist Office (Office Rwandais du Tourisme et des Parcs Nationaux), B.P. 905, Kigali, tel: 76512, provides information on the parks.

THE WEST

VOLCANO NATIONAL PARK
(PARC NATIONAL DES VOLCANS)

Volcano National Park is home to the mountain gorilla, discovered by Europeans in the early 1900's. The peaks of the Virunga Mountains, heavily forested extinct volcanoes, serve as a border with Zaire and Uganda and are part of the watershed between the Zaire and Nile river systems.

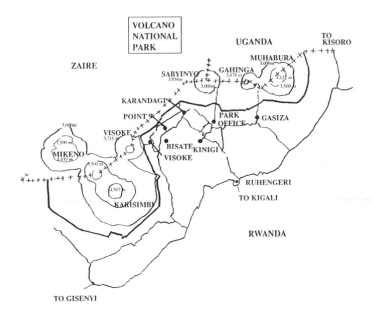

This 46-square-mile park supports several vegetation zones from lowland forest to luxuriant mountain forest to Afro-alpine. From 8500-11,000 feet primary forest is dominated by hagenia trees growing 30-60 feet in height. Hagenia have twisted trunks with low branches covered with luchen out of which parasitic orchids often grow.

Volcano National Park borders Virunga National Park in Zaire and the Gorilla Sanctuary in Uganda. The park receives a high amount of rainfall, averaging 40 inches per year. Daytime temperatures average about 50° F.

The mountain gorilla is larger and has longer hair than the lowland gorilla. It grows to over six feet in height and weighs more than 440 pounds.

Mountain gorillas form themselves into groups of three to 30. They are active by day and sleep in nests at night. Females and their young usually make their nests in trees while the adult males make their nests on the ground.

Mountain gorillas eat leaves, buds and tubers (like wild celery). They are continuously on the move, looking for their favorite foods. They eat morning and afternoon, their dining habits interspaced with a midday nap.

Our guide approaching a mountain gorilla (silverback) in the Volcano National Park.

Fourteen species of primates are found in these forests, including the red colobus and the crested mangabey. Other wildlife in the park includes forest elephants, giant forest hog, black-fronted duiker (very common), yellow-backed duiker and buffalo. Over 90 species of birds have been recorded, including spectacular mountain touracos and black partridges.

Forest elephants are smaller than those found on the savannah and are most often found in the lower forest zone. Forest elephants do not hesitate to climb the steep slopes of the volcanoes and are known to climb to the bamboo zone where they eat the young bamboo shoots.

Gorilla Trekking

Searching for gorillas in the misty mountain air of volcanoes can be likened to an adventurous game of "hide and seek" in which the guides know where they were yesterday but must

Mountain gorilla (silverback) in Volcano National Park.

find their trail again today and follow it. Finding gorillas can almost be guaranteed for those willing to hike one to four hours in search of them.

Each group of visitors is led by a park guide. Porters may be hired (their services are included in most package tours) to carry lunch, drinks, etc., and to assist anyone who may wish to return early.

The search often involves climbing down into gullies, then pulling yourself up steep hills by holding onto vines and bamboo. Even though the pace is slow, you must be in good condition to keep up; the search may take you to altitudes from 7500 to 9800 feet. While this sounds difficult, almost anyone in good physical condition without a heart problem can do it.

Once the gorilla group has been located, the guide communicates with them by making low grunting sounds and imitates them by picking and chewing bits of foliage. Juvenile gorillas are often found playing and tend to approach within a few feet of their human guests. Occasionally our guides had to keep them from jumping into our laps!

Adult females are a little more cautious but may still approach within several feet of you. The dominant male, called a silverback because of the silvery-grey hair on his back, usually keeps more than 20 feet from its human visitors.

Gorilla-viewing "etiquette" is important. Do not make eye contact with a silverback. If a silverback begins to act aggressively, look down immediately and take a submissive posture by squatting or sitting, or he may take your staring as aggression and charge. The key is to follow the directions of your well-trained guide. Gorillas are herbivores (vegetarians) and will not attack a human unless provoked. Please do not touch the gorillas as they are very susceptible to catching human colds and diseases.

After spending up to 60 minutes visiting with these magnificent animals, visitors descend to a more open area for a picnic lunch.

The groups visited by tourists have been numbered or named by the researchers studying them. Gorilla groups 9 and 11 may be visited by up to six tourists each day, and Groups 13 and Susa may be visited by up to eight. However, conservation groups are exerting pressure to keep the maximum number of visitors for all the gorilla groups limited to six persons per day.

Group 13 tends to be the easiest to find; Groups 9 and 11 may take a few hours. Visitors to Group 11 meet at the Visoke departure point. Muside has two departure points for visitors to Group 13, Karandagi or Kanuma, so be sure to learn which is your departure point at Park Headquarters.

Group 9 divides its time between Rwanda and Zaire and therefore permits are sold only at the Park Headquarters at Kinigi up to one day in advance. The trek to visit the Susa Group is demanding and is recommended for very fit hikers only.

Groups 11, 13 and Susa must be booked in advance at the tourist office in Kigali. Children under 15 years of age are not allowed to visit the gorillas.

Visitors must check in at Park Headquarters near Kinigi village, about a 45-minute drive from Ruhengeri, between 7:00-8:00 a.m. Be sure to have your voucher before making the 30-40 minute (up to ten-mile) drive to departure points where the searches begin. Visitors must meet their guides at designated departure points no later than 9:00 a.m.

The most popular time to visit the gorillas is during the dry seasons, mid-June through September and December-March. Use 400 ASA film or higher as gorillas are often found in the shadow of the forest. You will probably want to "push" 400 ASA to 800 ASA to get enough light. 1000 and 1600 ASA films are used by many trekkers. Bring several rolls of film on the trek — you very well may need it!

Mornings are almost always cool and misty; even if it doesn't rain, you will undoubtedly get wet from hiking and crawling around wet vegetation. Wear a waterproof jacket (or poncho) and pants (preferably gortex), leather gloves to protect your hands from stinging nettles, waterproof light or medium weight hiking boots to give you traction on muddy slopes and keep your feet dry, wool socks and wool hat. Bring a waterproof pouch for your camera and plenty of film, water bottle and snacks. Do not wear bright clothes, perfumes, colognes or jewelry as these distractions may excite the gorillas.

Visiting the gorillas is one of the most expensive yet most rewarding safaris in Africa. At present, the cost of a permit for one gorilla visit is approaching U.S. $200, which must be paid in addition to the regular park entrance fee. It is very difficult to get to the park and departure points unless you join a tour (the best option) or rent your own vehicle. There is no public transportation from Ruhengeri to the Park Headquarters or to the trek departure points.

Mountain Climbing

Hiking in the beautiful Virunga Mountains is in itself an adventure. Trails lead to the craters or peaks of the park's five volcanoes, upwards through the unique high-vegetation zones of bamboo, hagenia-hypericum forests, giant lobelia and senecio, and finally to alpine meadows. Views from the top, which overlook the lush Rwandan valleys and into Zaire and Uganda, are spectacular.

Some travelers spend a day or two searching for gorillas interspaced with hikes to one or more of the volcanoes.

Karisimbi (14,786 ft./4507 m.) is Rwanda's highest and occasionally snow-capped mountain. It is the most arduous ascent, requiring two days from the Visoke departure point. The night may be spent in a metal hut at about 12,000 feet (3660 m.).

Visoke (12,175 ft./3711 m.) has a beautiful crater lake and requires four hours of hiking up a steep trail to reach the summit from the Visoke departure point. The walk around the crater rim is highly recommended. Allow seven hours for the entire trip.

Lake Ngezi (9843 ft./3000 m.), a small, shallow crater lake, is the easiest hike in the park, taking only three to four hours round-trip from the Visoke departure point.

Sabinyo (11,922 ft./3634 m.) can be climbed in five to six hours starting at Park Headquarters near Kinigi. A metal hut is located just before you reach the lava beds. The final section is along a narrow rocky ridge with steep drops on both sides.

Gahinga (11,398 ft./3474 m.) and **Muhabura** (13,540 ft./4127 m.) are both reached from the departure point at Gasiza. The trail rises to a hut in poor condition on the saddle between the two mountains. Gahinga's summit can be reached in four hours, while two days are recommended to reach the summit of Muhabura.

A park guide must accompany each group. Porters are optional. Should you encounter gorillas on your hikes, you may not leave the path to follow them. You may only track gorillas if you have previously purchased the proper permits.

ACCOMMODATION — DELUXE: see GISENYI.

TOURIST CLASS: * *Hotel Muhabura* is the best hotel in *Ruhengeri* and has the most convenient access to Volcano National Park. It is about a ten-mile/45-minute drive to Park Headquarters. Ten double rooms and two pavilions with bathrooms ensuite, plus popular bar, disco and dining room are available.

CLASS F: Very basic bungalows located at Park Headquarters have two bunkbeds per room (about 40 beds total) with separate shower and toilet facilities.

CAMPING: The campsites at Park Headquarters near Kinigi have cold shower and toilet facilities. Beware of thieves.

GISENYI

Gisenyi is a picturesque resort on beautiful Lake Kivu with sandy white beaches believed to have little or no bilharzia. Crocodiles are absent from the lake due to volcanic action eons ago which wiped them out, making swimming safer.

ACCOMMODATION — DELUXE: * *Hotel Izuba Méridien* is an excellent hotel with 68 double rooms and four suites with private facilities: it is located 1 3/4-hours drive from Volcano National Park. Situated on Lake Kivu, the hotel has a swimming pool, tennis courts and solarium.

TOURIST CLASS * *Hotel Palm Beach* has rooms with private facilities and is located on the lakeshore drive.

KIBUYE

Kibuye, located on Lake Kivu midway between Gisenyi and Cyangugu, is a small town with an attractive beach. Be sure not to miss the over 330-feet-high **Ndaba Waterfall** (Les Chutes des Ndaba), not far from Kibuye.

ACCOMMODATION — TOURIST CLASS: * *Kibuye Guest House* is located on Lake Kivu and has 18 double rooms with private facilities, tennis courts and sports activities on the lake.

LA FORET DE NYUNGWE (NYUNGWE FOREST RESERVE)

The Nyungwe Forest is one of the most biologically diverse high-altitude rain forests in Africa. Located in southwestern Rwanda bordering the country of Burundi, this 375-square-mile reserve is home for 12 species of primates including a rare subspecies of black and white colobus monkey, the rare golden monkey, blue monkeys and mangabeys.

In addition to a variety of butterflies and orchids, over 200 species of birds have been recorded.

Although Nyungwe Forest Reserve is situated at a lower altitude and is dryer (receives less rain) than Volcano National Park, hiking is more difficult in Nyungwe. The vegetation at Nyungwe is much thicker and many slopes are steeper, if not impossible to ascend. Colobus and the other primates are often difficult to approach closely. However, this will hopefully change with time.

ACCOMMODATIONS: Day trips to Nyungwe Forest Reserve can be made from Butare. See "Accommodations" under "Butare" below.

CAMPING: Campsites have no facilities.

BUTARE

Located in southern Rwanda not far from the border with Burundi, Butare is the intellectual capital of Rwanda. Here you find the National Museum (good archaeology and ethnology exhibits) and the National University and National Institute of Scientific Research (ask about folklore dances). Several craft centers are located in villages within ten miles of Butare.

ACCOMMODATION — TOURIST CLASS: * *Hotel Faucon* and *Hotel Ibis* have rooms with facilities ensuite.

CENTRAL AND EAST

KIGALI

The capital of Rwanda, Kigali is the commercial center of the country and has little of interest for the tourist. There are very good restaurants in the deluxe hotels. The National Tourist Office, or Office Rwandais du Tourisme et des Parcs Nationaux (ORTPN), is located near the post office on Place de l'Independence.

ACCOMMODATION — DELUXE: * *Hotel des Diplomats* has 24 double rooms and 16 apartments, all with ensuite facilities, video and private terraces, and tennis. * *Hotel des Mille Collines* has 112 rooms with private facilities and video, and swimming pool. * *Umubano Méridien* is located a few miles outside the city center.

TOURIST CLASS: * *Hotel Kiyovu* has rooms with facilities ensuite. * *Chez Lando* has rooms with private facilities.

AKAGERA NATIONAL PARK
(LE PARC NATIONAL DE L'AKAGERA)

Akagera National Park is located in northeastern Rwanda along the Akagera River (a Nile affluent) bordering Tanzania. Over 500,000 animals of great variety inhabit the park, including some of the largest buffalo in Africa, along with zebra, giraffe (recently introduced), hippo, crocodile, lion, leopard, impala, Defassa waterbuck, eland, sable, bushbuck, oribi, roan and black-backed jackal.

Akagera is the best place in Africa to see sitatunga, which are often seen from towers overlooking the swamps. Rhino, elephant and leopard are rarely seen. Birdlife is excellent with 525 species of birds recorded — a record for any park or region of this size.

Akagera National Park covers 980 square miles (10% of the country's area) and can be divided into three regions.

The northern part of the park is predominantly low, tree-less hills interspaced with both dry and marshy valleys. Buffalo, zebra, waterbuck, topi, and many other species of herbivore prefer this region. Herds of animals numbering in the thousands can be seen, especially in the dry season.

African buffalo.

Interestingly enough, buffalo, zebra and topi are much larger here than those found in East Africa. Some buffalo males weigh in excess of 2200 pounds with shoulder heights of 6 feet and horn widths of 3.5 feet. In addition, isolation from other populations in East Africa has caused inbreeding, which has resulted in some buffalo with horns twisted and turned in an ungainly fashion and some zebra trading in their stripes for spots — blotches of black and white.

The second region is the most unique and is possibly the best preserved and most diverse swamp in terms of both flora and fauna in East and East-Central Africa. It is composed of three large swamps separated by lakes along the eastern border of the park. Papyrus dominates the swamps. Large numbers of waterfowl, including herons, ducks, storks, waders and plovers can be seen in areas with floating ferns, swamp grasses and water lilies.

At the fishing station (Pêcherie) on Lake Ihema, the largest of the lakes, boats can be rented, or you may join irregularly scheduled group departures to the islands and far shores of the lake. Fresh fish is fried there almost every afternoon and is some of the best I've ever eaten. Plage aux Hippos (Hippo Beach) on Mihindi Lake has picnic facilities and is a great spot for watching hippos, crocodiles and waterfowl.

The third region covers the central and southern areas lying west of the swamps and is characterized by more trees and thicker vegetation than the northern region.

Two hundred and eighty miles of relatively good all-weather tracks run through the park; these tracks are marked with numbered crossroads. Stay in your vehicle, except at marked picnic spots, camping or hotel grounds. Remember, this is not a zoo — the wildlife is wild! French-speaking guides (no English) are available for hire at the gate.

The best time to visit the park is during the dry season, July to September, while February, June and October are also good. Tsetse flies can be a nuisance, but without them the land would probably be used for farming.

ACCOMMODATION - CLASS A: * *Hotel Akagera* is a modern lodge overlooking Lake Ihema with 54 double rooms and six apartments with private facilities and private terraces, video and swimming pool. *Gabiro Guest House*, a rustic lodge located at Byumba at the edge of the park, has 60 double rooms with private facilities.

CAMPING: Several sites are within the park. Permits have to be obtained in advance from the Rwanda Tourist Office in Kigali.

Even in the simplest bush camp, the food is most often very good.

SOUTH AFRICA

SOUTH AFRICA

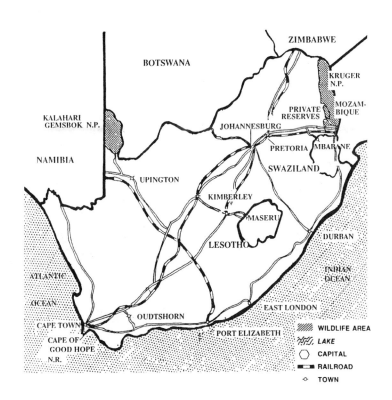

FACTS AT A GLANCE

AREA:	437,900 SQUARE MILES
APPROXIMATE SIZE:	THREE TIMES THE SIZE OF TEXAS OR FIVE TIMES THE SIZE OF GREAT BRITAIN
POPULATION:	32 MILLION (1990 EST.)
CAPITAL:	PRETORIA (POP. EST. 850,000)
OFFICIAL LANGUAGES:	ENGLISH AND AFRIKAANS

Johannesburg skyline. Photo: SATOUR.

SOUTH AFRICA

South Africa is a large country rich in natural beauty and wildlife whose actual size has been made much larger by the news. Actually, it covers less than 3.8% of the continent.

Seventy percent of the total population belongs to four ethnic groups: Zulu (the largest), Xhosa, Tswana and Bapedi. Fifteen percent of the population is white, of which 60% are Afrikaners. English and Afrikaans are spoken throughout the country.

In 1488 the Portuguese navigator Bartholomew Dias discovered the Cape of Good Hope. The first Dutch settlers arrived in 1652 and the first British settlers in 1820. To escape British rule, Boer (meaning farmer) Voortrekkers (meaning forward marchers) moved to the north and east, establishing the independent republics of Transvaal and Orange Free State.

Two very big economic breakthroughs were the discovery of diamonds in 1869, and even more importantly, the discovery of gold in Transvaal shortly thereafter. Conflict between the British and Boers resulted in the Anglo-Boer War from 1899 until British victory in 1902.

In 1910 the Union of South Africa was formed and remained a member of the British Commonwealth until May 31, 1961, when the Republic of South Africa was formed outside the British Commonwealth.

WILDLIFE AND WILDLIFE AREAS

Kruger National Park and Kahalari-Gemsbok National Park are the premier reserves of South Africa. Several private re-

African elephant. Photo: Mike Appelbaum.

serves adjacent to Kruger National Park offer the best options for international visitors, providing excellent accommodations, day and night game drives, and walks.

The parks, reserves and sanctuaries in South Africa are very well organized and maintained, and in many ways are similar to those in North America. National Park accommodations are clean and inexpensive. Campers share ablution blocks with running hot and cold water, and many sites have laundromats. The facilities and infrastructure make this country an excellent choice for self-drive safaris.

Generally speaking, the major roads in the parks are tarred with the minor ones constructed of good quality gravel, allowing for comfortable riding. Tourists must stay in their vehicles, except where specifically permitted, and cannot leave the roads in search of game. Open vehicles are not allowed in the parks, and roof hatches on vehicles must remain closed. Reservations for all national parks can be made by contacting the Chief Director, National Parks Board, P.O. Box 787, Pretoria 0001; tel: (012) 343-1191; fax (012) 343-0907; telex: 32-1324 SA.

Burchell's zebra. Photo: Mike Appelbaum.

THE NORTH AND EAST

Johannesburg began as a mining town when the largest deposits of gold in the world were discovered in the Witwatersrand in 1886. One-third of the gold mined in the world since the Middle Ages has come from the Witwatersrand field.

This "City of Gold" is now the country's largest commercial center and city (pop. two million) and is the main gateway for overseas visitors. Attractions include the Africana Museum, the Gold Mine Museum, and Gold Reef City — a reconstruction of Johannesburg at the turn of the century. The Johannesburg Zoo has a few very rare white lions.

ACCOMMODATION — Deluxe: * *Johannesburg Sun*, the largest hotel in Africa, has 792 air-conditioned rooms with private facilities, swimming pool, gym, squash courts and jogging track. * *Sandton Sun* is located 10 miles from Johannesburg in one of the country's finest shopping malls. The hotel has 334 spacious air-conditioned rooms with private facilities and refrigerator; there is also a health club, swimming pool, and five restaurants, including the exquisite "Chapters." * *Carlton Hotel* is located in a large mall (Carlton Center) and has 463 air-conditioned rooms with facilities ensuite, swimming pool and health club.

FIRST CLASS: * *Gold Reef City Hotel* has 45 rooms (facilities ensuite) beautifully decorated with turn-of-the-century furniture reflecting the Victorian era. * *Braamfontein Protea Hotel* is an air-conditioned, all-suite hotel with swimming pool and gym located on the edge of downtown Johannesburg within walking distance of air and train terminals. All rooms have facilities ensuite. * *Rand International*, located in the center of town, has 143 air-conditioned rooms with private facilities. TOURIST CLASS * *Holiday Inn-Downtown* is centrally located with 258 air-conditioned rooms with private facilites. * *Airport Sun Hotel*, located less than a mile from Jan Smuts International Airport, has 238 air-conditioned rooms with facilities ensuite, swimming pool and sauna.

KRUGER AND THE PRIVATE RESERVES

The most popular area of the country for wildlife safaris is Kruger National Park and the private reserves that lie along its western border. The best game viewing for this region is June-September (the very best is July-August) during the sunny, dry winter season when the grass has been grazed down and the deciduous plants have lost their leaves. This is also the best time to hike the wilderness trails in Kruger and take foot safaris in the private reserves. Calving season is in early spring (September-October) for most game species.

Winter days are usually warm with an average maximum of 73° F. and clear skies. Late afternoons are cool, while temperatures at night and early morning sometimes drop below freezing. From October to February there are light rains, with December, January and February receiving the heaviest downpours with temperatures sometimes rising to 104° F. March and April are cooler as the rains begin to diminish.

The best time to look for over 450 bird species in this region is from October to March — just the opposite from the best game-viewing periods. However, bird watching is good year-round since less than half the bird population is composed of seasonal migrants.

To get to the area, many people take about a one-hour flight to Skukuza, Phalaborwa or directly to their camp. Avis auto rentals are available at Skukuza. Alternatively, the drive from Johannesburg to Kruger (Skukuza) is about 250 miles northeast on tarred roads and takes five to six hours.

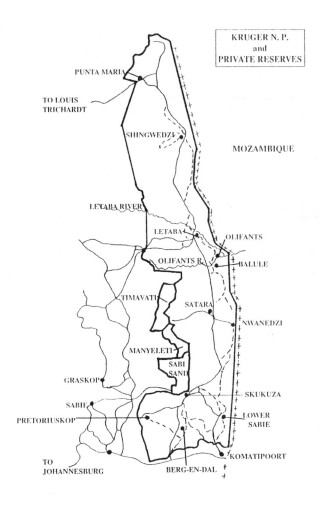

KRUGER N. P.
and
PRIVATE RESERVES

KRUGER NATIONAL PARK

Kruger is the largest South African park and has more species of wildlife than any other game sanctuary in Africa: 130 species of mammal, 114 species of reptile, 48 species of fish, 33 species of amphibians, and 468 species of birds.

The park is home to large populations of elephant (over 8000), buffalo (over 25,000), Burchell's zebra (over 25,000), greater kudu, giraffe, impala, white rhino, black rhino, hippopotamus, lion, leopard, cheetah, wild or cape hunting dog, and spotted hyena, among others.

Kruger's 7700 square miles make it nearly the size of the state of Massachusetts. The park is 55 miles wide at its widest point and 220 miles long. It is totally fenced, cutting off the annual winter migration routes of antelope, zebra and various other species in search of water and better grazing. Several hundred windmills and artificial water holes have been constructed to provide the water so desperately needed in the dry season.

The park can be divided into three major regions: northern, central/southeastern, and southwestern. Altitude varies from 650 feet in the east to 2950 feet at Pretoriuskop in the southwest. Summer temperatures may exceed 105° F. while winter temperatures seldom drop below freezing.

The northern region from the Letaba River to the Limpopo River is the driest. Mopane trees dominate the landscape with the unique baobab (upside-down) trees becoming increasingly numerous towards Pafuri and the Limpopo River. From Letaba to Punda Maria is the best region for spotting elephant, tsessebe, sable and roan antelope. Elephant prefer this area since it is less developed than the other regions, making it easier to congregate away from roads and traffic, and mopane trees (their preferred source of food) are prevalent.

The central/southeastern region is situated south of Letaba to Orpen Gate and also includes the eastern part of the park from Satara southward covering Nwanedzi, Lower Sable and Crocodile Bridge. Grassy plains and scattered knobthorn, leadwood, and marula trees dominate the landscape. Lion inhabit most areas of the park but are most prevalent in this region where there is also an abundance of zebra and wildebeest — their favorite prey. Cheetah and black-backed jackal are best spotted on the plains. Wild or cape hunting dogs are mainly scattered through flatter areas, with possibly a better chance of finding them in the Letaba-Malopene River area and northwest of Malelane.

The southwestern part of the park, including a wide strip along the western boundary from Skukuza to Orpen Gate, is more densely forested with thorny thickets, knobthorn, marula and red bush-willow. This is the most difficult region in which to spot game — especially during the rainy season. Many of the park's 600 white rhino prefer this area.

Black rhino are scattered throughout the southern and central areas, often feeding on low-lying acacia trees. Leopard

are rarely seen. Buffalo roam throughout the park while hippo prefer to inhabit the deeper parts of Kruger's many rivers by day.

Four different wilderness trails (walking safaris) are conducted twice weekly by experienced game rangers: Olifants, Nyalaland, Wolhuter and Bushman Trails. These walks take an easy pace, as you explore the natural beauty of the bush and spot game on foot. A maximum of eight participants between 12 and 60 years of age are allowed per safari. Trails begin at their respective meeting places at 3:00 p.m. on Mondays or Fridays and end after breakfast on the third day.

Travelers wishing to participate in walking safaris but who also prefer their creature comforts should stay at camps in the private reserves (see "Private Reserves" below).

The Automobile Association of South Africa patrols the park, assisting its membership. During school holidays and long weekends, the number of day visitors to the park is limited, so be sure to reserve in advance.

ACCOMMODATION — CLASS C, D & CAMPING: There are 16 *National Park Rest Camps* offering a wide range of accommodations including cottages with private bath, thatched huts with or without private facilities, and campsites. The larger rest camps have licensed restaurants. Many of the cottages and huts have cooking facilities and refrigerators.

THE PRIVATE RESERVES

Along the western border of Kruger lie a number of privately owned wildlife reserves. These reserves are associations of ranchers who have fenced around the reserves but have not placed fences between their individual properties, allowing game to roam throughout the reserves. The private reserves, in general, have exceptionally high standards of accommodation, food and service.

A very important advantage private reserves have over national parks is that private reserves use open vehicles which give not only a better view but also a much better feel of the bush. At most reserves, a game tracker sits on the hood or the back of each vehicle. Drivers are in radio contact with each other, greatly increasing the chances of finding those species that guests want to see most.

Vehicles may leave the road to pursue game through the

At most camps and lodges in the private reserves, a game tracker sits on the hood or at the back of each vehicle. Photo: Sabi Sabi.

bush. Night drives, which are not allowed in Kruger, provide an opportunity to spot game rarely seen during the day. Walking is also allowed.

ACCOMMODATION — SABI-SAND PRIVATE GAME RESERVE

Sabi-Sand Private Game Reserve is situated to the north and northwest of Skukuza and includes Sabi Sabi Game Reserve (Bush Lodge and River Lodge), Mala Mala Game Reserve (Mala Mala, Kirkman's and Harry's Camps), Londolozi (Main Camp, Treehouse and Bush Camp) and Inyati.

Almost all camps offer day and night game drives and walks. Many guests fly via Comair to Skukuza and are transferred to their respective camps, while some guests drive to the camp of their choice or travel by tour bus.

CLASS A: * *Mala Mala* is a very expensive camp (50 beds) with a swimming pool and with air-conditioned thatched rondavels — each with two bathrooms. * *Sabi Sabi* offers deluxe air-conditioned rooms with private facilities and a swimming pool at both of their camps — Bush Lodge and River Lodge. *Bush Lodge* (25 doubles) overlooks a water hole while River Lodge (20 doubles) is set on a riverbank. * *Inyati Game Lodge* has nine thatched chalets (doubles) with ensuite facilities and swimming pool.

CLASS B: * *Londolozi* Game Reserve has three camps, Tree

Camp, Bush Camp, and Main Camp. * *Tree Camp*, the most exclusive of the three properties, is built around a giant ebony tree and has four rooms (doubles). * *Bush Camp* has four rock bungalows. Rooms in all three camps have ensuite facilities. * *Main Camp* accommodates 24 guests in rondavels and luxury suites. * *Kirkman's Camp* has air-conditioned cottages with ensuite facilities and swimming pool. * *Harry's Camp* has seven air-conditioned thatched rondavels with private facilities and swimming pool.

ACCOMMODATION — TIMBAVATI AND MANYELETI GAME RESERVES.

Guests of Tanda Tula (Timbavati Private Nature Preserve), Khoka Moya and Honeyguide (Manyeleti Game Reserve) fly with Comair to Phalaborwa or by charter aircraft directly to Tanda Tula; some guests drive to their respective camps. Each camp has a splash pool (small swimming pool) in which to cool off on hot days. Day game drives and walks are offered.

CLASS A: * *Tanda Tula*, on the Timbavati Game Reserve, has seven air-conditioned thatched brick bungalows (14 beds) with ensuite facilities. * *Khoka Moya Trails Camp* is situated on the Manyeleti Game Reserve and caters to only eight guests in four rustic wood and thatch bandas with facilities ensuite. Daily walking trails and night game drives are offered. * *Honeyguide Safari Camp* is also located on the Manyeleti Game Reserve and caters to a maximum of 12 guests in luxury tents with private facilities. Daily walking trails and night game drives are offered.

SUN CITY

Sun City is a premier entertainment vacation complex with Las Vegas-style floor shows, casino, golf, tennis, and water sports. Sun City is located in Bophuthatswana; it's a two-hour drive by car or a short flight from Johannesburg.

ACCOMMODATION — DELUXE: * *The Cascades* is a luxurious hotel with 245 rooms with facilities ensuite, spectacularly designed and landscaped with lush gardens, waterfalls, and swimming pool; the cuisine is fit for a king. All rooms have ensuite facilities.

FIRST CLASS: * *Sun City Hotel* has 340 rooms with private facilities and swimming pool. * *Sun City Cabanas* has 284 cabanas with facilities ensuite.

Cascades Hotel at Sun City. Photo: Sun International.

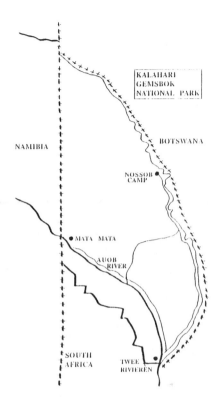

THE WEST AND SOUTH

KALAHARI-GEMSBOK NATIONAL PARK

Located in the northwest corner of South Africa and sharing borders with Namibia and with Gemsbok National Park in Botswana, this 3700-square-mile park is predominantly semi-desert and part desert. Scattered thorn trees and grasses lie between red Kalahari sand dunes. Bushmen inhabited the area as much as 25,000 years ago.

The park features large herds of blue wildebeest, eland, springbok, and the stately gemsbok with their long, straight spear-like horns. Also present are red hartebeest, duiker, steenbok, Kalahari lion, cheetah, brown hyena, and wild dog.

Summer temperatures can exceed 104 ° F. Winter days are pleasant but temperatures can drop below freezing at night.

Gemsbok can survive for long periods of time without drinking.
Photo: SATOUR.

Wells provide water for the animals which have adapted to desert conditions by eating plants with high water content such as wild cucumber and tsamma melon.

Cars may be hired from the Parks Board but must be reserved in advance. Visits to the park by vehicle are arranged by the Town Council of Upington. The southern entrance to the park is about 215 miles north of Upington.

ACCOMMODATION — CLASS D: There are three rest camps with self-contained cottages with kitchens, huts with and without bathrooms, camping sites, stores, petrol and diesel. * *Twee Revieren* is located at the southern entrance of the park. The camp has a swimming pool and a landing strip for small aircraft. A barbecue is served every evening. * *Nossob* is located in the northeastern part of the park near the Bot-

The Big Hole at Kimberly. Photo: SATOUR.

swana border. The camp has an information center about the plant and animal life of the park and a landing strip for small aircraft. * *Mata Mata* is located on the western border of the park.

KIMBERLEY

Kimberley is the "diamond city" where one of the world's biggest diamond strikes occurred in 1868. Visit the open air museum and the "Big Hole" where over three tons of diamonds were removed from the largest man-dug hole on earth.
ACCOMMODATION — FIRST CLASS: * *Kimberley Sun Hotel* has 114 rooms with private facilities and swimming pool.

CAPE TOWN

Sir Francis Drake once said of the Cape Town area: "The fairest cape we saw in the whole circumference of the globe." Today Cape Town is thought to be by many well-traveled people one of the most beautiful settings in the world. The

Seal colonies off Cape Town.

On the Champagne Cruise, Cape Town.

Table Mountain, Cape Town.

Cape reminds me of the California coast — stark, natural beauty and a laid-back atmosphere.

The cable ride (or three-hour hike) up **Table Mountain** with breathtaking views is a must. Bring warm clothing since it is usually much cooler and windier on top. An afternoon **Champagne Cruise** past islands with hundreds of seals, rocky cliffs and sandy beaches allows a delightful perspective of the area.

The one-day drive down the Cape Peninsula to the **Cape of Good Hope Nature Reserve** and **Cape Point** is one of the finest drives on the continent. The reserve has a population of bontebok, as well as other species, and a variety of beautiful wild flowers. Some people say this is where the Atlantic meets the Indian Ocean, while others say it is at Cape Agulhas, the southernmost point of Africa.

Sea Point is bustling with nightlife, with many distinctive restaurants, bistros and bars. **Kirstenbosch National Botanical Gardens**, one of the finest gardens in the world, has 9,000 of the 21,000 flowering plants of Southern Africa.

February-March is the best time to visit the Cape when

Cape Point, where the Atlantic Ocean meets the Indian Ocean.
Photo: SATOUR.

there is very little wind; October-January is warm and windy;
May-August, rainy.

Stellenbosch is the center of the wine industry, and a half
to a full day should be taken to visit a few wineries
such as Blaauklippen.

Some of the finer restaurants include Belvedere House, La
Vita, and La Perla (in Sea Point). The Wooden Bridge, situated
across Table Bay, is exceptionally nice in summer; guests may
watch the sun set behind Table Mountain.

ACCOMMODATION — DELUXE: * *Cape Sun* is a modern hotel
with a great view of the harbor; it has 362 rooms with facilities
ensuite, pool, health club and gym. * *Mount Nelson* is an old-
world British hotel set on seven landscaped acres. The hotel
has rooms with facilities ensuite and swimming pool. * *President Hotel*, located on the beachfront about a 10-minute drive
from central Cape Town, has 153 rooms with facilities ensuite,
swimming pool, tennis courts and sauna. * *St. George's* is a

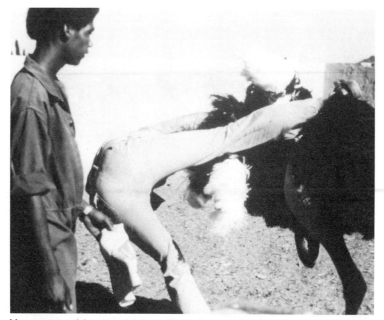

How not to ride an ostrich at Oudtshoorn. Photo: Maryann Watson.

sophisticated British-style hotel located in the center of the business district, has 137 rooms with private facilities and swimming pool.

FIRST CLASS: * *Inn on the Square*, located on the 18th century Greenmarket Square, has 170 air-conditioned rooms with facilities ensuite. * *Townhouse Hotel* has 104 rooms with private facilities, swimming pool, and gym.

GARDEN ROUTE

One of the prettiest drives on the continent, the Garden Route, runs from Jeffrey's Bay to Swellendam between Fort Elizabeth and Cape Town. Rain falls throughout the year, keeping the route luxuriously green.

OUDTSHOORN

Oudtshoorn is where you go to ride an ostrich — or at least watch them race — and tour an ostrich farm.

How <u>to</u> ride an ostrich at Oudtshoorn. Photo: SATOUR.

A lounge on the Blue Train.

THE BLUE TRAIN

The world-renowned luxurious Blue Train offers an experience that has all but disappeared in modern times. The train is promoted as "A Five-Star Hotel on Wheels," and that it is.

Two identical Blue Trains were built in South Africa and put into service in 1972. Each train has 16 permanently coupled passenger coaches accommodating a maximum of 107 guests. The trains are air-conditioned and carpeted, with individually controlled music and radio channels as well as hot, cold and iced water taps in all compartments. Five-star meals are served in the beautifully appointed dining car with its exquisite table settings. Most passengers dress elegantly for dinner.

The train runs from Cape Town to Johannesburg and Pretoria, and vice-versa, year-round. Four types of compartments are available, ranging from small rooms to luxury suites. All compartments have private baths except D-Class, whose guests may use showers at the end of their car. Book well in advance as reservations are often difficult to obtain.

Ride the "Five Star Hotel on Wheels" from Cape Town to Johannesburg and Pretoria (or vice versa). Photo: SATOUR.

SWAZILAND

SWAZILAND

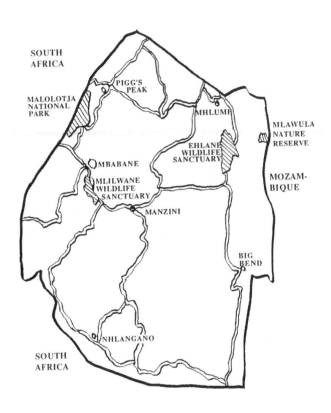

FACTS AT A GLANCE

AREA:	6704 SQUARE MILES
APPROXIMATE SIZE:	NEW JERSEY OR WALES
POPULATION:	712,000 (1990 EST.)
CAPITAL:	MBABANE (POP. EST. 60,000)
OFFICIAL LANGUAGES:	ENGLISH AND SISWATI
	ENGLISH IS WIDELY SPOKEN

Impala. Photo: Mike Appelbaum.

SWAZILAND

Swaziland, along with Lesotho and Morocco, is one of the last three remaining kingdoms in Africa. The country is deeply rooted in tradition - an important part of present-day life. Although Swaziland is the second smallest country in Africa, within its boundaries lie every type of African terrain except desert. Swaziland has several small wildlife reserves, bushmen paintings, international-class resorts, and superb scenery.

Unlike most African countries, Swaziland has never been a totally subject nation. Although the British administered the country for 66 years, the people have always been governed by their own rulers according to their own traditions.

Swaziland has an excellent climate; the higher altitudes have a near temperate climate while the rest of the country has a subtropical climate. Summers (November-January) are rainy, hot and humid. Winters (May-July) are crisp and clear, with occasional frosts in the highveld (higher altitudes). July is usually windy and dusty.

Geographically, the country is divided into four belts of about the same width, running roughly north to south: the mountainous highveld in the west, the hilly middleveld, the Lubombo Plateau along the eastern border, and the lowveld bush.

Swaziland may have been inhabited since the early Stone Age, and later by Bushmen. In the fifteenth century descendants of the Nguni migrated to what is now Maputo, Mozambique, from the great lakes of Central Africa. About 1700 the Nkosi Dlamini settled within the present-day borders

Common waterbuck can be easily identified by the white circle on their buttocks, as if they had sat on a wet toilet seat.
Photo: Mike Appelbaum.

of Swaziland.

Mswati the Second was proclaimed king of the people of the Mswati in 1840, forming the seed of a Swazi nation. By this time the kingdom had grown to twice its present size, and whites began to obtain valuable commercial and agricultural concessions.

Dual administration of the country by British and Boer (Transvaal) governments failed. The Boers took over from 1895 until the Anglo-Boer War broke out in 1899. Swaziland became a High Commission Territory under the British after the war in 1903.

In 1921 Sobhuza the Second became king and remained on the throne until his death in 1982, making him the longest ruling monarch in the world. This long reign gave his country a higher level of political stability than experienced by most of the world.

Swaziland gained its independence on September 6, 1968, making it the last directly administered British colony in Africa. The Queen Regent, Indlovukazi, ruled after the death of Sobhuza, until Prince Makhosetive was crowned king in 1986. Sobhuza had over 600 children through numerous wives, and Makhosetive was chosen from more than 200 princes.

The mining of the highland's (Ngwenya's) iron ore deposits

began as early as 26,000 B.C., until 1980, when supplies were exhausted. In the late 1800's the Swazi gold rush centered around Piggs Peak and Jeppe's Reef, and lasted for 60 years.

The people are called Swazi(s), most of which are subsistence farmers, following a mixture of Christian and indigenous beliefs. About 95% are of Swazi descent, with the rest of the population composed of Zulu, European, Mozambiquean and mulatto. Most live in scattered homesteads instead of concentrating themselves in villages and cities.

More than 15,000 Swazis work outside the country, primarily in South African gold and platinum mines. Much of Swazi tradition revolves around the raising of cattle.

The country's main crops are maize, sugar, citrus, cotton, pineapples, and tobacco. Seventy-five percent of the population works in agriculture.

The combination of friendly people, interesting culture, beautiful countryside and small game reserves make Swaziland an attractive country to visit.

WILDLIFE AND WILDLIFE AREAS

Less than 100 years ago, Swaziland was abundant in most forms of wildlife. But much wildlife was exterminated by hunters in the years to follow. Hunting is now illegal, and conservation programs have partially revived this nation's wildlife heritage.

Swazi reserves are among the smallest on the continent, but for their size contain a great variety of species. The parks are ideal for horseback or walking safaris, providing close contact with nature. Open vehicles are most often used.

The country is prolific in birdlife, hosting more than 450 different species; these include such rarities as the bald ibis and blue crane. Other more common species include the glossy starling, lilac-breasted roller, hamerkop, sunbirds, kingfishers, geese and guineafowl.

In the country's wide range of altitude grow over 6000 different species of flora, including 25 varieties of aloes and six species of cyclads.

Cyclads, often called "living fossils", are the oldest known seed-bearing plants in the world. According to carbon dating, these plants have changed very little during the last 50 million years, and are presently protected by law.

The Swaziland National Trust Commission (P.O. Box 75, Mbabane, tel: 42579) is in charge of the national parks and may be contacted for further information and assistance.

THE NORTH

MALOLOTJA NATIONAL PARK

This is the country's largest park, covering 70 square miles of mountains and gorges harboring unique highveld flora and fauna. Rock faces, rapids, waterfalls, grasslands, impenetrable riverine forests, and mountains rising to an altitude of 5900 feet, provide scenic backdrops for game. Tree cyads over 20 feet may be found in the valleys.

Malolotja Falls with a 300-foot drop are the highest in the country. Wildlife includes oribi, vaal rhebok, klipspringer, impala, red duiker, reedbuck, white rhino, wildebeest, aardwolf, black-backed jackal, honey badger, serval and zebra. Over 150 species of birds have been sighted. There are bald ibis colonies and blue cranes in the park November-February. Flora, characteristic only of this region of Southern Africa, include barberton, kaapsehoop and woolly cyclads.

Ngwenya Mine may be the site of the world's earliest known mine, thought to have been worked as early as 26,000 B.C.

With limited roads, the park is best suited for walkers and backpackers. Wilderness trails one to seven days in length are well marked and require a permit; day trails may be used without permit. Camping along the trail is only allowed at official sites; these sites have water but no facilities. Permits must be obtained for backpacking and for fishing at the Forbes Reef Dam and Upper Malolotja River from the tourist office.

The best time to visit is August-April; June-July is cold and windy. The main gate is located 22 miles northwest of Mbabane on the road to Piggs Peak.

ACCOMMODATION — CLASS C and D: * *National Park Cabins* have six fully furnished cabins, each with six beds, private facilities, crockery and cutlery. Bring your own food, bedclothes and towels.

CAMPING: Campsites with ablution blocks are available.

EHLANE WILDLIFE SANCTUARY

Located in the northwestern corner of the country about 44 miles from Manzini, this 55-square-mile sanctuary is composed of unspoiled acacia bushveld. Over 10,000 animals congregate here during the dry months, but move south with the coming of spring rains. Wildlife includes black-backed jackal, spotted hyena, giraffe, kudu, blue wildebeest, waterbuck, steenbok, and zebra.
ACCOMMODATION — CLASS F: Basic huts are available.
CAMPING: Camping is allowed.

MLAWULA GAME SANCTUARY

East of Ehlane Wildlife Sanctuary, Mlawula's lowveld and Lubombo mountainside support oribi, white rhino, leopard, ostrich, and red hartebeest, among other species.
ACCOMMODATION — CLASS F: Basic accommodation is available.
CAMPING: Campsites are available.

MLILWANE WILDLIFE SANCTUARY

Located in the Ezulwini Valley, Mlilwane means "little fire" from the lightning which often strikes a nearby hill where large deposits of iron ore exist. This 17-square-mile game sanctuary has a variety of wildlife including white rhino, giraffe, hippo, buffalo, zebra, crocodile, jackal, caracal cat, serval cat, civet, nyala, blue wildebeest, eland, sable antelope, kudu, waterbuck, blesbok, reedbuck, bushbuck, oribi, springbok, duiker, and klipspringer.

The sanctuary is composed of Middleveld and Highveld with altitudes ranging from 2200-4750 feet. It is located on an escarpment that was a meeting point of westerly and easterly migrations of animals, which resulted in the congregation of a large number of wildlife species.

The northern limits of Mlilwane are marked by the twin peaks of "Sheba's Breasts." "Execution Rock" is another legendary peak where common criminals were supposedly pushed to their deaths.

Over 60 miles of gravel roads run throughout the sanctuary. Visitors are not allowed out of their vehicles unless accompanied by a guide. Guided tours in open vehicles, on foot, or on horseback can be arranged in advance at the Rest Camp. Horseback-riding safaris are conducted along bridle trails through the park. The best time to visit is the dry season, May through September.

ACCCOMMODATION — DELUXE/FIRST AND TOURIST CLASS: see "Ezulwini Valley" below.

CLASS D: * *Park Bandas* and a dormitory are available. There is an ablution block with hot and cold running water.

CAMPING: Campsites are available.

EZULWINI VALLEY

The Ezulwini Valley, or "Place of Heaven", is the entertainment center of the country and is the most convenient area in which to stay when visiting the Mlilwane Wildlife Sanctuary.

ACCOMMODATION — DELUXE: * *The Royal Swazi Sun Hotel, Casino and Country Club*, situated on 100 acres, has 145 rooms with ensuite facilities, swimming pool, sauna, hot tub, casino, adult cinema, 72-par golf course, horseback riding, tennis, squash, mini-golf, lawn-bowling, casino, a discotheque, nightclub, and cabaret. Guests of the Ezulwini Sun Cabanas and the Lugogo Sun Cabanas may use the facilities of the more exclusive Royal Swazi; complimentary hotel bus transfer service is provided.

FIRST CLASS: * *Ezulwini Sun Cabanas* has 120 air-conditioned rooms with private facilities and swimming pool; traditional Swazi dance performances are held every Saturday. * *Lugogo Sun Cabanas* has 202 air-conditioned rooms with ensuite facilities and swimming pool.

LOBAMBA

Lobamba is the spiritual and legislative capital of the country. The Queen Mother's village is situated here. The National Museum, concentrating on Swazi culture and traditions, and the House of Parliament may be visited.

The country's two most important ceremonies are the Ncwala and Umhlanga, both of which take place at the Ludzidzini Royal Residence.

The most important of the two ceremonies is the **Ncwala** or First Fruit Ceremony, usually held in December and January;

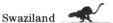

Swazi dancers.

its exact date depends on the phases of the moon as analyzed by Swazi astrologers. The Ncwala symbolizes the religious spirit identifying the Swazi people with their King. The Ncwala is spread over about a three-week period, and involves the entire Swazi nation.

The famous week-long Umhlanga **(Reed Dance)**, is a colorful ceremony in which hundreds of Swazi maidens gather reeds and march with them to the Royal Residence at Ludzidzini where the reeds are used to repair the windbreakers around the residence of the Queen Mother, Idlovukazi. The Umhlanga occurs in late August/early September.

Photographs of these two ceremonies can be taken only with permission from the Swaziland Information Services (P.O. Box 338, Mbabane, Swaziland, tel: 4-2761).

PIGGS PEAK

Piggs Peak, located in one of the most scenic areas of the country, was named after William Pigg who discovered gold there in January of 1884. Nearby is the country's most famous Bushmen painting, located at the **Nsangwini Shelter**. Ask the District Officer at Piggs Peak to find a guide to take you there.
ACCOMMODATION — FIRST CLASS: * *Protea Pigg's Peak Hotel & Casino*, located six miles north of Piggs Peak, has 106 rooms with facilities ensuite, swimming pool, gym, tennis and squash courts, cinema and casino.

Witch doctor's shop in Nhlangano.

THE SOUTH

MBABANE

Mbabane, the capital of Swaziland, is located in the mountainous highveld overlooking the Ezulwini Valley. Mbabne has a number of shops selling local crafts. Most international visitors stay in Ezulwini Valley instead of Mbabane. The international airport (Matsapha) is located about 15 miles from Mbabane, between Mbabane and the industrial city of Manzini.

NHLANGANO

Nhlangano means "The Meeting Place of the Kings" and commemorates the meeting between King Sobhuza the Second and King George the Sixth in 1947. Nhlangano is located in the southwestern part of the country in an unspoiled mountainous area and is the burial place of many Swazi kings.
ACCOMMODATION — FIRST CLASS: * The *Nhlangano Sun* is the best hotel in the area, with casino, disco bar, swimming pool, squash, tennis, and 47 comfortable chalets with ensuite facilities.

TANZANIA

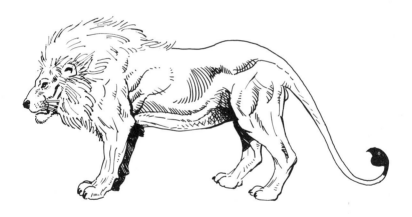

TANZANIA

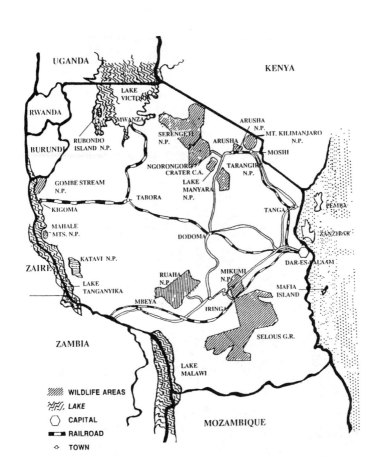

FACTS AT A GLANCE

AREA:	363,708 SQUARE MILES
APPROXIMATE SIZE:	TEXAS PLUS OKLAHOMA OR FRANCE
POPULATION:	24 MILLION (1990 EST.)
CAPITAL:	NOMINAL: DODOMA
FUNCTIONAL:	DAR ES SALAAM (POP. EST. 1,500,000)
OFFICIAL LANGUAGE:	SWAHILI; ENGLISH WIDELY SPOKEN.

Cheetah with cub. Photo: Mike Appelbaum.

TANZANIA

Between Africa's highest mountain (Kilimanjaro) and Africa's largest lake (Victoria) lies one of the best game-viewing areas on the continent. This region also includes the world's largest unflooded intact volcanic caldera or crater (Ngorongoro) and the most famous wildlife park (the Serengeti). To the south lies one of the world's largest game reserves — the Selous.

Volcanic highlands dominate the north, giving way southward to a plateau, then semidesert in the center of the country and highlands in the south. The coastal lowlands are hot and humid with lush vegetation. One branch of the Great Rift Valley passes through Lakes Manyara and Natron in northern Tanzania to Lake Malawi (Lake Nyasa) in the south while the other branch passes through Lakes Rukwa and Tanganyika in the west.

Heavy rains usually occur in April and May, and lighter rains in late October and November. Altitude has a great effect on temperature. At Arusha (4600 ft.) and the top of Ngorongoro Crater (7500 ft.), nights and early mornings are especially cool. Tanzania's highest temperatures occur in December-March and lowest in July.

Evidence suggests East Africa was the cradle of mankind. The earliest known humanoid footprints, estimated to be 3.5 million years old, were discovered at Laetoli by Dr. Mary Leakey in 1979; in 1957, Dr. Leakey also found the estimated 1.7 million-year-old skull *Zinjanthropus boisei* at Olduvai Gorge.

By the 13th century Arabs, Persians, Egyptians, Indians and Chinese were involved in heavy trading on the coast. Slave trade began in the mid-1700's and was abolished in 1873. British Explorers Richard Burton and John Speke crossed Tanzania in 1857 to Lake Tanganyika. Speke later discovered Lake Victoria which he felt was the source of the Nile.

The German East Africa Company gained control of the mainland (then called German East Africa) in 1885, and the German government held it from 1891 until World War One when it was mandated to Britain by the League of Nations. Tanganyika gained its independence from Britain in 1961 and Zanzibar in 1963. Zanzibar, once the center of the East African slave trade, was ruled by sultans until its union with Tanganyika in 1964, forming the United Republic of Tanzania.

There are 120 tribes in Tanzania. Bantu languages and dialects are spoken by 95% of the population, with Kiswahili the official and national language. Over 75% of the people are peasant farmers. The export of coffee, cotton, sisal, tea, cloves, and cashews bring 70% of the country's foreign exchange.

WILDLIFE AND WILDLIFE AREAS

Reserves cover over 95,000 square miles of area — probably more than any other country on earth. There are 11 national parks, 17 game reserves and one conservation area comprising over 15% of the country's land area. Tanzania's great variety of wildlife can be at least partially attributed to its great diversity of landscapes, with altitudes ranging from sea level to almost 20,000 feet.

Vehicles with roof hatches or pop tops are used on safari. Walking is not allowed in most of the national parks except Arusha, Gombe Stream, Mahale and Rubondo Island National Parks and the Selous Game Reserve where visitors must be accompanied by a national park guide.

The peak tourist seasons are from July through September and December-March. January, February and August are the busiest months. Heavy rains falling in April and May hamper travel and game viewing. Light rains are usually from late October-December.

The country contains 35 species of antelope and over 1.5 million wildebeest — over 80% of the population of this species in Africa. The calving season for wildebeest is from mid-January to mid-March.

Guides are available for hire at the gates of some reserves.

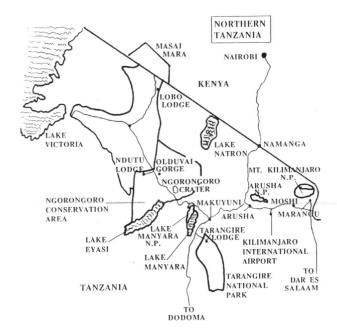

Information and booklets on the parks are available from the National Park Headquarters, Arusha International Conference Centre (AICC), P.O. Box 3141, Arusha, Tanzania.

THE NORTH

This region from Mt. Kilimanjaro in the east to Serengeti National Park in the west is the area most visited by tourists and contains the country's most famous parks.

Most visitors reach Arusha on a four-hour drive from Nairobi (Kenya) via Namanga or fly into Kilimanjaro International Airport where they are transferred to town. Kilimanjaro International Airport, located 34 miles east of Arusha and 22 miles west of Moshi, has a bank, bar and restaurant.

The Northern Circuit includes Lake Manyara National Park, Ngorongoro Conservation Area, Olduvai Gorge, Serengeti National Park and Tarangire National Park.

From Arusha, drive 45 miles west on a good, newly constructed tarmac road across the gently rolling Masai Plains with scattered acacia trees, to Makuyuni. You may then either continue on the main road towards Dodoma for another 20 miles to Tarangire National Park, or turn right (northwest) on an all-weather dirt road to Mto wa Mbu (Mosquito Creek).

In route you pass many Masai bomas (villages), Masai in their colorful traditional dress walking on the roadside, riding bicycles, herding their cattle, and driving overloaded donkey carts.

Masai Morani completing the circumcision ritual are sometimes seen clad in black with white paint on their faces. They leave the village as a child for a period of time for training and instruction by elders and return as men.

Mto wa Mbu is a village with many roadside stands filled with wood carvings and other local crafts for sale. Be sure to bargain. If you take a few minutes to walk into the village behind the stands, you will get a more realistic (and less touristic) view of village life.

Continuing west you soon pass the entrance to Lake Manyara National Park. The road becomes quite rough as it climbs up the Rift Valley escarpment past huge baobab trees and numerous baboons looking for handouts. Fabulous views of the valley and Lake Manyara Park below can be seen. You then pass through beautiful cultivated uplands and small villages past the turnoff to Gibb's Farm and on up the slopes of the Crater Highlands to Ngorongoro Crater. The road then follows the rim of the crater past the Wildlife Lodge, Rhino Lodge and Crater Lodge, and finally descends the western side of the crater to Olduvai Gorge and Serengeti National Park.

ARUSHA

This town is the center of tourism for northern Tanzania and is situated in the foothills of rugged Mt. Meru. Named after one of the Arusha tribes, it is located on the Great North Road midway between Cairo and Cape Town. There is little to do here except shopping for *makonde* carvings and other souvenirs in the numerous craft shops at the center of town. Walking around the Arusha Market, located behind the bus station, is an interesting way to spend a few hours.

ACCOMMODATION — Also see "Accommodation" under "Arusha National Park."

FIRST CLASS: * *Mt. Meru Hotel*, part of the Novotel chain, is a 200-room hotel with ensuite facilities, swimming pool and ten-

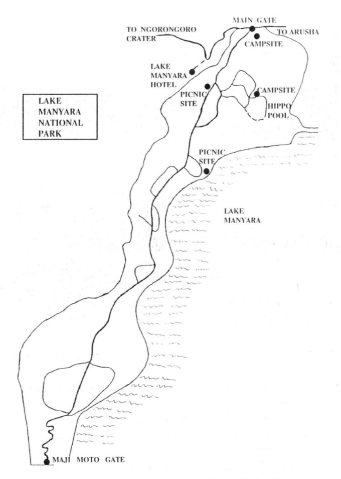

TO NGORONGORO CRATER
MAIN GATE
TO ARUSHA
CAMPSITE
LAKE MANYARA HOTEL
PICNIC SITE
CAMPSITE
HIPPO POOL
LAKE MANYARA NATIONAL PARK
PICNIC SITE
LAKE MANYARA
MAJI MOTO GATE

nis courts. The hotel is located at the foot of Mt. Meru on the outskirts of Arusha. * Newly built *Mountain Village* has 40 bungalows (doubles) and three triples with ensuite facilities and is six miles outside Arusha overlooking Lake Duluti. Horseback riding and fishing are available.

TOURIST CLASS: * *New Arusha Hotel,* located in the center of town, has 72 rooms and attractive gardens. * *Hotel 77* is Tanzania's largest hotel, with 400 double rooms with private facilities.

LAKE MANYARA NATIONAL PARK

Once one of the most popular hunting areas of Tanzania,

Hippo and white pelicans at Lake Manyara National Park.

this 123-square-mile park has the Great Rift Valley escarpment for a dramatic backdrop. Two-thirds of the park is covered by alkaline Lake Manyara, which is situated at an altitude of 3150 feet.

The turnoff to Lake Manyara is past Mto wa Mbu on the road from Makuyuni to Ngorongoro Crater, about 75 miles west of Arusha.

Five different vegetation zones are found in the park. The first zone reached from the park entrance is groundwater forest fed by water seeping from the Great Rift Wall, with wild fig, sausage, tamarind and mahogany trees. Elephants prefer these dense forests as well as marshy glades. The other zones include the marshlands along the edge of the lake, scrub on the rift Valley Wall, open areas with scattered acacia, and open grasslands.

Manyara, like Ishasha in the Ruwenzori National Park in Uganda, is well known for its tree-climbing lions found lazing on branches of acacia trees. Some people believe that lions climb trees in Manyara to avoid tsetse flies and the dense undergrowth while remaining in the cool shade, while lions of the Ruwenzori National Park in Uganda climb trees to gain a

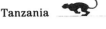

Lake Manyara National Park with the Great Rift Valley Wall in the background.

hunting advantage. Finding lion in the trees is very rare, so don't set your heart on it — look at it as an unexpected bonus.

Manyara features large concentrations of elephant and buffalo. Black rhino and leopard are rare. Other wildlife includes common waterbuck, Masai giraffe, zebra, impala, baboons, blue monkeys and Sykes monkeys. Over 380 species of birds, including over 30 birds of prey, have been recorded.

The traditional migration route to Tarangire National Park has been all but cut off by new villages. Much of the wildlife is resident year-round, making this a good park to visit anytime. The best time to visit is December-February and May-July; August-September is also good.

On a recent visit to the hippo pool, we saw over 20 gregarious hippos lying all over each other in a pile on the bank. Something finally spooked them, and a mad rush ensued as they joined other hippos in the pool. In a matter of minutes we spotted over 20 species of birds without moving from that spot.

Birds spotted included white-breasted cormorants, red-billed oxpeckers, African spoonbills, lesser flamingos, white pelicans, grey-headed gulls, wood sandpipers, black-winged stilts, white-faced ducks, white-crowned plover, blacksmith plover, long-toed plovers, avocet, water dikkops, cattle egrets, black-winged white terns, common sandpiper, painted snipe and sacred ibis.

As we were rounding a bend, we almost ran right into two huge bull elephants that were sparring with tusks locked, pushing each other from one side of the road to the other, trumpeting and kicking up mounds of dust in their fight for dominance.

Roads are good year-round and four-wheel drive is not needed, although in the rainy season some side tracks may be temporarily closed. There is a small museum with a large number of mounted birds commonly seen in the park at the gate. Booklets to the parks are also sold.

ACCOMMODATION — CLASS B: * *Lake Manyara Hotel*, magnificently set on the Rift Valley Escarpment overlooking the park and the Rift Valley 1000 feet below, has 212 rooms with private facilities, swimming pool and airstrip.

CLASSES D & F: * *National Park Self-Service Bandas* (ten doubles) are located near the park entrance. Some bandas have private facilities and everyone shares a communal kitchen.

CAMPING: Two campsites are located near the park entrance, both with toilet and shower facilities. One campsite is situated within the park with no facilities; this latter site requires a special permit.

GIBB'S FARM

Located between Lake Manyara National Park and the Ngorongoro Conservation Area, Gibb's Farm (Class A/B) has 12 attractively decorated cottages (30 beds) and the best food on the Northern Circuit. Many tour groups stop here for lunch.

This is a working farm that produces coffee and most of the food it serves its guests. The attractive brick-and-stone colonial house is set in spacious, beautifully landscaped gardens on a hill overlooking coffee plantations. Walks to nearby waterfalls can be arranged.

Gibb's Farm is located near the village of Karatu, 15 miles

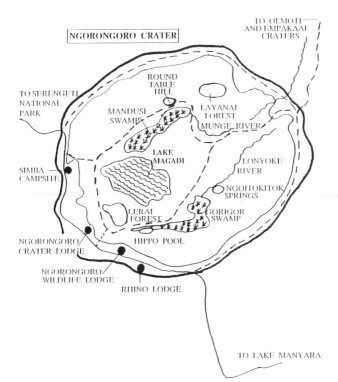

from Lake Manyara National Park and 25 miles from the Ngorongoro Crater.

NGORONGORO CRATER CONSERVATION AREA

Ngorongoro Crater is the largest unflooded, intact caldera (collapsed cone of a volcano) in the world. Known as the eighth wonder of the world, its vastness and beauty is truly overwhelming and is believed by some to have been the proverbial Garden of Eden. Many scientists suggest that before its eruption, this volcano was larger than Mt. Kilimanjaro.

Ngorongoro contains possibly the largest permanent concentration of wildlife in Africa with an estimated average of 30,000 large mammals. In addition, this is probably the best park in Africa to see black rhino.

Large concentrations of wildlife make Ngorongoro Crater their permanent home. Game viewing is good year-round. Because there is a permanent source of fresh water, there's

Ngorongoro Crater is the largest intact unflooded caldera in the world.

no reason for the wildlife to migrate as they must do in the Serengeti.

The 102-square-mile crater itself is but a small portion of the 3200-square-mile Ngorongoro Conservation Area, which is characterized by a highland plateau with volcanic mountains as well as several craters, extensive savannah and forests. Altitudes range from 4430-11,800 feet.

The Serengeti Plains cover the western part of the conservation area. Since this is classified as a conservation area and not a national park, wildlife, human beings and livestock exist together. Ground cultivation is not allowed.

The 10,700-foot-high **Empakaai Crater**, situated 20 miles northwest of Ngorongoro Crater, is known for its scenic beauty. The drive through Masailand offers great views. Hiking is allowed if accompanied by an armed wildlife guard.

Ngorongoro Crater is about 12 miles wide and its rim rises 1200-1600 feet off its expansive 102-square-mile floor. From the crater rim, elephant appear as small dark specks on the grasslands. The steep decent into the crater along a narrow rough, winding road takes 25-35 minutes from the crater rim. The crater floor is predominantly grasslands (making game

Ngorongoro is one of the best parks in Africa to see black rhino.

easy to spot) with two swamps fed by streams and the Lerai Forest. The walls of the crater are lightly forested.

Once on the floor, your driver will more than likely turn left and travel clockwise around the crater floor. Lake Magadi, also called Crater Lake and Lake Makat, is a shallow soda lake near the entry point of the crater which attracts thousands of flamingos and other water birds. The Masai are allowed to bring in their cattle for the salts and permanent water available on the crater floor, but must leave the crater at night.

The dirt road continues past Mandusi Swamp. Game viewing is especially good in this area during the dry season (July-October) as some wildlife migrates to this permanent source of fresh water. Hippo, elephant and reedbuck among many other species can usually be found here.

You then come to Round Table Hill which provides a good view and excellent vantage point to get one's bearings. A road continues to the Layanai Forest where it dead ends near the crater wall. The circular route continues over the Munge River, whose source is in the Olmoti Crater north of Ngorongoro Crater, to Ngoitokitok Springs. From there, you journey past Gorigor Swamp, fed by the Lonyokie River, to the Hippo Pool, which is probably the best place to see hippo.

Cheetah.

The Lerai Forest, primarily composed of fever trees (a type of acacia) is a good place to spot elephant, and, if you are very lucky, leopard. There are two picnic areas and campsites here with long-drop toilets and running water. The exit road climbing the wall of the crater is behind the forest.

On a full-day's game drive during my most recent visit, we saw seven black rhino, including one mother with her baby, 27 lion, several golden jackal and spotted hyena, and numerous elephant, buffalo, zebra, wildebeest, ostrich, flamingos, baboons, monkeys, kori bustards and a host of other species. Elephant are also found in the wooded areas and on the slopes of the crater. Cheetah are present, but there are no giraffe or topi.

Over 350 species of birds have been recorded. Birds commonly sighted include ostrich, crown cranes, Egyptian geese, and pelicans.

At the picnic site vervet monkeys are very aggressive in getting at your food. Kites (a species of bird) made many swooping attempts at our lunches. You may wish to eat inside your vehicle. Overnight camping is allowed in the crater for those who are equipped and have a permit. A Ngorongoro Conservation guide is required and will accompany the group for a small fee. Camping sites should be reserved well in advance — at least one year in advance for high season.

One important thing to remember: game is not confined to the crater; wildlife is present throughout the conservation area including near hotels and lodges. This I learned the hard way on my first visit to Ngorongoro some years ago. One evening just outside of the Ngorongoro Wildlife Lodge, blindly I walked within 20 feet of three large buffalo. One buffalo appeared as if it was going to charge, then fortunately the buffalo ran off. Welcome to Africa! I thought, relieved beyond words. Certainly, I would have been no match for one charging buffalo, let alone three of the huge beasts.

Game viewing in the Ngorongoro Conservation Area west of the crater bordering the Serengeti is best between November and May when the Serengeti migration is in the area.

Ngorongoro Crater is about 118 miles west of Arusha. At Ngorongoro Village there is a garage with petrol. An airstrip is located further along the crater rim. A guide is no longer required and any four-wheel-drive vehicles are allowed. Visitors arriving in two-wheel-drive vehicles (i.e., minivans) must

Kongoni.

hire four-wheel-drive vehicles to go for game drives into the crater.

About 30 miles west of Ngorongoro Crater and a few miles off the road to the Serengeti is **Olduvai Gorge**, site of many archeological discoveries including the estimated 1.7-million-year-old *Zinjanthropus boisei* fossil. The fossil is housed in the National Museum in Dar es Salaam.

A small museum overlooks the gorge itself, and a guide there will tell you the story of the Leakeys' research and findings. For a small tip the guide will take you down into the gorge and show you where the *Zinjanthropus boisei* fossil was found.

ACCOMMODATION — CLASS B: * *Ndutu Safari Lodge* — see "Accommodation" under "Serengeti National Park." Ndutu is in the Ngorongoro Conservation Area but is on the Serengeti Plain on the border of Serengeti National Park.

CLASS B/C: * *Ngorongoro Wildlife Lodge*, an attractive 78-room hotel with spectacular views of the crater, has a large lounge and dining area, veranda with telescopes and good service. * *Ngorongoro Crater Lodge*, a rustic lodge with panoramic views of the crater, has individual cottages and blocks of cottages with ensuite facilities (134 beds). There is a large double fireplace between the bar and dining room.

CLASS C: * *Ngorongoro Rhino Lodge* is a small lodge with no view of the crater. Two rooms share one toilet and bathroom.

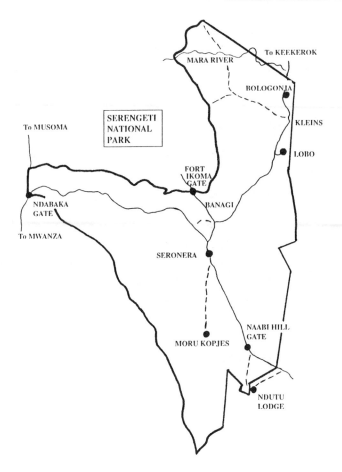

To KEEKEROK

MARA RIVER

BOLOGONJA

To MUSOMA

SERENGETI
NATIONAL
PARK

KLEINS

LOBO

FORT
IKOMA
GATE

BANAGI

NDABAKA
GATE

To MWANZA

SERONERA

NAABI HILL
GATE

MORU KOPJES

NDUTU
LODGE

CAMPING: * *Simba Campsite*, on the crater rim, has faulty Asian toilets and shower facilities (usually cold). Campsites on the floor of the crater should be reserved well in advance since camping is very popular. Campsites are also available at Lake Ndutu.

SERENGETI NATIONAL PARK

This is Tanzania's largest and most famous park and has the largest concentration of migratory game animals in the world. It is also famous for its huge lion population and is one of the best places on the continent to see them. The park has received great notoriety through Professor Bernard Grzimek's

Serengeti Migration. Photo: Mike Appelbaum.

book, *Serengeti Shall Not Die.*

Serengeti is derived from the Masai language and appropriately means "endless plain." The park's 5700 square miles make it larger than the state of Connecticut. Altitude varies from 3000-6000 feet.

The park comprises most of the Serengeti ecosystem, which is the primary migration route of the wildebeest. The Serengeti ecosystem also includes Kenya's Masai Mara National Reserve, bordering on the north, the Loliondo Controlled Area, bordering on the northeast, the Ngorongoro Conservation Area, bordering on the southeast, the Maswa Game Reserve, bordering on the southwest, and the Grumeti and Ikorongo Controlled Areas, bordering on the northwest. The "western corridor" of the park comes within a few miles of Lake Victoria.

Nearly 500 species of birds and 35 species of large plains animals can be found in the Serengeti. The park may contain as many as 13 million wildebeest, 250,000 Thompson's gazelle, 200,000 zebra, 70,000 topi, 30,000 Grant's gazelle, 20,000 buffalo, 9,000 eland, 8,000 giraffe, 1500 lion and 800 elephant. The

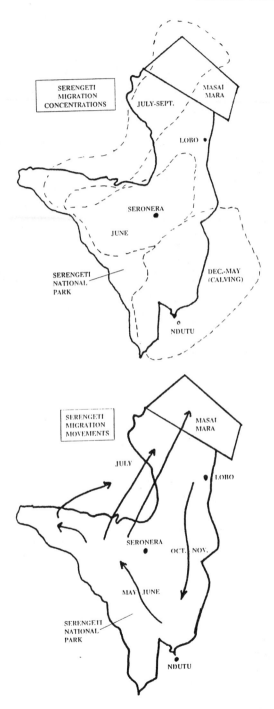

Black-backed jackal are seen in many reserves in Africa.

best time to visit is December-May when game is most highly concentrated in the southern part of the park.

Most of the Serengeti is a vast open plain broken by rocky outcrops (kopjes). There is also acacia savannah, savannah woodland, riverine forests, some swamps and small lakes.

The north is more hilly with thick scrub and forests lining the Mara River, where leopard are sometimes spotted sleeping in the trees. Acacia savannah dominates the central region, with short and long grass open plains in the southeast, and woodland plains and hills in the western corridor.

It is impossible to predict the exact time of the famous **Serengeti Migration**, which covers a circuit of about 500 miles. From December-May wildebeest, zebra, eland and Thompson's gazelle usually concentrate on the treeless short grass plains in the extreme southeastern Serengeti and western Ngorongoro Conservation Area near Lake Ndutu in search of short grass which they prefer over the longer dry-stemmed variety. This is the best time to visit the Serengeti. In April and May, the height of the rainy season, a four-wheel-drive vehicle is highly recommended.

Masai giraffe.

Other species common to the area during this period are Grant's gazelle, eland, hartebeest, topi and a host of predators including lion, cheetah, spotted hyena, honey badger and black-backed jackal. Kori bustards and yellow-throated sand-grouse are also common.

During the long rainy season (April-May), nomadic lions and hyena move to the eastern part of the Serengeti. The migration, mainly of wildebeest and zebra, begins in May or June. Once the dry season begins wildebeest and zebra must migrate from the area. There is no permanent water, and both of these species must drink on a regular basis.

The mating season is concentrated over a three-week period, and generally occurs in May or June. After a gestation period of eight and a half months the calves are born, usually on the short grass plains.

Wildebeest move about six to ten abreast in columns several miles long towards the western corridor. Zebra do not move in columns but in family units.

As a general rule, by June or July the migration has progressed west of Seronera. The migration then splits into three separate migrations: one west through the corridor toward permanent water and Lake Victoria, then northeast; the second one due north, reaching the Masai Mara of Kenya around mid-July; and the third northward between the other two to a region west of Lobo Lodge where the group disperses. At present, there are no roads in the region where the third group disperses; however, this may soon change.

During July-September, the Serengeti's highest concentration of wildlife is in the extreme north. The first and second groups meet and begin returning to the Serengeti National Park around the end of September/early October; the migration then reaches the southern Serengeti by December.

Short grass plains dominate the part of the Ngorongoro Conservation Area bordering the Serengeti. As one moves northwest into the park, the plains change to medium-grass plains and then into long-grass plains around Simba Kopjes north of Naabi Hill Gate. Topi, elephant, Thompson's and Grant's gazelles, bat-eared fox and warthogs are often seen here.

Seronera

Seronera Lodge, Park Headquarters and the Park Village are located together in the center of the park. Game is plentiful in the Seronera Valley, which is famous for lion and leopard. Other wildlife includes hyena, jackal, topi, Masai giraffe, and Thomson's gazelle. This is the best part of the park to find

cheetah, especially in the dry season. In the wet season, many cheetah are found in the short-grass plains. They are, however, found throughout the park.

Banagi Hill, eleven miles north of Seronera on the road to Lobo, is a good area for Masai giraffe, buffalo and impala. Four miles from Banagi on the Orangi River is a hippo pool.

Lobo

From Banagi northward to Lobo and the Bologonja Gate are rolling uplands with open plains, bush, woodlands and magnificent kopjes. This is the best area of the park to see elephant. Forests of large mahogany and fig trees are found along the rivers where Patas monkeys, kingfishers, fish eagles and turacos may be seen. Other wildlife found in the Lobo area includes grey bush duiker, Cotton's oribi and mountain reedbuck. Large numbers of Masai giraffe are permanent residents.

Large herds of wildebeest are often in the region from August till the rains begin, usually in November. During this period many wildebeest drown while attempting to cross the Mara River.

Western Corridor

Beginning three miles north of Seronera, the western corridor road passes over the Grumeti River and beyond to a central range of hills. Eighteen miles before Ndabaka Gate is an extensive area of black cotton soil which makes rainy season travel difficult. This area is best visited June-October during the dry season. Colobus monkeys may be found in the riverine areas. Other wildlife includes roan, Patterson's eland, topi, impala and crocodile.

The granite kopjes or rocky outcrops that dot the plains are home to rock hyrax, Kirk's dikdik and klipspringer. Banded, dwarf and slender mongoose are occasionally seen nearby. Verreaux's eagle and black rhino are sometimes sighted near the Moru Kopjes.

There are two saline lakes in the south of the park, *Lake Magadi* and *Lake Lagaja*, known mainly for their populations of lesser and greater flamingos.

Three species of jackal occur in the Serengeti: black-backed, side-striped and golden. Side-striped jackal are rare; golden jackal are usually found in the short-grass plains; and black-backed jackal are quite common. The six species of vultures occurring in the park are white-backed, white-headed, hooded, lappet-faced, Ruppell's and Egyptian. At the time of this writing, the border with Kenya between Serengeti National Park and the Masai Mara is closed. There is a dry weather road (often impassable in the rainy season) from Mwanza and Musoma (Lake Victoria) to the west through Ndabaka Gate. The main road from the Ngorongoro Conservation Area via Naabi Hill Gate is open year-round.

Vehicles must stay on the roads within a ten-mile radius of Seronera. Travel in the park is only allowed from 6:00 a.m. till 7:00 p.m. Visitors may get out of the vehicle in open areas if there are no animals present. Do stay close to the vehicle and keep a careful lookout.

From July to October, when the migration is usually in Kenya, you may want to pass up the Serengeti and spend your time in Tarangire National Park, which is excellent that time of year.

Guides, garage facilities and petrol are available at Seronera and Lobo. A guide must be taken if you are driving to the Moru Kopjes.

ACCOMMODATION — CLASS B: * *Ndutu Safari Lodge* is a rustic lodge located on the edge of the park in Ngorongoro Conservation Area. Wildlife is most heavily concentrated in this area December-May. Rooms with private facilities are available. Five tents provide additional accommodation during high season (January-March). Campsites are also available.

CLASS B/C: * *Lobo Wildlife Lodge*, a dramatically beautiful lodge in the north of the park 43 miles north of Seronera, is uniquely designed around huge boulders and has a swimming pool carved out of solid rock. All seventy-five double rooms have private facilities. * *Seronera Wildlife Lodge*, situated in the center of the park 90 miles from Ngorongoro Crater at an altitude of 5700 feet, has 75 double rooms with private facilities, swimming pool (often empty of water) and airstrip. The lodge sometimes experiences water problems.

CAMPING: There are four campsites at Seronera and one each at Naabi Hill Gate, Moru Kopjes, Kirawira and Lobo. Camping in other areas requires permission from the warden and higher fees. It is best to book well in advance.

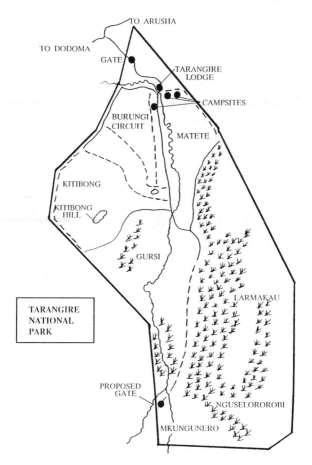

TARANGIRE NATIONAL PARK

Large numbers of baobab trees dotting the landscape give the park a prehistoric look the likes of which I have never seen. This park has a different feel to it than any other northern park — and an eerie feeling at that, making it one of my favorites.

Tarangire is the best park on the northern circuit to see elephant. On my last visit Cynthia Moss, author of *Elephant Memories* and *Portraits In The Wild*, identified over 500 individual elephants within the park in a week!

Fewer tourists visit this park than Manyara, Ngorongoro and Serengeti, allowing a better opportunity to experience it

Wildebeest among baobab trees in Tarangire National Park.

as the early explorers did — alone. This park should not be missed; wildlife viewing is excellent, especially from July through October when many migratory animals return to the only permanent water source in the area: the Tarangire River and its tributaries.

At the beginning of October/November during the short rainy season, migratory species including wildebeest and zebra, soon followed by elephant, buffalo, Grant's gazelle, Thomson's gazelle and oryx begin migrating out of the park. However, as more and more migration routes are cut off from the expansion of man's presence, more and more animals are remaining in the park. Giraffe, waterbuck, lesser kudu and other resident species tend to remain in Tarangire. At the end of the long rains in June, the migratory species return to the park.

Tarangire wildlife populations include approximately 30,000 zebra, 25,000 wildebeest, 5,000 buffalo, 5,000 eland, 3000 elephant, 2500 Masai giraffe and 1000 oryx. Other prominent species include Grant's and Thomson's gazelle, hartebeest, impala, lesser and greater kudu, reedbuck and gerenuk. Lion are often seen. Cheetah, spotted hyena and leopard are also present, as are the banded, black-tipped, dwarf, and marsh mongoose.

The **Lemiyon region**, the northernmost region of the park which includes Tarangire Safari Lodge, is characterized by a high concentration of baobab trees unmatched in any park I've seen. This unique landscape is also dotted by umbrella acacia trees with some open grasslands and wooded areas. Elephant, wildebeest and zebra are often seen. On my last visit a zebra was killed by lion less than 200 yards from the lodge. Visitors with little time for game viewing may want to concentrate on the Matete and the Lemiyon areas including the Tarangire River.

The **Matete region** covers the northeastern part of the park and is characterized by open grasslands with scattered umbrella acacia and baobab trees and the Tarangire River. Lion, fringe-eared oryx and klipspringer are seen quite often. Bat-eared fox are also present.

On the 50-mile **Burungi Circuit**, you pass through acacia parklands and woodlands. You are likely to see a number of species including elephant, eland and bushbuck.

The eastern side of the **Kitibong area** is a good place to find large herds of buffalo. The eastern side is mainly acacia parklands and the western side, thicker woodlands.

The **Gursi section** is similar to the Kitibong area with the addition of rainy season wetlands, which are home to large populations of water birds. African wild dogs are sometimes seen.

Hippo are found in the extensive swamps of the **Larmakau region** located in the central eastern part of the park. **Nguselo-rorobi**, in the south of the park, is predominantly swamp with some woodlands and plains. The **Mkungunero section** has a few fresh water pools and a variety of birdlife.

On my most recent visit, we spotted eland, giraffe, buffalo, a few lion, oryx, elephant, impala, Grant's gazelle, zebra, hartebeest, warthog, baboon, and ostrich. We met one group of game viewers that kept their fires burning all night to keep three lions they had heard near the camp at bay!

Elephants have destroyed many baobab trees. A baobab tree with a huge hole through the center of its trunk can be seen near the lodge.

Game viewing is excellent in this 1000-square-mile park during the dry season from July-September/October, which happens to be the worst months for viewing game in the Serengeti. Consequently, visitors to Tanzania during those months

Baobab tree near Tarangire Safari Lodge.

might consider substituting Tarangire for the Serengeti should there not be time for both, or at least try to add Tarangire to their itinerary. Over 300 species of birds have been recorded in the park. Bird watching is best December-May.

During the rainy seasons many roads become impassable. There are garage facilities at Park headquarters, but no petrol is available.

ACCOMMODATION — CLASS B: * *Tarangire Safari Lodge*, an excellent lodge situated high on a bluff overlooking the park, has 35 tents and six bungalows (doubles) with private facilities, a large swimming pool and wading pool for children, and large boutique. Wildlife viewing is excellent in the late afternoon from the veranda.

CAMPING: There are three campsites overlooking the Tarangire River with no facilities.

MOUNT KILIMANJARO

Known to many through Ernest Hemingway's book, *The Snows of Kilimanjaro*, Mount Kilimanjaro is the highest mountain in the world that is not part of a mountain range and is definitely one of the world's most impressive mountains. Kilimanjaro means "shining mountain;" it rises from an average altitude of about 3300 feet on the dry plains to 19,340 feet, truly a world-class mountain. On clear days the mountain can be seen from over 200 miles away.

The mountain consists of three major volcanic centers: Kibo (19,340 ft.), Shira (13,650 ft.) to the west and Mawenzi (16,893 ft.) to the east. The base of the mountain is 37 miles long and 25 miles wide. The park covers 292 square miles of the mountain above 8856 feet (2700 m.). The park also has six corridors that climbers may use through the Forest Reserve.

Hikers pass through zones of forest, alpine, and semidesert to its snowcapped peak, situated only three degrees south of the equator. It was once thought to be an extinct volcano; but due to recent rumblings, it is now classified as dormant.

Climbing Mt. Kilimanjaro was definitely a highlight of my travels. For the struggle to reach its highest peak, I was handsomely rewarded with a feeling of accomplishment and many exciting memories of the climb.

Kilimanjaro is in fact the easiest mountain in the world to ascend to such heights. But it is still a struggle for even fit adventurers. On the other hand, it can be climbed by people from all walks of life who are in good condition and have a strong will. Mind you, reaching the top is by no means necessary; the flora, fauna and magnificent views seen en route are fabulous.

The first written record of Kilimanjaro was by Ptolemy 18 centuries ago. A Christian missionary, Johann Rebmann, reported his discovery of this snowcapped mountain, but the Europeans didn't believe him. Hans Meyer was the first European to climb Kilimanjaro in 1889.

The most unique animal in this park is the Abbot's duiker, which is found in only a few mountain forests in northern Tanzania. Other wildlife includes elephant, buffalo, eland, leopard, hyrax, and black and white colobus monkeys. However, very little large game is seen.

The best time to climb is January, February, August and September during the dryer seasons when the skies are fairly clear. January and February are warmer while September is cooler.

July, November and December are also good, while April

and May should be avoided because of heavy rains and overcast skies. I, of course, happened to be in Tanzania in April, but I still made the climb and thoroughly enjoyed it.

From March-May, during the long rainy season, the summit is often covered in clouds with snow falling at higher altitudes and rain at lower altitudes. The short rains (between October-December) bring afternoon thunderstorms, but evenings and mornings are often clear.

Many routes to the summit require no mountaineering skills. Mountaineers wishing to ascend by technical routes may wish to contact the Mountain Club of Kenya for advice and get a copy of *Guide to Mt. Kenya and Kilimanjaro* published by the club and edited by Iain Allan (P.O. Box 45741, Nairobi, Kenya).

Registration and payment of fees for all routes must be made at the Park Headquarters in Marangu. The Park Headquarters are located about a seven-hour drive from Nairobi, two and one-half hours from Arusha. Children under ten years of age are not allowed over 9843 ft. (3000 m.).

Zones

Mt. Kilimanjaro can be divided into five zones by altitude: 1) Cultivated lower slopes, 2) Forest, 3) Heath and Moorland/-Lower Alpine; 4) Highland Desert/Alpine; and 5) Summit. Each zone spans approximately 3300 feet (1000 m.) in altitude. As the altitude increases, rainfall and temperatures decrease; this has a direct effect on the vegetation each zone supports.

The rich volcanic soils of the **lower slopes** of the mountain around Moshi and Marangu up to the park gate (6000 ft./1830 m.) are intensely cultivated, mostly with coffee and bananas.

The **forest zone** (5900-9185 ft./1800-2800 m.) receives the highest rainfall of the zones, with about 80 inches (2000 mm.) on the southern slopes and about half that amount on the northern and western slopes. The upper half of this zone is often covered with clouds, and humidity is high with day temperatures ranging from 60-70° F. Don't be surprised if it rains while walking through this zone; in fact, expect it.

In the lower forest there are palms, sycamore figs, bearded lichen and mosses hanging from tree limbs, tree ferns growing to 20 feet in height, and giant lobelia, which grow to over 30 feet. In the upper forest zone, giant groundsels appear. Unlike many East African volcanic mountains, no bamboo belt surrounds Kilimanjaro.

Black and white colobus and blue monkeys, olive baboons and bushbuck may be seen. Elephant, eland, giraffe, buffalo and suni may be seen on the northern and western slopes. Also present but seldom seen are bush pig, civet, genet, bush duiker, Abbot's duiker and red duiker.

Zone three is a lower alpine zone ranging from 9185-13,125 ft. (2800-4000 m.), and is predominantly **heath** followed by **moorlands**. Rainfall decreases with altitude from about 50 inches to 20 inches per year. Giant heather (10-30 ft. high), grasslands with scattered bushes and beautiful flowers, including "everlasting" flowers, protea and colorful red-hot pokers, characterize the lower part of this zone.

You then enter the moorlands with tussock grasses and groups of giant senecios and lobelias — weird prehistoric-looking Afro-alpine vegetation that would provide a great setting for a science fiction movie. With a lot of luck, you may spot eland, elephant, buffalo or klipspringer.

The **highland desert/alpine** zone is from around 13,125-16,400 ft. (4000-5000 m.) and receives only about ten inches of rain per year. Vegetation is very thin and includes tussock grasses, "everlasting" flowers, moss balls and lichens. The thin air makes flying too difficult for most birds, and the very few larger mammals that may be seen do not make this region their home. What this zone lacks in wildlife is compensated by the fabulous views. Temperatures can range from below freezing to very hot, so be prepared.

The **summit** experiences arctic conditions and receives less than four inches of rain per year, usually in the form of snow. It is almost completely void of vegetation.

Kibo's northern summit is covered by the Great Northern Glacier. On Kibo there is an outer caldera about one and a half miles in diameter. Uhuru peak is the highest point on the outer caldera and also the highest point on the mountain.

Within the outer caldera is an inner cone which contains the Inner or Reusch Crater, which is about a half-mile in diameter. Vents (fumaroles) spewing steam and sulfurous gasses are located at the Terrace and the base of the crater. Within the Inner Crater is an ash cone with an ash pit about 1100 feet across and about 400 feet deep.

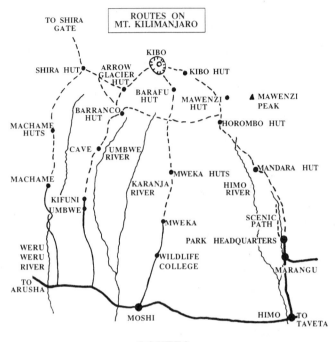

ROUTES

Climbing Kibo via the routes described below requires no mountaineering skills. A guide for each climbing party is required. Porters are optional, though highly recommended. It is more interesting (and more expensive) to take other routes up and return via the Marangu Route, offering additional variety to the climb.

Little firewood is available. Do bring fuel for cooking and heating. The national park guides are not qualified to lead glacier or ice climbing routes. The services of a professional guide must be arranged in advance.

The Park has a rescue team based at the Park Headquarters with immediate response to emergencies on the Marangu Route. If using another route, descend the mountain and contact Park Headquarters (tel: Marangu 50), and they will send a rescue team to assist.

Marangu (Tourist) Route

The Marangu (Tourist) Route is probably the least scenic

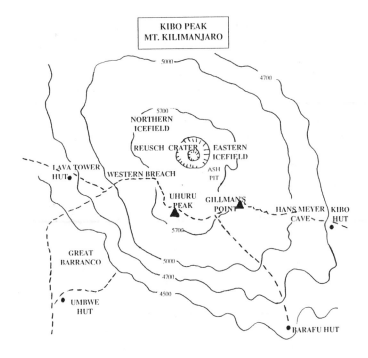

KIBO PEAK
MT. KILIMANJARO

5000

4700

5700
NORTHERN
ICEFIELD

REUSCH CRATER   EASTERN
                 ICEFIELD

LAVA TOWER   WESTERN BREACH   ASH
HUT   PIT

UHURU
PEAK   GILLMAN'S
        POINT   HANS MEYER KIBO
                 CAVE   HUT

5700

GREAT
BARRANCO   5000

4700

4500

UMBWE
HUT

BARAFU HUT

route up the mountain, but it is the most often used. Marangu has the best accommodations and is the easiest (most gradual) route to the summit.

This route may be completed in five days, but it's best to take six days, spending an extra day at Horombo hut to allow more time to acclimatize to the altitude. The huts are dormitory-style with common areas for cooking and eating.

Most climbing tours originate in Nairobi, Arusha or Kilimanjaro Airport and are for seven or eight days. The night before and the night after the climb are usually spent in the village of Marangu at either Kibo or Marangu Hotel.

DAY ONE: MARANGU (6004 ft./1830 m.) to MANDARA HUT (8856 ft./2700 m.) REGULAR ROUTE: THREE-FOUR HOURS; FOREST ROUTE: FOUR-FIVE HOURS. ALTITUDE GAIN: 2854 ft. (870 m.).

An hour or two is spent at Park Headquarters at Marangu Gate handling registration, paying park fees and arranging the loads for the porters. Try to leave in the morning to allow a leisurely pace and to avoid afternoon showers.

The fastest route and the one most often taken is along an

old vehicle track. The forest trail takes longer but has much less traffic than the main trail; this trail veers off to the left a short way past the gate and runs along a stream. You have a choice of rejoining the main trail about half way to (about one hour before) arriving at Mandara Hut. Both paths are often muddy.

Mandara has a number of small wooden A-frame huts sleeping eight persons each, four to a room, and a main cabin with a dormitory upstairs and dining room downstairs, for a total of 200 beds. Kerosene lamps, stoves and mattresses are provided.

DAY TWO: MANDARA to HOROMBO HUT (12,205 ft./3720 m.): FIVE-SEVEN HOURS. ALTITUDE GAIN: 3346 ft. (1020 m.).

On Day Two you pass through the upper part of the rain forest to tussock grassland and fascinating Afro-alpine vegetation of giant groundsels and giant lobelias to the moorlands. Once out of the forest, you begin to get great views of the town of Moshi and Mawenzi Peak (16,893 ft./5149 m.).

If you can spare an extra day for acclimatizing, Horombo is the best hut for this. There are some nice day hikes that will help you further acclimatize. Kibo is too high to allow a good night's sleep. Horombo also has 200 beds and is similar to Mandara.

DAY THREE: HOROMBO HUT to KIBO HUT (15,430 ft./4703 m.): FIVE-SIX HOURS. ALTITUDE GAIN: 3225 ft. (983 m.).

On the morning of Day Three, the vegetation begins to thin out to open grasslands. You pass "Last Water" (be sure to fill your water bottles as this is last source of water). The landscape becomes more barren as you reach "the saddle," a wide desert between Kibo and Mawenzi Peak. Kibo Hut does not come in view until just before you reach it. Kibo Hut has 120 beds and is located on the east side of Kibo Peak.

With the wind-chill factor, it can be very cold so dress warmly. This is the day many hikers feel the effects of the altitude and may begin to experience some altitude sickness. Most people find it impossible to sleep at this height because of the lack of oxygen and the bitter cold, not to mention the possibility of altitude sickness. Get as much rest as you can.

DAY FOUR: KIBO HUT to GILLMAN'S POINT (18,635 ft./5680 m.) and UHURU PEAK (19,340 ft./5895 m.) AND DOWN TO HOROMBO HUT. TEN TO TWELVE HOURS.

Your guide will wake you shortly after midnight for your

ascent, which should begin around 1:00 a.m. Be sure not to delay the start; it is vital that you reach the summit by sunrise. The sun quickly melts the frozen scree, making the ascent all the more difficult.

The steep ascent to Gillman's Point on the edge of the caldera is a grueling four-to-five-hour slog up scree. Hans Meyer Cave is a good place to rest before climbing seemingly unending switchbacks past Johannes Notch to Gillman's Point.

Uhuru Peak is a fairly gradual climb of 705 ft. (215 m.). It will take another hour to hour and a half. Uhuru Peak is well-marked and there is a book in which you may sign your name.

If you are still feeling strong, ask your guide to take you down into the caldera to the inner crater which has some steam vents. You return to Gillman's Point by a different route.

On my climb our guide woke us late, and we didn't start the climb until after 2:00 a.m. We made it all right to Gillman's Point, but the final hike to Uhuru (Freedom) Peak was a killer. Instead of walking across the frozen crust, I fell through knee-deep snow on every step. Had we arrived an hour earlier, this may not have been a problem.

The feeling of accomplishment upon reaching the summit was one of the highlights of my life. I was amazed at the tremendous size of the glaciers so close to the equator. Standing over 16,000 feet above the surrounding plains, the views were breathtaking in every direction. Sunrise over Mawenzi is a beautiful sight. You truly feel you're on the top of the world!

Shortly after sunrise you begin the long walk down the mountain to Kibo Hut for a short rest, then continue onward to Horombo Hut. Provided you are not completely exhausted, the walk down is long but pretty easy going. From Gillman's Point to Horombo takes about four hours and from Uhuru Peak about five.

The entire descent is made in two days, and one's knees take a hard pounding; you may want to wrap your knees with elastic bandages or use elastic knee supports.

DAY FIVE: HOROMBO HUT to MARANGU.

Another long day of hiking as you descend past Mandara Hut to Park Headquarters where you receive a diploma certifying your accomplishment. Most climbers spend the night at Kibo or Marangu Hotel and have the pleasure of sharing their experiences with unwary visitors planning to begin their Kilimanjaro adventure the following day.

Mweka Route

This is steepest and most direct route to Uhuru Peak. It starts at Mweka village near the College of Wildlife Management (4593 ft./ 1400 m.) and runs along an old logging road through banana and coffee plantations for about three miles, then along a seldom-used path for another three and a half miles to Mweka Hut at 9515 ft. (2900 m.). This hike takes six to eight hours. There is water nearby.

After a five-to-six-hour climb the following day through heathlands and alpine desert, you reach Barafu Hut (14,435 ft./4400 m.). The third day is a steep climb between Ratzel and Rebmann Glaciers to Kibo Rim (six to seven hours) and Uhuru Peak (one more hour).

Umbwe Route

This is a spectacular route but very steep and strenuous. The route begins at Umbwe (about 4600 ft./1400 m.), a village ten miles from Moshi. Walk two miles to Kifuni village and into the forest. Follow the path for another three and a half miles and then branch left into a mist-covered forest until you reach the forest cave (Bivouac #1) at 9515 ft. (2900 m.), six to seven hours from Umbwe. Overhanging cliffs extending about five feet from the cliff provide reasonable protection for about six people; however, it is recommended you use your own tents. The wood is usually very damp and water is available, but not close by.

Continue through moorlands and along a narrow ridge with deep valleys on either side. The thick mist and vegetation covered with "Old Man's Beard" moss creates an eerie atmosphere. The second caves at 11,483 ft. (3500 m.) are still another two- to three-hour hike from Bivouac #1. The vegetation thins out, and you branch right shortly before arriving at Barranco Hut (12,795 ft./3900 m.) about two hours later.

From Barranco you can backtrack to the fork and turn right (North) and hike for three hours to where Lava Tower Hut (15,092 ft./4600 m.) used to stand. From there the climb is up steep scree and blocks of rock to the floor of the crater and Uhuru Peak via the Great Western Breach. The climb from Lava Tower Hut to the caldera takes about nine hours. An

Burchell's zebra.

alternative from Barranco Hut is to traverse the mountain eastward and join the Mweka Route.

Shira Plateau Route

This is a very scenic and yet seldom-used route, providing great views of Kilimanjaro and the Rift Valley and probably the best wildlife viewing on the mountain. A four-wheel-drive vehicle is needed and the roads may be impassable in the rainy seasons. The route is hard to find. Be sure to have a guide that knows the way.

Drive north from the Moshi-Arusha road at Boma la Ng'ombe to Londorossi Gate, located on the western side of Kilimanjaro. Continue on to a campsite. The track ends shortly thereafter, at 12,270 ft. (3720 m.). The defunct Shira Hut (12,467 ft./3800 m.) is only one-and-a-half hour's walk away. You may want to take two days to acclimatize before continuing on.

From Shira Hut it is about a four-hour hike to the remains of Lava Tower Hut. The vegetation changes on the Shira Plateau are fabulous as you walk through open grasslands and moorlands dotted with giant senecios over 30 feet high and past the impressive Shira Cone, Cathedral and Needle Peaks.

From Lava Tower Hut follow the directions from the Umbwe Route to the summit.

Machame Route

This relatively easy route is possibly the most beautiful route up the mountain. The park gate is located a few miles above Machame village. Hike four to six hours through rain forest to Machame Huts (9843 ft./3000 m.). The following day hike, five to seven hours to the defunct Shira Hut (12,467 ft./3800 m.) on the Shira Plateau (see Shira Route for description of the area). Continue hiking about four hours to Lava Tower Hut. From Lava Tower Hut follow the directions from the Umbwe Route to the summit.

Summit Circuit

There is a circuit between 12,139-15,092 ft. (3700-4600 m.) completely around the base of Kibo peak. Horombo, Barranco and Moir Huts are on the circuit, while Lava Tower, Shira, Kibo and Mawenzi Huts are on side trails not far from the circuit. A tent is needed since there is no hut on the northern side of Kibo. Be sure to bring a well-insulated pad for your sleeping bag.

Huts

Mandara, Horombo and Kibo Huts are described under the "Marangu/Tourist Route" above. The other huts are prefab metal huts, either 10 or 15 feet in diameter in varying states of disrepair; some are basically uninhabitable. Many of the wooden floors have been ripped up and used for firewood. It is best to bring your own tents and let the guides and porters use the huts. Drinking water should be filtered, treated and/or boiled as some sources on the mountain are polluted.
MAWENZI HUT (15,092 ft./4600 m.). From "The Saddle" on the Marangu route just after passing East Lava Hill, hike one and a quarter miles east-northeast (050 degrees) to the hut at the base of the West Corrie. Mawenzi Hut sleeps five and is about a three-hour hike from Horombo or Kibo Huts. There are no toilets. Mawenzi Peak should only be attempted by well-equipped, experienced mountaineers.

Male lion. Photo: Mike Appelbaum.

MAWENZI TARN HUT (14,206 ft./4330 m.). This hut is situated northeast of Mawenzi Hut; it is an easy hike around the foot of the peak. The hut sleeps six.

MWEKA HUTS (9515 ft./2900 m.). There are two large huts sleeping 12 persons each. A stream and firewood are available nearby.

BARAFU HUT (15,092 ft./4600 m.). The hut sleeps twelve and there is no wood or water.

BARRANCO HUT (12,795 ft./3900 m.). The hut sleeps eight and there is a bivouac site about a 600-foot walk above the hut under a rock overhang. Plenty of wood is available in the vicinity and a stream is nearby.

MOIR HUT (13,780 ft./4200 m.). This hut is located on the northwest side of Kibo north of the Shira; it sleeps ten and there is water nearby.

Climbing Tips

Here are a number of ways of increasing your chances of making it to the top. One of the most important things to remember is to *take your time*. *Polepole* is Swahili for "slowly" which is definitely the way to go. There is no prize for being the first to the hut or first to the top.

Pace yourself so that you are never completely out of breath. Exaggerate your breathing, taking deeper and more frequent breaths than you feel you actually need. This will help you acclimatize and keep you from exhausting yourself prematurely, or developing pulmonary or cerebral edema.

Ski poles make good walking sticks, can be rented at Park Headquarters, and are highly recommended. Bring a small backpack to carry the items you wish to have quick access to along the trail, such as a water bottle and camera. Most importantly, listen to what your body is telling you. Don't over do it! Many people die each year on the mountain because they don't listen or pay attention to the signs and keep pushing themselves.

On steep portions of the hike, use the "lock step" method to conserve energy. Take a step and lock the knee of the uphill leg. This puts your weight on your leg bone, using less muscle strength. Pause for a few seconds, letting your other leg rest without any weight on it, and breath deeply. Then repeat. This technique will save vital energy that you may very well need in your quest for the top.

Some climbers take the prescription drug diamox, a diuretic which usually reduces the symptoms of altitude sickness, but there are side effects from taking the drug, including increased urination. You should discuss the use of diamox with your doctor prior to leaving home.

Drink a lot more water than you feel you need. High-altitude hiking is very dehydrating, and a dehydrated body weakens quickly. Climbers should drink three to four liters (quarts) of liquids daily.

Most hikers find it difficult to sleep at high altitude. Once you reach the hut each afternoon, rest a bit, then hike to a spot a few hundred feet in altitude above the hut and relax for awhile. Acclimatizing even for a short time at a higher altitude will help you get a more restful night's sleep. Remember, "Climb high, sleep low!"

Consume at least 4000 calories per day on the climb. This can be a problem. Most climbers loose their appetite at high altitude. Bring along trail mix (mixed nuts and dried fruit), chocolate and other goodies that you enjoy to supplement the meals prepared for you. Forget about drinking alcoholic beverages on the climb. Altitude greatly enhances the effects of alcohol. Meanwhile, alcohol causes dehydration. Headaches caused by altitude sickness can be bad enough without having a hangover on top of it.

Equipment Checklist

The better equipped you are for the climb, the higher your chances of making the summit. When it comes to clothing, the "layered effect" works best. Bring a duffle bag to pack your gear in for the climb. Wrap your clothes in heavy garbage bags to keep them dry. Keep the weight under the porter's maximum load of 33 pounds (15 kg.).

Here's a checklist of items to consider bringing:
CLOTHING —
    Gortex jacket (with hood) and pants
    polypropylene long underwear — tops and bottoms, medium and heavyweight
    wool sweater (one or two)
    Gortex gaiters (to keep the scree out of your boots at higher altitudes)
    tennis shoes or ultralight hiking boots (for lower altitudes)
    medium-weight insulated hiking boots for warmth and to help dig into the scree during the final ascent
    heavy wool or down mittens with Gortex outer shell and glove liners
    several pairs of wool socks and polypropylene liner socks
    several pairs of underwear
    track or warm-up suit (to relax and sleep in)
    long trousers or knickers (wool or synthetic)
    light, loose-fitting cotton trousers
    shorts (with pockets)
    wool long-sleeve and cotton long-sleeve shirts
    T-shirts or short-sleeve shirts

turtleneck shirt
down vest
balaclava (wool or synthetic)
wide-brimmed hat or cap for protection from the sun
bandana
wool hat
sleeping pad (for all routes except the Marangu Route)

MISCELLANEOUS —
day pack large enough to carry extra clothing, rain gear, plastic water bottle (1 litre/quart), camera and lunch.
sleeping bag (rated at least to 0 degrees F.)
pocket flask for summit climb
flashlight with extra bulb and batteries. Some prefer head lamps.
light towel
sunglasses and mountaineering glasses
camera and film
strong sun block
chapstick
body lotion (otherwise skin may get dry and itchy)
water purifiers
duffle bag
half-dozen heavy garbage bags in which to wrap clothes
toilet paper
Wash-n-Drys
pocket knife with scissors
granola bars, trail mix and sweets that travel well
powdered drink mix

FIRST AID KIT —
malaria pills
moleskin
Band-Aids (plasters)
Ace (elastic) bandages
gauze pads (4" x 4")
diuretics (diamox) — by prescription from your doctor
broad-spectrum antibiotics (pills)
laxative
antihistamine tablets

Spotted hyena are scavengers as well as efficient hunters.

antibiotic cream
anti-diarrhoea — Imodium or Lomotil
iodine
headache pills, i.e., Tylenol
throat and cough lozenges
decongestant
analgesic
Buprofen tablets (such as "Motrine") for muscle
cramps and sore joints

Park Headquarters are located in Marangu (Kilimanjaro National Park, P.O. Box 96, Marangu; tel: Marangu 50), 29 miles from Moshi, 63 miles from Kilimanjaro Airport and 75 miles from Arusha.

Equipment is available for rent from Park Headquarters, Kibo and Marangu Hotels, but it is often heavily worn or of low quality. I recommend that you bring your own gear.

ACCOMMODATION — CLASS C: * *Kibo Hotel* — Situated less than a mile from Marangu village, this lodge has rooms with private facilities (150 beds). * *Marangu Hotel* — Located a mile and a half from Marangu village, this rustic lodge has 29 double rooms with private facilities.

ARUSHA NATIONAL PARK

Arusha National Park is predominately inhabited by forest animals while in the other northern parks savannah animals are the most prevalent. This is the best place in northern Tanzania to spot black and white colobus monkeys and bushbuck, and to photograph larger species with Mt. Kilimanjaro in the background. Early mornings are best for this since Mt. Kilimanjaro is less likely to be covered with clouds.

Wildlife is more difficult to spot here than in the other northern parks; do not expect to see large herds of game. However, you are allowed to walk in this park when accompanied by a park ranger, and there are a number of hides and picnic sites to enjoy. The best time to visit is July to March.

This 53-square-mile park is actually the merger of three regions: Meru Crater National Park, Momela Lakes, and Ngurdoto Crater National Park. The wide range of habitats from highland rain forest to acacia woodlands and crater lakes host a variety of wildlife. Armed park guides are required to accompany you for walks in the park or for climbing Mt. Meru; guides are available at Park Headquarters at Momela Gate.

The turnoff to the park entrance is 13 miles east of Arusha and 36 miles west of Moshi. The park is a nice day trip from Arusha.

On the open grassland near the entrance to the park, Burchell's zebra are often seen. High in the forest canopy of the Ngurdoto Forest is a good place to find black and white colobus monkeys. Olive baboons are common and red duiker is sometimes seen.

It is not allowed to walk in the two-mile-wide Ngurdoto crater, which is in essence a reserve within a reserve. However, there are good views of the crater, Momela Lakes and Mt. Kilimanjaro (on clear days).

Driving north from Ngurdoto, you pass Ngongongare Spring, the Senato Pools (sometimes dry) and Lokie Swamp and are likely to see common waterbuck and maybe Bohor reedbuck. Buffalo are often seen around Lake Longil.

As you continue past Kambi Ya Fisi (hyena's camp), the landscape becomes more open, and elephant and giraffe may be seen. Hippo, and a variety of waterfowl may be seen at the shallow, alkaline Momela Lakes.

From Kitoto a four-wheel-drive vehicle is needed to reach

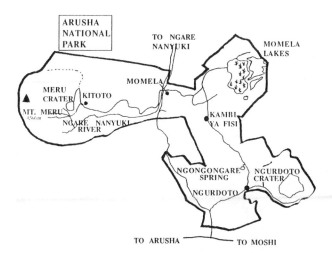

Meru Crater. Better yet, take an hour or so and walk to the river, then to the crater. The shear cliff rises almost 5000 feet and is one of the highest in the world.

At the base of Mt. Meru, you may encounter elephant and buffalo. Kirk's dikdik, banded mongoose and klipspringer may also be seen in the park. Over 400 species of birds have been recorded.

Mt. Meru (14,980 ft./4566 m.) is an impressive mountain classified as a dormant volcano; its last eruption was just over 100 years ago. The mountain can be climbed in one day, but it is far more enjoyable to take three days, allowing more time for exploration.

On the morning of the first day of a three-day climb, walk for about three hours from Momela Gate (about 5000 ft./1500 m.) to Miriakamba Hut. In the afternoon, hike to Meru Crater. On the second day, hike three hours to the Saddle Hut and in the afternoon walk for about one and a half hours to Little Meru (12,533 ft./3820 m.). On Day Three, reach the summit and return to Momela Gate.

The best months to climb are October and December-February. Bring all your own gear and book a park guide in advance.

ACCOMMODATION — CLASS B: * *Oldoinyorok Lodge* — A small lodge with six bungalows (doubles) and ensuite facilities

The dikdik is Africa's smallest antelope.

located on the edge of Arusha National Park.

CLASS D: — * *Momela Game Lodge* has rondavels (40 beds) outside the gate of Arusha National Park.

CLASS F: One self-service resthouse (five beds) is located near Momela Gate. Book through the Warden, Arusha National Park, P.O. Box 3141, Arusha.

CAMPING: One campsite is located near Ngurdoto Gate in the forest and three are at the foot of Tululusia Hill. All have water, toilet facilities and firewood.

RUBONDO ISLAND NATIONAL PARK

Located in the southwestern part of Lake Victoria, the main attraction of this 93-square-mile island is sitatunga, which is indigenous to Rubondo. In addition, walking is allowed and the

African Elephant. Photo: Mike Appelbaum.

wildlife may be approached very closely.

Also indigenous to the park are hippo, bushbuck, crocodile, marsh mongoose and python. Chimpanzee, black and white colobus monkey, black rhino, giraffe and roan antelope have been introduced. There are no large predators. Bird watching, especially for waterfowl, is very good here.

In addition to the main island, there are about a dozen small islands that make up the park. Habitats include papyrus swamps, savannah, open woodlands and dense evergreen forests. Visitors accompanied by a guide who is usually armed may walk along forested trails in search of wildlife or wait patiently at a number of hides. The best time to visit is November-February. A few boats are available for hire.

Flying is the only easy way to get to the park. An airstrip is located at Park Headquarters. By vehicle it is a seven-hour drive and two-hour boat ride by one route and a ten-hour drive and half-hour boat ride by another route. Visitors are not allowed to bring their vehicles to the island.

ACCOMMODATION — CLASS F: A few self-service bandas are available; bring your own food.

CAMPING: Sites are available; but bring your own supplies.

THE SOUTH

The "Southern Circuit" of wildlife reserves includes the Selous Game Reserve, Ruaha National Park and Mikumi National Park. The Selous and Ruaha are seldom visited and offer a great opportunity to explore wild and unspoiled bush.

SELOUS GAME RESERVE

This little-known reserve happens to be the largest game reserve in Africa. Over 21,000 square miles in area, the Selous is more than half the size of the state of Ohio, twice the area of Denmark and three and three-fourths times larger than Serengeti National Park. Unexploited and largely unexplored, no human habitation is allowed in this virgin bush except for limited tourist facilities.

The Selous is a stronghold for over 50,000 elephant (recently down from 100,000 due to rampant poaching), 150,000 buffalo (herds often exceed 1000), and large populations of lion, leopard, sable antelope, Lichtenstein's hartebeest, greater kudu, hippo, crocodiles, and numerous other species including black rhino, giraffe, zebra, wildebeest, waterbuck, wild dog and impala. Over one million large animals live within its borders. Over 350 species of birds and 2000 plant species have been recorded.

Game is plentiful but more patience is required to spot them than in the northern parks. The wildlife is truly wild (unaccustomed to humans) and, as a result, it is more difficult to approach closely.

Almost 75% of this low-lying reserve (360-4100 ft.) is composed of miombo woodlands with the balance being grasslands, flood-plains, marshes and dense forests. The extensive miombo woodlands are a favorite habitat for tsetse flies, which are more prevalent here than in the northern parks. The

Selous has been spared encroachment by man because the presence of tsetse flies prevent grazing of domestic animals and because the soil is too poor to farm.

Walking safaris accompanied by an armed ranger are very popular and are conducted by all the camps. This reserve will give you the feeling of exploring the bush for the first time as you will encounter few, if any, other visitors during your safari.

The Rufiji River, the largest river in East Africa, roughly bisects the park as it flows from the southwest to the northeast. The Rufiji and its tributaries, including Great Ruaha and Luwego, have high concentrations of hippos and crocs. Fish eagles are numerous.

Exploring the Rufiji River, its channels, swamps and lakes by raft or boat and running the rapids of Stiegler's Gorge by raft are other adventurous ways of exploring the reserve. Fishing is also popular.

All tourist activities are restricted to the northern region. The best time to visit the park is during the dry season, June-October. During the two rainy seasons, November-January (short rains) and February-May (long rains), many of the roads are impassable and wildlife is scattered. The reserve is usually closed March-May.

Most visitors fly to camps in the Selous from Dar es Salaam by charter aircraft. Access by road is difficult and only possible in the dry season. The **Tazara Railway** (Dar es Salaam to Zambia) passes through the northern part of the Selous about four hours after departing Dar es Salaam, and an abundance of game is usually seen. This railway also serves as the border between the Selous and Mikumi National Parks. Some travelers disembark at Fuga Halt where they are taken (by prior arrangement) to the camps.

ACCOMMODATION — The camps are located from about 160-235 miles from Dar es Salaam, requiring a six-to-ten-hour drive in a four-wheel-drive vehicle. All camps have private airstrips and flying is highly recommended.

CLASS B/C: * *Mbuyu Safari Camp* — This comfortable tented camp on the banks of the Rufiji River has 15 tents with private facilities. Game drives, walking and boat safaris are offered. * *Selous Safari Camp*, also called *Beho Beho Camp*, is located north of the Rufiji River. The camp has bandas with private facilities and offers game drives and walking. * *Stiegler's Gorge Lodge* has chalets with private facilities overlooking the gorge.

CLASS C: * *Rufiji River Camp*, a basic tented camp with ten tents (doubles), offers game drives, fishing, walking and boat safaris.

CAMPING: Sites are available.

RUAHA NATIONAL PARK

Ruaha, known for its great populations of elephant, greater and lesser kudu, hippo, crocs and magnificent scenery is one of the country's newest and best national parks, and because of its location, it is one of the least visited.

Ruaha's scenery is spectacular and its 5000-square-mile area makes it almost as large as Serengeti National Park. The landscape is characterized by miombo woodland with rocky hills on a plateau over 3300 feet in altitude. Park elevation ranges from 2460 feet in the Ruaha Valley to 6230-foot Ikingu Mountain in the west of the park.

The Great Ruaha River with its impressive gorges, deep pools and rapids runs for 100 miles close to the park's eastern boundary and is home to many hippo and crocodiles. The best place in the park to see elephant is from the track that runs along the Ruaha River downstream from Msembe.

The dry season, June-November, is the best time to visit the park when game is concentrated along the Ruaha River. Large numbers of greater and lesser kudu, elephant, wildebeest and impala can be seen along with eland, sable antelope, roan antelope, buffalo, Defassa waterbuck, ostrich and giraffe. Lion, leopard, spotted and striped hyena, black-backed jackal, bat-eared fox and African wild dog are also present in significant numbers. Black rhino are present but seldom seen. Over 370 species of birds have been recorded.

Many tracks become impassable during the wet months January-March and the wildlife is scattered. Game viewing February-June is difficult due to high grass. Tsetse flies are present, especially in the miombo woodlands.

There are a number of photographic hides (blinds) and tree-houses overlooking watering areas allowing close views of wildlife undisturbed by the presence of man.

The park is about a four-hour drive from Iringa through the villages of Mloa and Idodi and across the Ruaha River via the Ibuguziwa Ferry. Park Headquarters and an airstrip are located at Msembe, 70 miles from Iringa and 385 miles from

Greater kudu.

Dar es Salaam.
ACCOMMODATION — CLASS C: * *Ruaha River Camp*, located in the park six miles south of Msembe, has rondavels and tents.
CLASS D: Several basic hotels are located at Iringa, 70 miles east of the park.
CLASS F: * *National Park Rondavels* (self-service) are situated at Msembe.
CAMPING: Campsites available. Book self-service rondavels and campsites through the Park Warden, Ruaha National Park, P.O. Box 369, Iringa.

Lion cub.

MIKUMI NATIONAL PARK

Mikumi is the closest park to Dar es Salaam (180 miles) and takes four hours to drive on tarmac from Dar via Morongoro.

The park covers 1266 square miles and borders the Selous Game Reserve to the south along the Tazara Railroad line. There is a hippo pool on the main highway which runs to Zambia and divides the park.

The park is dominated by the Mkata River flood plain with swamps and grasslands dotted with baobab trees and miombo woodlands at an average altitude of 1800 feet above sea level. Elephant, buffalo, lion, hippo, zebra, wildebeest and Masai giraffe are prevalent. Sable antelope, common waterbuck, Lichtenstein's hartebeest, eland, Bohor reedbuck and impala may also be seen. Black and white colobus monkeys are frequently seen in the south of the park.

During our two-day stay, we saw elephant, zebra, six lion, giraffe, buffalo, impala, ground hornbill and guinea fowl, among other species. There is a variety of birdlife as Mikumi is in the transition zone between north and south.

The long rains are March-May and the short rains from

November-December. Rainfall within the park ranges from 20-40 inches yearly.

It is difficult to say what is the best time to visit Mikumi. Unlike most parks, wildlife is concentrated in this park in the wet season when the vegetation is the thickest, making game viewing more difficult. Fewer animals are present in the dry season, but the ones present are easier to spot. Considering this, the best time to visit is June-February.

This park is open all year although some roads are closed during the rainy season. There is an airstrip, petrol station and garage at Park Headquarters.

ACCOMMODATION — CLASS B/C: * *Mikumi Wildlife Lodge* has 50 double rooms with private facilities and a swimming pool.

CLASS D: * *Mikumi Wildlife Camp* has self-contained bandas, restaurant and bar.

CAMPING: Campsites available.

THE WEST

LAKE TANGANYIKA

Lake Tanganyika forms much of the western border of Tanzania and is indeed an "inland sea." This is the world's longest lake (446 miles) and the world's second deepest lake (over 4700 feet). Only Lake Baikal in Russia is deeper, at over 5700 feet. More than 400 species of fish inhabit its clear waters — more than any other body of water in the world. Easiest access to the lake is by flying to Kigoma.

KIGOMA

Kigoma is the country's major port on huge Lake Tanganyika. From here you can catch a steamer to Burundi or Zambia. Kigoma is the closest town to Gombe Stream National Park and many travelers stay here while in transit to and from the park. Kigoma can be reached by air, by road or by a pleasant two-and-one-half-day train ride from Dar es Salaam.

Ujiji, a small town six miles south of Kigoma, is where the line, "Dr. Livingstone, I presume" was spoken by Stanley in 1872. Buses run there regularly from the Kigoma Rail Station.

ACCOMMODATION — CLASS D: * *New Kigoma Railway Hotel*

overlooks the lake and has rooms with private facilities. * *Lake View Hotel* has no view of the lake and is second choice to the Railway Hotel.

GOMBE STREAM NATIONAL PARK

Gombe Stream is the setting for Jane Goodall's chimpanzee studies, her films and books, including *In The Shadow of Man*. This remote 20-square-mile park is situated along the eastern shores of Lake Tanganyika ten miles north of Kigoma in remote northwestern Tanzania.

This tiny park covers a thin strip of land three miles wide and stretches for ten miles along Lake Tanganyika. A mountain range ascends steeply from the lake at an altitude of 2235 feet to form part of the eastern wall of the western branch of the Great Rift Valley, rising to 5000 feet.

Thick gallery forests are found along Gombe Stream and many other permanent streams in the valley and lower slopes of the mountains. Higher up the slopes are woodlands with some grasslands near the upper ridges.

The experience of seeing chimpanzees in the wild is by far the major attraction of this park. Other primates include red colobus monkey, blue monkey and baboon. Other wildlife of note includes buffalo, Defassa waterbuck and leopard.

Chimpanzees can usually be found around the research station and are quite habituated to humans. Also, ask a park ranger to take you up into the forest to track them. The Kakombe Waterfall is worth a visit. There is also a nice walk along the lake shore northward from the guesthouse.

The easiest access is by water taxi (three hours) which departs Ujiji in the morning every day except Sunday.

ACCOMMODATION — CLASS F: A basic self-service hostel with 15 beds is located a little over a mile from the research station. Bring your own food, cooking utensils, gas stove and linens. Book well in advance or bring a tent as the guesthouse may be full. Only basic supplies are available in Kigoma.

CAMPING: Allowed on special request.

MAHALE MOUNTAINS NATIONAL PARK

Like Gombe Stream, the main attraction of this remote park, which was only recently gazetted in 1985, is being

Warthog family.

able to walk among large populations of chimpanzees. The chimps have been studied by Japanese researchers for the last 20 years, and over 100 of them have been habituated to humans.

Located about 95 miles south of Kigoma, this 609-square-mile park is situated on the eastern shores of Lake Tanganyika. The Mahale Mountains with deep ravines, permanent streams and waterfalls run through the center of the park, forming the eastern wall of the Great Rift Valley with altitudes up to 8075 feet above sea level.

The area surrounding Park Headquarters is predominantly acacia woodland, changing to lowland forest and then montane forest as one progresses inland and gains altitude.

In addition to over 1,000 chimpanzees, the park is also home to the red colobus monkey, Angolan black and white colobus monkey, banded mongoose, Sharpe's grysbok and blue duiker. Bushbuck and warthog are commonly seen around Park Headquarters.

Seasons are relatively unpredictable. The dry season usually runs from May-October while rainy seasons are usually November-January and March-May. Nights are often cool and rainfall ranges within the park from 60-100 inches per year. The best time to visit is May-October.

There is no easy way to reach this seldom visited park.

Easiest access to the park is by boat from Kigoma. Take the weekly steamer *MV Liemba* for six hours to the village of Lagosa (Mugambo). You usually arrive in the middle of the night and must be transferred ashore. From here charter a boat for a three-hour ride to Kasoge (Kasiha village) in the park. Small boats make this journey in 12-16 hours. The park may also be reached by four-wheel-drive vehicle on a dirt track from Mpanda via Mwesi, but this route is not advised.

ACCOMMODATION — CLASS F: The is a basic guesthouse, but you will need to bring your own food, crockery and cutlery, bed linens and stove. No supplies are available in the park.

CAMPING: Camping sites available.

KATAVI NATIONAL PARK

This undeveloped 870-square-mile park is located between the towns of Mpanda and Sumbawanga on the main road running through western Tanzania from north to south.

Lake Katavi and its extensive flood plains are in the north of this park that is about 2950 feet above sea level. To the southeast is Lake Chada which is connected with Lake Katavi by the Katuma River and its extensive swampland. Miombo woodlands dominate most of the dry areas except for acacia woodlands near Lake Chada.

Wildlife includes hippo, crocs, elephant, zebra, lion, leopard, eland, puku, buffalo, roan and sable antelope. Over 400 species of birds have been recorded.

The long rains are March-May. The best time to visit is July-October.

ACCOMMODATION — CLASS F: There are only a few huts for shelter. Very basic hotel accommodation is available in Mpanda and Sumbawanga.

CAMPING: Sites are available in the park. Campers must be self-sufficient as there are no facilities.

THE COAST

DAR ES SALAAM

Dar es Salaam, meaning "haven of peace" in Arabic, is the functional capital, largest city, and commercial center of Tanzania. Many safaris to the southern parks begin here. Among

Burchell's zebra.

the more interesting sights are the harbor, National Museum, Village Museum and the Kariakoo Market. Ask at your hotel about traditional dancing troops that may be performing during your stay.

Once the German capital, hub of the slave trade and end-point of the slave route from the interior, **Bagamoya** is an old seaport 46 miles north of Dar es Salaam. Fourteenth century ruins, stone pens and shackles that held the slaves may be seen.

ACCOMMODATION — FIRST CLASS: * *The Kilimanjaro Hotel* is a large air-conditioned hotel with ensuite facilities, swimming pool and fabulous view of the harbor.

TOURIST CLASS: * The *New Africa Hotel* is air-conditioned with ensuite facilities and has popular terrace coffee shop.

* *Oyster Bay Hotel* is four miles from town on the coast.

ZANZIBAR

Zanzibar and its sister island, Pemba, grow 75% of the world's cloves. A beautiful island unspoiled by tourism, Zanzibar is only 22 miles from the mainland — a twenty-minute flight from Dar es Salaam or a five-to-seven-hour ride by motorboat. A more traditional, yet difficult-to-arrange way to reach the island is sailing by dhow from Dar es Salaam, usually with a return to Bagamoyo.

The narrow streets and Arabic architecture of historical Zanzibar City are exceptionally mystical and beautiful on a moonlit night. Main attractions include the Zanzibar Museum, the former British Consulate, Arab Fort, Anglican Cathedral built on the site of the old slave market, Sultan's Palace, clove market and Indian bazaar. Livingstone's and Burton's houses are near the picturesque Dhow Harbour. Visitors can take a short boat ride to Slave Island to see the slave trading ruins and a giant tortoise.

Scheduled flights to the island are often overbooked. Customs at Zanzibar may require visitors to change foreign currency on the island regardless of how much they may have previously changed on the mainland. The tourist office is in Livingstone House in Zanzibar City.

ACCOMMODATION — FIRST CLASS: * *Hotel Ya Bwawani* is a large hotel with private facilities, saltwater pool and disco.

TOURIST CLASS: * *Africa House*, an old hotel with traditional Arabic design, has rooms with private facilities.

MAFIA ISLAND

A forty-minute flight south from Dar es Salaam, this island offers some of the best big-game fishing in the world. Species caught include marlin, sailfish, tuna and shark.

ACCOMMODATION — CLASS C: * *Mafia Island Lodge* has rooms with private facilities.

UGANDA

UGANDA

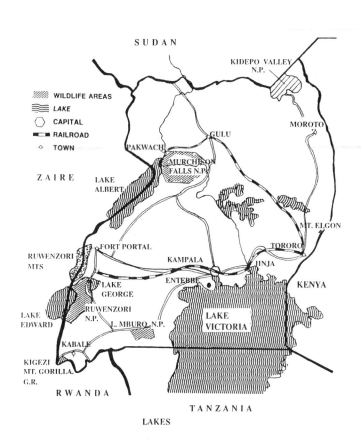

SUDAN

KIDEPO VALLEY
N.P.

MOROTO

WILDLIFE AREAS
LAKE
CAPITAL
RAILROAD
TOWN

GULU

PAKWACH

MURCHISON
FALLS N.P.

ZAIRE

LAKE
ALBERT

MT. ELGON

FORT PORTAL

TORORO

RUWENZORI
MTS

KAMPALA

JINJA

LAKE
GEORGE

ENTEBBE

KENYA

RUWENZORI
N.P.

LAKE
EDWARD

L. MBURO N.P.

LAKE
VICTORIA

KABALE

KIGEZI
MT. GORILLA.
G.R.

RWANDA

TANZANIA

LAKES

FACTS AT A GLANCE

AREA:	93,981 SQUARE MILES
APPROXIMATE SIZE:	OREGON OR GREAT BRITAIN
POPULATION:	17 MILLION (1990 EST.)
CAPITAL:	KAMPALA (POP. EST. 1,000,000)
OFFICIAL LANGUAGES:	ENGLISH. SWAHILI, LUGANDA AND ENGLISH ARE WIDELY SPOKEN.

Reticulated giraffe. Photo: Mike Appelbaum.

UGANDA

Uganda, once the "Pearl of the British Empire" in East Africa, is one of the most beautiful countries on the continent. One-sixth of its area is covered by water. Along its western boundary lies Africa's highest mountain range, Ptolemy's fabled "Mountains of the Moon." The Ugandans claim the source of the Nile is at Jinja where it leaves Lake Victoria.

The weather in Uganda is similar to Kenya's except that Uganda's is wetter. The driest time of the year is December-February and June-July, and the wettest is from mid-March to mid-May with lighter rains in October-November.

English is spoken as widely here as in Kenya or Tanzania. The main religions are Christianity and Islam.

In the 18th century, the Kingdom of Buganda became the most powerful in the region. Together with three other kingdoms and several native communities, it was made a British Protectorate in 1893 and achieved independence in 1962.

Over 90% of the population is employed in agriculture. Coffee is the major export.

Uganda has had more than its fair share of turmoil over the past 18 years; in spite of this, the people are among the friendliest on the continent.

Although I have traveled through many parts of Uganda and have met with only kindness and a genuine curiosity about myself and my country, as of this writing, travel here is still a bit risky. However, conditions have greatly improved over the last several years, and security is better than it has been in the last two decades. To be on the safe side, contact the Depart-

Elephant.

ment of State (see "Security" in The Safari Pages) for travel advisories and register with your embassy on arrival.

Uganda is not yet ready for the return of volume tourism. Yet smaller, adventurous groups are reappearing and seem to be enjoying their "pioneer" status.

WILDLIFE AND WILDLIFE AREAS

This country was once very rich in wildlife, but much of the larger game was killed during Idi Amin's rule and in the war to oust him in the late 1970s. However, wildlife populations are returning. A real plus is that one seldom meets another vehicle on game drives — in essence having the park to themselves.

Uganda has four national parks and 16 reserves. The calving seasons for hartebeest and Uganda kob are January-February and for oribi, February-March.

NORTHERN AND WESTERN

MURCHISON (KABALEGA) FALLS NATIONAL PARK

This park is named after the famous falls where the Victoria Nile rushes through a narrow, 20-foot-wide rock gorge with tremendous force to crash on the rocks 150 feet below. Fish dazed by this fall are easy prey to one of the largest concen-

Pale-chanting goshawk. Photo: Mike Appelbaum.

trations of crocodile on the continent.

Located in northwestern Uganda, this park covers approximately 1500 square miles of predominantly grassy plains and savannah woodlands with altitudes ranging from 1650-4240 feet. Riverine forest line some parts of the Victoria Nile, which traverses the park from east to west. The Rabongo Forest has a population of chimpanzees.

In addition to Murchison Falls, a highlight of the park is the three-hour, seven-mile launch trip from the Paraa Lodge to the foot of the falls. Numerous crocodiles and hippos in the river and along its banks, as well as buffalo, elephant, and prolific birdlife (over 400 species) can be approached closely. Check to be sure the launch is in operation, and if it is, bring along 30 liters of diesel, as fuel is often in short supply.

The park is also home to giraffe, waterbuck, oribi, and Uganda kob. Record Nile perch over 200 pounds have been caught in the Nile. Some of the best fishing is just below Karuma Falls near Chobe Safari Lodge and just below Murchison Falls.

The easiest time to spot animals is January-February; the short dry season from June-July is also good. From March to May the landscape is more attractive but the wildlife is less concentrated.

Park headquarters and the most extensive road system for

game viewing are near the Paraa Lodge. The Buligi Circuit takes one to the confluence of the Albert and Victoria Niles. Water fowl are especially abundant, along with a variety of game. Fuel is often not available.

ACCOMMODATION — At the time of this writing, none of the lodges in the park are operational and are in a state of disrepair. There are airstrips at all three lodges, but check their condition before departure.

CLASS F: * *Chobe Lodge* is located in the eastern part of the park and overlooks picturesque Victoria Nile. * *Paraa Lodge* is located in the western part of the park. Launch trips to Murchison Falls may be available.

CAMPING: Several sites available.

KIDEPO VALLEY NATIONAL PARK

Kidepo Valley National Park covers about 500 square miles and is located in the Karamoja district in extreme northeastern Uganda. The park borders Sudan on the north and the Kenyan border is just a few miles to the east.

The scenery is some of the wildest in Africa, with rolling grasslands and scattered acacia. The park is ringed by mountains, with altitude ranges from 2950-9025 feet. Two seasonal rivers, the Kidepo and Larus, are often dry except for a few pools.

This is the least visited national park in Uganda, due to its remoteness, heavy poaching and lack of security in this district as a whole. Last year only 20 people visited the park — and many of them were relief workers from Uganda.

Wildlife includes greater and lesser kudu, eland, roan, oryx, Burchell's zebra, ostrich, hartebeest, Grant's gazelle, klipspringer, oribi and giraffe. There are small numbers of elephant, lion, leopard and cheetah. Birdlife is good, especially birds of prey; over 50 species have been recorded.

The roads in the park have not been graded in years. Anthills have made many roads impassable and some bridges have been washed out.

The best time to visit is during the dry season December-April. Four-wheel-drive vehicles are needed. Park Headquarters and Kidepo Lodge are located at Apoka Hill. The park is about 400 miles from Kampala and may be reached via Gulu, Kitgum, Rom and Karenga, or via Moroto, Kotido and Kaabong.

ACCOMMODATION — CLASS F: * *Kidepo Lodge* has 16 bandas (doubles) with private facilities and small verandas.
However, at the time of this writing it is not operational.
Visitors must bring their own drinks and food (which the
cooks will prepare) and kerosene for the stove. There is no
electricity unless you bring diesel for the generator.
CAMPING: Campsites are available.

QUEEN ELIZABETH (RUWENZORI) NATIONAL PARK

The park contains about 770 square miles of tremendous
scenic variety, including volcanic craters and crater lakes,
grassy plains, swamps, rivers, lakes and tropical forest. The

snow-capped Ruwenzori Mountains lie to the north and are not part of the park itself. The park is being extended to give migratory species more protection while moving to and from Virunga National Park in Zaire.

The launch trip on the **Kazinga Channel**, which joins Lakes Edward (Lake Rutanzige) and George, affords excellent opportunities for viewing hippos and a great variety of waterfowl at close range; this is a trip that should not be missed.

The Katwe-Kikorongo area in the north of the park has several saline lakes. South of the Kazinga Channel, the **Maramagambo Forest** is home for large numbers of chimpanzees, black and white colobus monkeys, rare red colobus monkeys, blue monkeys, red-tailed monkeys and baboons. The Ishasha region in the south of the park is famous for its tree-climbing lions.

Elephant were heavily poached but are slowly recovering. Other wildlife includes buffalo, leopard, sitatunga, Uganda kob, topi, and Defassa waterbuck. Over 540 species of birds have been recorded, including the rare prehistoric-looking whale-headed stork which is often sighted along the shores of Lake George.

Interestingly enough there are no giraffe, zebra, impala, rhino, or crocodiles in the Kazinga Channel or Lakes Edward and George. The crocodiles are believed to have been killed long ago by volcanic activity.

From Kampala the park is 260 miles via Mbarara and 285 miles via Fort Portal. A landing strip is located at Mweya for light aircraft; larger planes can land at Kasese. Guides are available for hire at park headquarters at Mweya.

ACCOMMODATION — CLASS C: * *Mweya Lodge* is situated on a high bluff overlooking the Kazinga Channel and Lake Edward. All rooms have private facilities.

CLASS F: * *Institute of Ecology Hostel.*

CAMPING: Sites are available near Mweya Lodge and along the Kazinga Channel.

RUWENZORI MOUNTAINS

This is the highest mountain range in Africa and home of the legendary "Mountains of the Moon." They rise 13,000 feet above the western arm of the Rift Valley to 16,762 ft. (5109 m.) above sea level just north of the equator and are usually

Secretary Bird.

covered in mist. See "Ruwenzori Mountains" in the chapter on Zaire for a general description.

Hikers in good condition can enjoy walking strenuous trails rising to over 13,000 feet in altitude through some of the most amazing vegetation in the world. There is a circuit with huts that takes a minimum of five days to hike — preferably six or seven.

The main trailhead begins near Ibanda. Drive six miles north from Kasese on the Fort Portal road, then turn left (west) for eight miles. John Matte and his son can outfit you with guides and porters. Bring all your own equipment. You will have to provide food for the guide and porters, rent or buy a sweater and blanket for each of them, and pay hut fees.

The Bujuku Circuit

On day one follow a dirt road from Ibanda three miles to Nyakalengija (5250 ft./1600 m.), then take the path to the Nyabitaba Hut (8700 ft./2651 m.). Many climbers prefer staying in a nearby rock shelter instead of the aluminum hut which can sleep up to 12 persons. Water and firewood are not available near the hut. Tent spaces are located nearby.

Day two is the most grueling of the circuit. Climbers pass heather and groundsel before reaching Nyamiliju Hut (10,900 ft./3322 m.). Again, the rock shelter is often preferred over the hut. Water is available nearby; there is no room for tents. On a clear day you can see Mt. Stanley and Mt. Speak and numerous glaciers.

On day three, hike through giant heather and groundsel forest with colorful mosses and through a muddy bog to Bigo Hut (11,300 ft./ 3444 m.). The hut sleeps up to 12, and it is in good condition. A good rock shelter is nearby. Water and firewood are available. From Bigo Hut, you may hike northeast to Bukurungu Pass, north to Roccati Pass, or southwest to Lake Bujuku.

On day four, cross the Kibatsi Bog to Cooking Pot Cave. The left fork of the path leads to Scott Elliot Pass. Take the right fork and hike northwest to Bujuku Hut (13,000 ft./4281 m.), near Lake Bujuku, offering great views of Mt. Baker and Mt. Stanley. Two huts in fair condition can hold up to 14 people. Water is available. A rock shelter for the porters is not far from the hut.

On day five, return to Cooking Pot Cave, take the fork to Scott Elliot Pass and continue past Mt. Baker to Lake Kitandara and Kitandara Hut (13,200 ft./4023 m.). Continue on to Kabamba Rock Shelter (12,400 ft./3779 m.).

On day six, descend to Kichuchu (a rock shelter) and onward through a bog and across the Mubuku River to Nyabitaba Hut and back to Ibanda. The best time to climb is December-early February and June-July during the dry season. However, no matter when you climb, you will still get wet. Wood found on the mountain is usually wet, so a camp stove and fuel is highly recommended. For information on climbing the summits and glaciers, I recommend the books, *East Africa International Mountain Guide* by Andrew Wielochowski (1986) and *Guide to the Ruwenzori* by Osmaston and Pasteur (1972), both published by West Col Productions in England. The best maps of the area are "The Central Ruwenzoris" with a scale of 1:250,000, and "Margherita" with a scale of 1:50,000.

For additional information write John Matte, P.O. Box 33, Kasese, Uganda, and enclose an international reply coupon to cover their mailing costs. International reply coupons are available at most post offices.

ACCOMMODATION — CLASS F: * A few huts with dirt floors are available for rent at Ibanda. All the huts on the hiking trails are in poor condition. Bring a ground sheet and insulated pad for your sleeping bag. It is best to bring your own tent.

KASESE

Kasese is the largest town situated near Ruwenzori National Park and the Ruwenzori Mountains, and is a good place to purchase supplies. Kasese can be reached by train or by road from Kampala.

ACCOMMODATION — CLASS D: * *Margherita Hotel* has rooms with private facilities and is located two miles out of town.

CENTRAL AND SOUTHERN

KAMPALA

Kampala, the capital of Uganda, is built on seven hills. Points of interest include the Uganda Museum and the Kasubi Tombs of the Kabakas — a shrine to the former Baganda kings and a fine example of Baganda craftsmanship.

The international airport is at Entebbe, about a 20-minute

drive from Kampala.
ACCOMMODATION — DELUXE: * *Kampala Sheraton Hotel*, situated in a magnificent park setting, has 279 air-conditioned rooms with private facilities, health club, several restaurants and swimming pool.
FIRST CLASS: * *Nile Hotel* contains the International Conference Center and has air-conditioned rooms with private facilities. * *Hotel Diplomate*, located on Tank Hill, has air-conditioned rooms with private facilities.
TOURIST CLASS: * *Fairway Hotel* is a basic hotel with private facilities overlooking the Kampala Golf Course.

LAKE MBURO NATIONAL PARK

Uganda's newest national park and formerly a game reserve, Lake Mburo National Park is located in southwestern Uganda between Masaka and Mbarara. This approximately 200-square-mile park is named after Lake Mburo, the largest of the park's fourteen lakes.

The park is characterized by open plains in the north, acacia grassland in the center and lakes and marshes in the south, and is bounded by the Kampala-Mbarara road on the North, Lake Kachera on the east and the Ruizi River on the west.

Wildlife includes hippo, buffalo, zebra, eland, roan antelope, reedbuck, topi, bushbuck, and klipspringer. Impala, which do not exist in any other park in Uganda, are numerous. There are some lion and leopard.
ACCOMMODATION — There is no accommodation in the park. The closest accommodation is the Katatumba Resort Hotel in Mbarara.
CAMPING: Campsites are available in the park.

KABALE

Kabale is Uganda's highest town, situated in a beautiful area called "The Little Switzerland of Africa" in southwestern Uganda.
ACCOMMODATION - CLASS D: * *White Horse Inn* has rooms with private facilities.

KIGEZI MOUNTAIN GORILLA GAME RESERVE

The Kigezi Mountain Gorilla Game Reserve is situated on the slopes of Mts. Muhabura and Gahinga in the southwestern corner of Uganda, bordering Rwanda and Zaire. A Joint Commission has been set up by Uganda, Rwanda and Zaire to protect the mountain gorilla in the Virunga Mountains where the borders of the three countries meet.

Gorillas are less likely to be sighted here than in the Volcano National Park in Rwanda or in Kahuzi-Biega National Park or Djomba Gorilla Sanctuary in Zaire. The Ugandan side of the mountains is dryer, providing less moisture to grow the vegetation gorillas prefer eating. However, the clearer skies provide breathtaking views of this, the most beautiful part of Uganda.

Zacharias has been leading groups up the mountain in search of gorillas for over 20 years. Request his services at the Traveller's Rest Hotel in Kisoro at least 24 hours in advance.

Gorillas are usually not spotted in one day; you must allow three days of searching to better insure success. If gorillas are found, it is difficult to approach closely or to spend much time with them; they are not habituated to humans as are gorillas in Rwanda and Zaire. Even if gorillas are not encountered, the hike through this peaceful scenic region of friendly people is well worth the effort.

From Kisoro, Zacharias will lead you to his home at the village of Giterderi, about a two-hour walk from Kisoro. Most people camp there for the night. The following morning, hike for about two hours to the area where the gorillas may be found. Return to camp just before dark.

This trek is recommended for only the hardiest of travelers. The hike from base camp can take up to ten hours and all participants must be in good shape. However, the cost of the treks is a mere fraction of that charged in Rwanda and Zaire.

Other wildlife in this 17-square-mile reserve includes blue monkey, black and white colobus monkey, buffalo and bushbuck.

ACCOMMODATION — CLASS D: * *Traveller's Rest* is the best hotel in the area, providing basic rooms with private facilities.

CAMPING: Zacharias will allow travelers who have hired him as a guide to camp near his home. There are no facilities. Bring your own food and water.

A lion pride rests in the tall grass.

ZAIRE

ZAIRE

SUDAN

EASTERN ZAIRE

UGANDA
LAKE MOBUTU
SESE-SEKO

EPULU OKAPI
STATION

BUNIA

MAMBASA

KISANGANI

MOUNT HOYO

BENI

RUWENZORI MTS.

BUTEMBO

VIRUNGA N.P.
LAKE EDWARD

RWINDI

NYAMULAGIRA VOLCANO
NYIRAGONGO VOLCANO
GOMA

LAKE KIVU

RWANDA

KAHUZI-
BIEGA N.P.

TANZANIA

BUKAVU

BURUNDI

UVIRA

LAKE
TANGANYIKA

///// WILDLIFE AREAS
~~~ LAKE
◯ CAPITAL
■▬■ RAILROAD
◇ TOWN
MOUNTAINS

FACTS AT A GLANCE

AREA:	905,000 SQUARE MILES
APPROXIMATE SIZE:	U.S.A. EAST OF THE MISSISSIPPI RIVER OR TEN TIMES THE SIZE OF GREAT BRITAIN
POPULATION:	33 MILLION (1990 EST.)
CAPITAL:	KINSHASA 3,500,000 (1990 POP. EST.)
LANGUAGES:	OFFICIAL: FRENCH NATIONAL: SWAHILI, TSHILUBA, KIKONGO, LINGALA.

Herd of elephant in the Rwindi area of Virunga National Park.

ZAIRE

The Republic of Zaire, formerly the Democratic Republic of the Congo, is the third-largest country in Africa. The name Zaire comes from the Kikongo word *nzadi*, meaning "river". The Congo or Zaire River, the tenth longest river in the world, winds 2880 miles through the Zaire basin, the world's second-largest drainage basin (the Amazon is the largest), and finally empties into the Atlantic ocean.

Of all the countries listed in this guide, Zaire is closest to "Tarzan's Africa." One can very easily imagine him swinging on a vine right in front of you as you travel through this country, visited more by adventurers than tourists.

Kivu Province, the most beautiful region of Zaire, holds the country's most exciting attractions. This province is situated along the western borders of Rwanda and Uganda in the region of the great lakes: Lakes Tanganyika, Kivu, Edward (Idi Amin), and Mobutu (Albert). This is an important agricultural area with large tobacco, coffee, tea and banana plantations. There are no paved roads in Kivu Province.

Due to the altitude, the region has an agreeable Mediterranean-type climate. In general, the best time to visit eastern Zaire is during the dry seasons from December-February and mid-June-August.

Of the 200 or so tribal or ethnic groups, four-fifths are Bantu. Physically, tribal groups range from the Tutsi, some of the tallest people on earth, to pygmies. About 80% of the population is Christian with the balance having Muslim or traditional beliefs.

What is now Zaire remained virtually unknown until Henry

Morton Stanley traveled from East Africa to the mouth of the Congo (Zaire) River (1874-1877). Belgian King Leopold II claimed what became the Congo Free State as his personal property until he ceded it to Belgium in 1907, and it was renamed the Belgian Congo. Zaire achieved independence on June 30, 1967.

Zaire is a country of gigantic untapped resources. Fifty percent of the land is arable and scarcely 2% is under cultivation or used as pasture. The country holds 13% of the world's hydroelectric potential. Copper accounts for about half of the country's exports, followed by petroleum, diamonds and coffee.

WILDLIFE AND WILDLIFE AREAS

Eight reserves cover 15% of the country's area. Virunga National Park is one of the finest reserves in Africa and contains the world's largest concentration of hippo. Over 1,000 species of birds have been recorded in Zaire, many in the Virunga National Park. In addition, Zaire is also a home of the rare okapi (antelope).

Like Rwanda, gorillas are a major attraction in Zaire. Mountain gorillas may be visited in Virunga National Park and eastern lowland gorillas may be seen in Kahuzi-Biega National Park.

The parks and reserves in Zaire are much less crowded than the ones in East Africa. During my latest visit, there were only four visitors staying at Virunga National Park's Rwindi Lodge, and I was the only visitor to Mt. Hoyo and the Ruwenzori Mountains in two weeks.

The world has not yet discovered that these are among the continent's finest attractions, making a visit here all the more inviting and adventurous. However, travel on your own is very difficult and often exasperating, even if you speak French.

THE NORTHEAST

GOMA

Goma is the tourist center for eastern Zaire, and fortunately tourism has done little to change this typical African town. Goma is situated on the northern shores of Lake Kivu, one of the most beautiful lakes in Africa, with Mt. Nyiragongo (volcano) forming a dramatic backdrop to the north.

Goma is the administrative center for Virunga National Park and Nyiragongo and Nyamulagira Volcanoes. The National Parks Office (Institut Zairois pour la Conservation de la Nature) is where you buy permits to climb the volcanoes and make reservations to visit the mountain gorillas at Djomba or Rumangabo.

Three boats per week depart Goma for Bukavu across Lake Kivu. The *Matadi* departs Goma on Wednesdays and Saturdays at 7:30 a.m. and takes about six hours. In addition to passengers, the *Karisimbi* takes cargo, departs Goma Saturday mornings and takes about 12 hours. However, departure days and times can vary, so don't depend on these boats if you have a tight schedule.

Le Nyira is a good restaurant in town. Goma has an international airport. Air charters are available.

ACCOMMODATIONS — FIRST CLASS: * *Hotel Karibu* has rooms with private facilities and is located six miles outside of Goma on Lake Kivu.

TOURIST CLASS: * *Hotel des Grand Lacs* also has rooms with private facilities. * *Masques Hotel* is located in town and has rooms with private facilities.

NORTH OF GOMA

On the drive from Goma northward one passes over the dramatic Kabasha Escarpment to Butembo. The route from the Kabasha Escarpment to Beni is one of the most beautiful in Africa and is properly named the "Beauty Route". The road passes through many picturesque villages, coffee, tea and banana plantations — the Africa that many of us have pictured in our minds.

VIRUNGA NATIONAL PARK
(PARC NATIONAL DE VIRUNGA)

Virunga National Park, previously called Albert Park, is the oldest reserve in Africa. It is the best game park in Zaire and one of the finest and least known parks in all of Africa. With approximately 4600 square miles in area, it is one of the largest on the continent as well. Altitudes range from 3000 feet on the grassy savanna to 16,794 feet in the Ruwenzori Mountains, resulting in a tremendous variety of topography, flora and fauna. Virunga is about 185 miles long and 25 miles wide and is divided into several sections, each requiring separate entrance fees. From south to north: the Nyiragongo and Nyamulagira volcanoes, Rumangabo Station, Djomba Gorilla Sanctuary, Rwindi, the Ruwenzori Mountains, and Mt. Hoyo. Guides are compulsory and their services are included in the park entrance fees.

The European Economic Community (EEC) has recently committed millions of dollars to upgrading the accommodations, facilities and administration of Virunga National Park. These changes are bound to attract many international visitors who would otherwise not venture to this world-class park.

VOLCANOES

The region around Goma is a highly volcanic area of constant activity. On my first visit here, I discovered that a new volcano had been born recently, and we hiked ten miles into the bush to see it. In the event of an eruption, we camped uphill from the volcano, which was scarcely 300 feet high and watched the fabulous fireworks all night. For some unknown reason a new volcano usually pops up in this active region about every other year between December and April. I just missed visiting another lava-filled caldera in 1984, which cooled a few weeks before my arrival.

In the southern part of the park near Goma lies the active volcanoes of Nyiragongo and Nyamulagira, which do not require technical mountaineering skills to climb. If the volcanoes are active at the time of your visit, you may want to spend a night near the crater rim to enjoy the remarkable fireworks display.

The best time to climb is December-January and June when the weather is clearest. February, July and August are also good.

NYIRAGONGO

Nyiragongo (11,384 ft./3470 m.) erupted in 1977, spewing

The silverback mountain gorilla Marcel (Rugabo), in the Djomba Gorilla Sanctuary. Photo: Ruppert Starr.

out miles of molten lava which destroyed villages within its path. I visited the area three months later and could still feel the heat radiating from the newly hardened lava.

Nyiragongo can be climbed in one day if you begin climbing early in the morning. The guide and porter station is located at Kibati (6400 ft./1950 m.), eight miles north of Goma on the Rutshuru road. Hike four to five hours through forest and Afro-alpine vegetation and past lava flows to the summit. Have lunch on the crater rim while watching sulfurous gases escape from the crater below. Allow two to three hours to return to Kibati before dark.

It is better to take two days for the climb, overnighting at a hut (in poor condition) about a 30-minute walk below the summit. At dawn the next morning, hike to the crater rim and enjoy breathtaking views of Lake Kivu, Goma and the surrounding countryside.

Bring a sleeping bag, insulated pad, warm clothing, fuel, food and water. A guide is required and porters are optional.

NYAMULAGIRA

If you are looking for a real safari experience, this is the better of the two volcanoes to climb. An armed guide accompanies each group, and porters may be hired. With luck, you will see forest elephant, chimpanzees, buffalo and antelope. Nyamulagira (10,023 ft./3055 m.) is best climbed in three days. On the first day, hike about six hours through dense upland jungle, passing numerous lava flows to a basic lodge at 8200 feet (2500 m.) altitude. Water is available at the lodge but must be purified.

On day two you reach the tree line after about an hour's hike and the crater rim about an hour after passing the tree line. The crater itself is about a mile and a half in diameter. Within the crater is a blowhole with a huge 1300-foot diameter shaft. Descend into and explore the crater, then return to the same lodge you slept in the night before. Hike down the mountain on the third day.

Nyamulagira is reached via Kakomero (5900 ft./1800 m.), 24 miles north of Goma. Bring your own food and equipment. ACCOMMODATIONS: CAMPING: Campsites are available at the Nyamulagira base camp.

DJOMBA GORILLA SANCTUARY

The Djomba Gorilla Sanctuary covers much of the Zaire side of the Virunga Mountains, which are shared with Rwanda and Uganda, and is the best place to see mountain gorillas in Zaire.

Here, three groups of mountain gorillas have also been habituated to man's presence. Each group is named after its leader (a silverback) and may be visited by up to six persons each at a time. National Parks guides must accompany each group.

Djomba Camp is the base from which gorilla trekking begins. To reach Djomba (sometimes spelled Jomba), drive about 40 miles north from (Goma past Nyiragongo and Nyamulagira volcanoes. Two miles before reaching Rutshuru, turn right and continue 19 miles to Park Headquarters. From there, visitors must hike for 30-45 minutes to Djomba Camp. Porters are available to carry luggage.

Two gorilla groups, Oscar (Rugendo) and Marcel (Rugabo), are the closest of the three groups to Djomba Camp and are most often visited by international guests. These two groups are normally found in less than one or two hours, but occasionally it can take as long as four or five.

Rwindi has the greatest concentration of hippo in the world —
about 23,000!

The Oscar and Marcel groups are most always found at
lower altitudes than the mountain gorillas of Rwanda, and the
terrain is not as steep as in Volcano National Park in Rwanda.
The gorilla search, therefore, is usually less physically demanding here than in Rwanda. In addition, trekkers may visit with
the gorillas up to two hours at Djomba, allowing plenty of time
to enjoy the experience, whereas in Rwanda, visits are limited
to one hour. However, Djomba is more difficult (and more
expensive) to reach than Volcano National Park.

The Faida group lives at higher altitudes than the Marcel
and Oscar groups, and the trek can be very demanding. In
addition, the Faida group spends part of its time in Uganda
and cannot be tracked over the border.

Buffalo and elephant are also present in the sanctuary, so
keep an eye out for them. For a description of gorillas and
gorilla trekking in general, see "Volcano National Park" in the
chapter on Rwanda.

Reserve your permit in advance for the Marcel and Oscar
groups at the National Parks Office in Goma or through a travel
agent specializing in Africa. Permits for the Faida group are not
sold in advance, since it spends part of its time in Uganda.
ACCOMMODATION — CLASS B: * *Djomba Camp* has several
cabins, each with two double rooms with private facilities and

a shared sitting room with fireplace.
CLASS F: A self-service hut with two bedrooms (12 beds total) is available. Bring your own food.
CAMPING: Campsites are available.

RUMANGABO STATION

Mountain gorillas may also be seen at Rumangabo Station, which is closer to Goma than Djomba. However, two days are required to visit the gorillas here. To reach Rumangabo, drive 28 miles north of Goma on the Goma-Rutshuru road and turn off to Park Headquarters. From here a park guard will lead you on about a three-to-four-hour walk to the village of Bukima where you spend the night. Your gorilla trek to see the Bukima (Zunguruka) group begins the following morning. As with the Djomba Gorilla Sanctuary, reservations must be made in advance.
ACCOMMODATION — CLASS F: At present there is only a basic tented camp. Bring a sleeping bag and food.

RWINDI

Continuing north towards Rwindi are the **Rutshuru Water-falls** and **Maji Ya Moto** hot-water springs, both near Rutshuru.
Rwindi is the chief game-viewing region of Virunga National Park. Predominantly composed of savannah plains and swamps, Rwindi has the greatest concentrations of hippo in the world (about 23,000).
The Kabasha Escarpment rises up to 6000 feet above the plains below and provides a dramatic backdrop for wildlife which includes elephant, buffalo, hippo, lion, hyena, jackal, waterbuck, reedbuck, bushbuck, topi, Thomas kob, Defassa kob, crocodiles and numerous aquatic birds.
The fishing village of Vitshumbi, located on the southern shores of Lake Edward (Lake Idi Amin), is worth a stop. Visit the fishery to enjoy the taste of delicious barbecued tilapia with pilipili (hot sauce).
Most game viewing is from mini-buses with roof hatches. Vehicles must stay on the park tracks. The main road from Goma to Butembo passes right through the park.
The best time to visit is during the dry season. Roads and tracks are poor in the rainy season. Rwindi Lodge, park head-

quarters and camping sights are located at Rwindi, 81 miles
north of Goma.
ACCOMMODATION CLASS C: * *Rwindi Lodge* has rondavels
with private facilities (130 beds total), and swimming pool.
CAMPING: Camping is not allowed.

RUWENZORI MOUNTAINS

The third highest mountains in Africa (behind Mts. Kilimanjaro and Kenya), the "Mountains of the Moon" are the highest
mountain chain on the continent. Permanently snow-covered
at altitudes over 14,800 feet (4500 m.), these jagged mountains
are almost perpetually covered in mist.

The mountain chain is approximately 60 miles long and 30
miles wide and the highest peak, Margherita, is 16,762 feet
(5109 m.) in altitude. A number of permanent glaciers and
peaks challenge mountaineers. However, mountaineering skills
are not needed for the hike itself — only for climbing the glaciers or peaks.

Unlike Mt. Kilimanjaro and many other mountains in east
and central Africa, the Ruwenzoris are not volcanic in origin.
The range forms part of the border with Uganda and can be
climbed from either the Zaire or Ugandan side. The trail on the
Zaire side of the Ruwenzoris is much steeper than the Ugan-

Hiking in the Ruwenzori Mountains is almost like visiting another planet. Photo: Jürg and Barbara Lictenegger.

Thick vegetation along the trail through the Ruwenzori Mountains.
Photo: Jürg & Barbara Lichtenegger.

dan side. Allow five days for the climb and longer if any peaks
are to be attempted.

The vegetation zones one passes through on the Ruwenzoris
are the most amazing I have seen in the world. Colorful mosses
look solid, but when probed with a walking stick (or your foot)
often prove to cover a tangle of roots more than six feet deep.
Several plants that are commonly small in other parts of the
world grow to gigantic proportions.

Park Headquarters are at the village of Mutsora, two miles
from Mutwanga, which is 30 miles east of Beni. From the road
junction near Beni, drive 28 miles east to Mutwanga, then two
miles to Mutsora.

The Butawu Route

The Butawu Route is the only route regularly used on the
Zaire side of the Ruwenzoris. All other routes are so overgrown
with vegetation that they are virtually impossible to climb.

On the first day, it takes five to six hours of hiking from the

Green Lake in the Ruwenzori Mountains.
Photo: Jürg and Barbara Lichtenegger.

Park Headquarters at Mutsora (5600 ft./1700 m.) through small fields of bananas, coffee, and other crops to reach Kalonge Hut (7015 ft./2135 m.). The hut sleeps 16 persons and there is room for tents nearby.

On the second day, one passes through areas with giant stinging nettles and bamboo forest over 100 feet high. Soon you come to a resting spot where offerings are left for the mountain gods. Your guide will expect you to leave something, (i.e., a few coins).

At about 8500 feet (2600 m.), the sides of the slick, muddy path become lined with spongy mosses and heather 25 feet tall. After about five hours of hiking (actually the most difficult part of the climb), one reaches Mahangu Hut (10,860 ft./3310 m.). The hut has room for 16 persons, and there is room for camping.

The third day one finally hikes past the upper tree line at about 12,500 feet (3800 m.) and enters a zone of giant groundsels over 16 feet high and giant lobelia over 25 feet high. Before completing the five-hour hike to Kiondo Hut (13,780 ft./4200 m.), you hike along an open ridge with fabulous views of Lac Noir (Black Lake). Kiondo Hut has room for 12, and there is room for tents nearby.

On day four of the hike, the Butawu Route continues on to Wasuwameso Peak (14,600 ft./4450 m.) for some fabulous views of Mt. Stanley. Climbers then return to Kiondo Hut and continue on down to Kalonge Hut for the night.

Alternatively, take a fabulous hike past Lac Vert (Green Lake) and Lac Gris (Grey Lake) to Moraine Hut (14,270 ft./ 4350 m.) at the foot of the glaciers. The hike to Moraine Hut from Kiondo Hut takes about five hours round-trip and requires a short bit of easy rock climbing with fixed ropes. Then return to either Kiondo Hut or Mahangu Hut for the night.

If you hike to Moraine Hut, be sure to return to Kiondo Hut early. My guide insisted there was plenty of time to reach Moraine Hut and return to Kiondo Hut the afternoon of the third day. We were so late returning we were forced to return in the dark. Had I not brought a flashlight, we might still be up there.

On the fifth day, return to Mutsora — hopefully for a hot bath and a soft bed!

Many hikers prefer camping at Grey Lake instead of using dilapidated Moraine Hut, which leaks. There is space for only one tent near Moraine Hut. Experienced mountaineers may press on to conquer the glaciers and peaks of the Ruwenzori from either location. Allow a minimum of six or seven days total for the climb if you wish to attempt any summits.

For information on climbing the summits and glaciers, I recommend the *East Africa International Mountain Guide* by Andrew Wielochowski (1986) and *Guide to the Ruwenzori* by Osmaston and Pasteur (1972), both published by West Col Productions in England.

The best time to climb is from December-February; June-August is also good. To reach the Ruwenzoris, travel north from Goma through Butembo, and just before Beni, turn east 28 miles to Mutwanga. Park headquarters are at Mutsora, about two miles from Mutwanga.

A guide at no charge is required; porters are available for a small fee. Both guides and porters expect cigarettes in addition to a tip. The guides know the path and where to find water en route — but little else. All guides speak French; an English-speaking guide may not be available. Guides who speak English tend to know only a few words.

Guides are not equipped for or experienced in glacier or rock climbing. Your group must be self-sufficient. There are no mountain rescue teams; bring a comprehensive medical kit. Accommodation on the mountain has recently been upgraded with funds from the EEC. Huts have fireplaces, bunk beds and wood stoves. Guides and porters love to smoke and often share the huts with you; consider bringing your own tent. Also, bring a warm sleeping bag, mattress, food, fuel, and enough water to last two days. Some of the windows may be broken; you may wish to bring some plastic with which to cover them.

See "Mt. Kilimanjaro" in the chapter on Tanzania for a more extensive equipment checklist and other preparations. Mt. Kilimanjaro is higher, but the trail up the Ruwenzoris is much steeper, slicker and more difficult to negotiate.

ACCOMMODATION — TOURIST CLASS: See "Butembo" or "Beni" below.

CLASS F: Rooms available at a basic lodge at Park Headquarters.

CAMPING: Camping is allowed at Park Headquarters.

ISHANGO

The Ishango region of Virunga National Park is situated at the northern end of Lake Edward (Idi Amin). This seldom-visited region of the park is predominantly open savannah similar to the Rwindi area and the southern shores of Lake Edward. Wildlife is also similar to what you find in the Rwindi region, except there are no elephants. Water birds are prolific, especially where the Semliki River empties into Lake Edward.

From Beni, travel east past the turnoff to the Ruwenzori Mountains and onward toward the Ugandan border to Kasindi. Then turn right (south) and continue to Ishango.

ACCOMMODATIONS: None.

CAMPING: Campsites are available.

MOUNT HOYO

Fifty-seven miles north of Beni and 12 miles south of Komanda, take the track to the east, uphill for nine miles to the colonial-style Mt. Hoyo Lodge (Auberge du Mount Hoyo). I was dropped off by a produce truck, loaded with bananas and goats at this intersection at 2:30 a.m., and hiked all night, pass-

A pygmy family in front of their hut near Mt. Hoyo.

ing Pygmy villages along the way to arrive at the lodge in time
for breakfast.

En route I came upon a line of millions of safari ants crossing the road. Thousands of ants had joined their legs and
formed a "cocoon" across the road, protecting those that
crossed beneath.

Mt. Hoyo has many attractions. The Cascades of Venus
(l'Escaliers de Venus) is a stepped waterfall in a thick jungle
setting of natural beauty. The cascades and the grottoes
(caves) with stalagmites and stalactites can be easily visited in
a half-day hike. Black and white colobus monkeys and chimpanzees may be seen in the forest.

A very interesting excursion is to join a few Balese (pygmy)
hunters on a mock antelope hunt. Armed with their bows and
arrows, groups of up to three visitors follow these hunters
through thick jungle vegetation in search of game. The pygmies
whistle to attract their "prey." Here, they proved the advantage
of being small — effortlessly walking under vines and limbs,
while I had to crawl on my hands and knees.

We feasted on honey which they fished from a bee's hive

with their arrows; and they enjoyed another delicacy — termites from a large mound.

Be sure to visit a pygmy village while in the area. Villages along the main roads have become a bit "commercialized," so if you have time, have a guide take you to a village off the beaten track.

ACCOMMODATION — CLASS C: * *Mount Hoyo Hotel* (Auberge du Mt. Hoyo) has rooms with private facilities and good views of the jungle below.

CAMPING: Campsites with basic shower and toilet facilities are available.

LOYA RIVER

The Loya River crosses the main road a few miles south of the turnoff to Mt. Hoyo. Take a ride in a piroque (dugout canoe) through the thick green Ituri Forest past artificial dams, created for fishing, and thick jungle. The Loya River flows into the Ituri River, which travels deep into the Ituri Forest.

Visit a pygmy village before returning. Be sure to bring a gift (i.e., tobacco), especially if you wish to take pictures.

BUTEMBO

This busy village with a population of over 100,000 is situated in the highlands along the "Beauty Route" just north of the equator, about halfway between Goma and Bunia. Many banana, coffee and tea plantations are in the area. Travelers driving from Rwindi often spend the night here before continuing on to Mt. Hoyo or the Ruwenzori Mountains.

ACCOMMODATION — TOURIST CLASS: * *Auberge* has rooms with private facilities. * *Kikyo Hotel* has rooms with private facilities.

EPULU OKAPI STATION

The Okapi Station at Epulu has guided tours of the rare Okapi antelope (ten at present), which roam several large pens set in natural surroundings. In addition, fourteen primate species have been seen in the forests near Epulu.

An interesting excursion for the adventurous is to go hunting with pygmies and camp in the forest for a night or two. The pygmies will build you a shelter for the night or you may bring your own tent. Guides and porters are available for hire.

Pygmy villages seldom visited by overseas visitors may also be visited by hiking into the jungle with a guide.

The Epulu Okapi Station is situated on banks of the Epulu River, a six-to-seven-hour drive from Mt. Hoyo in the dry season (December-February and June-August), which is the best time to visit. Roads are often impassable in the rainy season. From Mt. Hoyo, drive north to Komanda, then west past Mambasa to Epulu. Alternatively, charter a plane to Mambasa and hire a vehicle for the 50-mile drive to Epulu.

ACCOMMODATION — CLASS F: Three rondavels and a guest-house (20 beds total) with an ablution block with toilets and showers (cold water only).

CAMPING: Campsites available.

THE SOUTHEAST

KAHUZI-BIEGA NATIONAL PARK

This 2300-square-mile mountain sanctuary, located 17 miles northwest of Bukavu, is dedicated to preserving the eastern lowland gorilla (*Gorilla gorilla graueri*). Searching for these magnificent, rare and endangered animals is recommended only for travelers in good physical condition.

The search for gorillas usually takes less than an hour of hiking to altitudes from 7000 to 8200 feet through dense upland jungle and bamboo forests. However, it occasionally takes three or four hours to locate the gorillas. The park also includes swamp, woodland and extensive equatorial rainforest. The highest point in the park is Mt. Kahuzi at 10,853 feet.

On my visit to the park, I was the only tourist there to search for gorillas. I was accompanied by a guide and several cutters wielding pangas. As our search progressed, we found gorilla lairs where they had spent the previous night.

After four hours of following their trail and cutting our way through dense tropical foliage, we finally located them. The silverback (dominant male) was one of the largest I have seen — estimated by the guide to weigh over 450 pounds. Hanging vines and branches that blocked our view were cut until the silverback pounded his chest and charged — stopping just short of us, and established his well-earned territory. In the background an adult female and her young offspring were curiously watching us.

The park is managed by the Frankfurt Zoological Society. At present, there is a limit of eight people that may visit a gorilla group at one time. Children under 15 years of age are not allowed to visit the gorillas. In the rare event that gorillas are not sighted, visitors may return for another search the following day without paying additional fees.

Other wildlife present in the park includes elephant, giant forest hog, duiker, chimpanzee and colobus monkeys.

Daytime temperatures average 50-65° F., and yearly average rainfall is high — about 70 inches. The best time to visit the park is in the dry season. Bring waterproof light hiking boots (you may have to wade through water), a sweater, waterproof cover jacket, lunch, snacks and a canteen.

Silverbacks in Kahuzi-Biega cannot be approached as closely as those in the Djomba Gorilla Sanctuary and Volcano National Park (Rwanda). However, park fees for Kahuzi-Biega are less.

Book in advance with the National Parks Office (Institut Zairois pour la Conservation de la Nature) in Bukavu or through a travel agent or tour operator.

To reach the park, go north from Bukavu along the western side of Lake Kivu for 13 miles to Miti, then turn left (west), traveling for four miles to Station Tshivanga, the Park Headquarters.

ACCOMMODATION: The closest comfortable accommodation is in Bukavu.

CAMPING: Campsites are available at Park Headquarters.

BUKAVU

The region's capital, Bukavu, is a beautiful setting situated on the southern shores of Lake Kivu near the Rwanda border. The National Parks Office (Institut Zairois pour la Conservation de la Nature) is located at 185 Ave. President Mobutu, B.P. 2468; tel: 3001.

Boats for Goma depart Bukavu and cross beautiful Lake Kivu three times per week. The *Matadi* departs Bukavu Tues-

This riverboat cruises the Zaire River from Kinshasa to Kisangani.

days and Fridays at 7:30 a.m. and takes about six hours. In addition to passengers, the *Karisimbi* takes cargo, departs Bukavu Wednesday mornings, and takes about 12 hours.
ACCOMMODATION — TOURIST CLASS: * *Hotel Residence*, the best hotel in the region, has rooms with private facilities.

CENTRAL AND WESTERN

ZAIRE RIVER

Exploring the Zaire River by riverboat from Kinshasa to Kisangani is truly an adventure into the dark continent. The boat is slow, taking about 12 days upstream and eight downstream for the 1000-mile voyage — if no complications arise. You may also cruise from Lisala to Kisangani: this trip takes three to five days.

The riverboat is actually a motor boat with six barges tied on, with a dining room and bar on each barge. Local tribesmen paddle out to meet the riverboat in their dugout canoes, latch hold, and sell monkeys, crocodiles, huge juicy pineapples and other tropical fruits. One passes through the "mainstream" of

Zairian life on this river.

Deluxe and first class cabins are recommended for all but the most rugged of travelers. This riverboat is only for those with flexible schedules; it is not uncommon for it to be a week "off schedule."

KINSHASA

Situated in western Zaire near the mouth of the Zaire (Congo) River, Kinshasa is the country's capital. Points of interest include the Presidential Gardens and Zoo, the central market, and the National Academy of Fine Arts. Thieves Market is a good place to shop for malachite and wood carvings.

One of the greater attractions of this city are the numerous live bands playing the music of Zaire in clubs. Zaire music is extremely popular throughout most of sub-Sahara Africa.

The tourist office is located in Building La Rwindi on Boulevard du 30 Juin (tel: 25828). The airport is 18 miles from Kinshasa. More travelers reach Eastern Zaire from Nairobi (Kenya) or Kigali (Rwanda) than from Kinshasa.

ACCOMMODATION — DELUXE: The *Inter-Continental Hotel* is centrally located near the World Trade Center and has 510 air-conditioned rooms with ensuite facilities, swimming pool, tennis courts, squash, health club, casino and disco.

FIRST CLASS: *Hotel Le Memling* has 212 rooms with ensuite facilities.

ZAMBIA

ZAMBIA

FACTS AT A GLANCE

AREA:	290,585 SQUARE MILES
APPROXIMATE SIZE:	LARGER THAN TEXAS OR FRANCE
POPULATION:	7 MILLION (1990 EST.)
CAPITAL:	LUSAKA (POP. EST. 800,000)
LANGUAGES:	OFFICIAL: ENGLISH.

Leopard are often seen on night game drives in South Luangwa National Park. Photo: John Haupt.

ZAMBIA

A sparsely populated country rich in wildlife, Zambia was named after the mighty Zambezi River which flows through southern Zambia. The Zambezi River is fed by its Kafue and Luangwa tributaries. The three great lakes of Bangweulu, Mweru and Tanganyika lie in northern Zambia, and Lake Kariba lies along the southeastern border adjacent to Zimbabwe.

The country is predominantly a high plateau ranging in altitude from 3000-5000 feet, which is why it has a subtropical rather than a tropical climate. April-August is cool and dry; September-October is hot and dry; and November-March is warm and wet. Winter temperatures are as cool as 43° F. and summer temperatures as warm as 100° F. The dry season, with clear sunny skies, occurs May-October.

The Zambian people are predominantly composed of Bantu tribal groups who practice a combination of traditional and Christian beliefs. English is the official language and is widely spoken. Seventy-three other languages and dialects are also spoken. In contrast to most African countries, over 40% of the population live in urban areas, due mainly to the copper mining industry.

Cecil Rhodes obtained mineral right concessions in 1888 from the chiefs of what was proclaimed Northern Rhodesia, which came under British influence. In 1953 Northern Rhodesia, Southern Rhodesia and Nyasaland (now Malawi) were consolidated into the Federation of Rhodesia and Nyasaland. Northern Rhodesia succeeded from the Federation in 1963 and achieved its independence on October 24, 1964, as the Republic of Zambia.

Zambia's economy is based primarily on copper from the government-owned mines in the "copper belt" near the Zaire border. The price and subsequent production of copper has declined since 1975; this has brought on hardship and forced the economy to diversify. More emphasis is now being placed on developing agriculture (exporting fruit, coffee, sugar) and the tourism industry as a greater source of foreign exchange.

WILDLIFE AND WILDLIFE AREAS

Zambia boasts 19 gazetted national parks covering over 24,500 square miles, and with the 34 game management areas adjacent to the parks, Zambia has set aside 32% of its land to the preservation of wildlife. However, many national parks and reserves are not open to the general public.

Zambia's two major parks are South Luangwa National Park and Kafue National Park. South Luangwa is the more popular of the two, largely due to its high concentration of elephant and other game. In Kafue National Park the game is generally more scattered, but many of the species, such as greater kudu and sable antelope, are said to be substantially larger than elsewhere in the country. The red lechwe, unique to Zambia, is found in Kafue.

Going on safari in Zambia is different. In Kenya and Tanzania visitors are often rushed from park to park with only one or two nights in the same park. In Zambia the emphasis is on experiencing the bush and wildlife by participating in walking safaris (the biggest attraction), night safaris and boat safaris as well as day game drives. A tour of Zambia should at least consist of a visit to Victoria Falls and South Luangwa National Park. Travelers with more time may also wish to include a visit to Kafue National Park.

Zambia is excellent for walking safaris, which are operated in South Luangwa (my first choice), North Luangwa and Kafue National Parks. Most of the camps offer daily walks, and nearly all of them offer day and night game-viewing drives in open vehicles.

Fishing for tiger fish, lake salmon and Nile perch is excellent in Lake Tanganyika, Lake Kariba, and the Kafue River and is best April to November.

Visitors who have their own vehicles must be in the camps by nightfall and therefore cannot conduct night safaris on

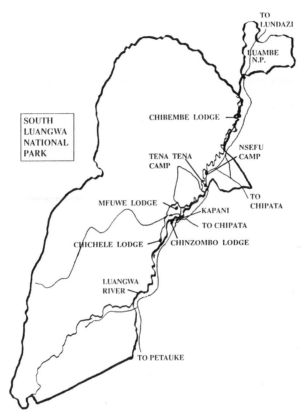

their own. Guests must not leave the roads in search of game or walk in the park without the company of an armed wildlife guard. I've been told that crocodiles in Zambia are responsible for more deaths than automobile accidents.

The best time to visit South Luangwa and Kafue National Parks is July-September, followed by June and October. November-April is the hot and humid rainy season when foliage becomes thicker, making wildlife more difficult to spot.

THE NORTH AND NORTHEAST

SOUTH LUANGWA NATIONAL PARK

The natural beauty, variety and concentration of wildlife make this huge 3500-square-mile park one of the finest in

African wild dog are rarely seen on safari.

Africa. Game is so prolific Luangwa is called "The Crowded Valley." The park has one of the highest concentrations of elephant on the continent.

South Luangwa is home to savannah, wetland and forest animals. The southern regions are predominantly woodland savannah with scattered grassy areas. Leopard, kudu and giraffe are numerous. To the north the woodlands give way to scattered trees and open plains where wildebeest and other savannah animals dominate the scene.

Thornicroft's giraffe are indigenous to the park. Lion, hyena, buffalo, waterbuck, impala, kudu, puku and zebra are plentiful. Small herds of Cookson's wildebeest may be seen. This is the best park in Zambia to see hippo completely out of the water. A few black rhino are present but are seldom seen. Leopard are most commonly sighted July-October and are frequently seen on night game drives. We saw at least one on each night drive during my recent visit.

Hippo and crocs abound in the muddy Luangwa River, a tributary of the Zambezi which runs along much of the park's eastern boundary and then traverses the southern part of the park.

Over 400 species of birds have been recorded, including

sacred ibis, saddle-billed storks, yellow-billed storks, Egyptian geese, spur-winged geese, fish eagles, crown cranes and long-tailed starlings.

A real advantage of this great park is that visitors can experience day and night game drives in open vehicles as well as participate in walking safaris ranging in length from a few hours to three days.

In the central eastern part of the park near Mfuwe Lodge, we saw lion, a pack of 21 African wild dogs, civet, buffalo, wildebeest, common waterbuck, greater kudu, puku, impala, crocs, hippos mating and fighting, Thorncroft's giraffes, elephant, zebra, monitor lizard, warthog, and the ever present baboons and vervet monkeys. Just before sunrise, elephants can sometimes be seen crossing the Luangwa River.

Driving from Masumba Airport at Mfuwe to Chibembe Lodge in the north, we sighted two African wild dogs, a spotted hyena, wildebeest, impala and warthog. As we were sipping whiskeys by the camp fire that night, we listened to baboon, hyena and hippo noises and watched honey badger (ratel) pass by within 20 feet of us.

Night Game Drives

There is no better park in Africa for night game drives than South Luangwa. On my most recent visit, the night game drive started out slowly until we almost ran over a lion lying in the middle of the road. What a shock! He was a member of a pride of seven that was hunting in thick bush. We followed them for awhile until the driver was afraid that we might accidentally get caught in the middle of the hunt and become the hunted!

We then followed a leopard at close range (20 feet) which all but ignored our presence. We had quite a thrill when the leopard jumped high into a bush after two dove that must have been sleeping. A close miss — lucky for the birds! Other sightings on the night game drives included spotted hyena, several more leopard and lion and a number of genet and civet.

Wildlife seen on one week's safari to South Luangwa included baboon, buffalo, bushbuck, civet, eland, elephant, large-spotted genet, Thornicroft's giraffe, hippo, honey badger, spotted hyena, impala, greater kudu, four leopard, over 20 lion, puku, vervet monkeys, warthog, common waterbuck, African wild dog, gnu, Burchell's zebra, banded mongoose, white-tailed mongoose, crowned crane, African darter, fish eagle, goliath heron, marabou stork, sacred ibis, long-tailed glossy starling, brown snake eagle and many other birds.

There are few all-weather roads in the park north of Mfuwe, so most of the northern camps are closed from November 1 through June 1. In May and early June the grass is still high. The northern part of the park is usually closed December through May.

Guests of most camps usually have a game drive or walk in the early morning, and in the afternoon, take either a day game drive departing about 3:30 p.m. and returning at dusk, or a late afternoon/night game drive, departing after 4:00 p.m. and returning around 8:00 p.m. Schedules will, of course, vary from camp to camp. Be sure to sign up for the option of your choice when checking in or as soon as possible thereafter.

Walking Safaris

Walking safaris are an excellent way to experience the bush, and are a major attraction of South Luangwa National Park. Walking safaris are only conducted from June-October during the dry season when the foliage has thinned out enough for safe walking. Walks may last from a few hours to three days, depending on the camp you visit. Many bush camps are rebuilt every year as they are often swept away during the rainy season.

Three-Day/Three-Night Walking Safaris

In addition to offering day and night game drives, Chibembe Lodge operates as the base camp for three-day/three-night walking safaris. This safari is the highlight of many visitors' trip to Africa and was certainly one of my favorite adventures. For those who are willing to rough it a bit and who would enjoy walking six to ten miles per day, it is highly recommended.

Groups of up to seven adults (children under 12 are not allowed) walk from bush camp to bush camp accompanied by a trail leader from Chibembe and an armed game scout from the national parks.

Guests overnight in two-bedded huts in simple camps. One shower with hot water heated with firewood and one long-drop toilet are shared by the group. Each hut has a lantern.

The beginning of an afternoon walk from a bush camp in South Luangwa National Park.

Bring spare batteries for your video recorder; no generators are available. Luggage and provisions are carried ahead to the next camp by porters who walk separately from the group. Guests usually carry only their cameras and a little water. Food is prepared by a resident cook, and the camp is stocked with cold drinks, wine and beer. Huts are cleaned by the staff, and laundry service is available.

Visitors usually fly from Lusaka to Mfuwe Airport and are driven to Chibembe where they spend the night. The next morning after a hardy breakfast, the group sets off walking about 6:30 a.m. The first adventure entails crossing the Luangwa River in a banana boat. Appropriately named, travel in this oddly shaped, oversized canoe is a precarious situation at best. One imagines the canoe will turn over at any minute as one passes numerous hippo and watches crocodiles on the river banks slither into the muddy river.

After crossing the river to the park, the group begins walking, escorted by a guide from Chibembe, the gun-bearing national park guide in the front and the tea-bearer bringing up the rear. The terrain is fairly flat, but often rugged. Large fields

Crossing the Luangwa River from a bush camp in South Luangwa National Park.

of ground holes are encountered — footprints of elephant, buffalo and antelope made during the rainy season. These holes harden in the dry season and make walking difficult.

On our first day we walked about two hours, and then our tea-bearer made hot tea. Our guide showed us how to make fire with a piece of wood, a stick and dried elephant dung. On the walk he did an excellent job answering our endless questions about spoor (footprints), animal droppings, flora and fauna of the bush.

After another one-and-a-half-hour's walk, we reached our first camp. Scenically situated on the banks of the Luangwa River, there were more than 40 hippo in the water below and numerous crocs on the far shore.

After much-welcomed cold drinks, lunch, and a short siesta, we regrouped at 3:30 p.m. for tea. At 4:00 p.m. we set off for another walk and returned just before dark (about 5:45 p.m.). After everyone had a hot shower, dinner was served. Then we sat around the campfire, listening to the mysterious sounds of the night and gazing up at millions of stars.

Hippo, lion, hyena and elephant often come into camp at night. So, it's not a good idea to leave your hut after everyone has gone to bed.

The lions' natural camouflage make them difficult to spot in high grass. Photo: Mike Appelbaum.

One night we were awakened by an elephant silhouetted in the moonlight and standing next to our hut. One of the group took a flash photo and spooked it, and it ran out of camp. But I would have loved to have watched it longer, to have more fully experienced this encounter with the wildlife that is Africa.

On an afternoon walking through an area with high golden grass, I commented to our guide that a lion could be 20 feet from the path and we might not see it. Just as the guide agreed with me, we turned around and there was a large female lion on the path not 50 feet behind us. Once the lion knew we were all aware of her presence, she ran off. That was our first lion sighting!

Days two and three on the walks have similar schedules. In the morning you walk to your next camp, then have another walk in the afternoon. On day four you leave camp very early, cross back over the Luangwa River in time for breakfast at Chibembe. Guests usually go on day and night game drives, spend the night, and fly back to Lusaka the following day.

An armed national park guide accompanies each walking safari.

On our walking safari we saw numerous herds of impala, Burchell's zebra, puku, elephant and buffalo, along with Thornicroft's giraffe, baboons and lion. Most importantly, we felt a sense of accomplishment from experiencing the bush on more intimate terms, in the way that Livingstone, Stanley and other early African explorers confronted the challenge of the continent on foot.

I suggest that guests stay an additional one or two nights in the park to go on vehicle safaris with day and night game drives to round out your experience of the park; more wildlife is usually seen from a vehicle than on a walking safari.

Shorter Walking Safaris

Visitors to South Luangwa do not have to go on a three-day walking safari to experience walking in the bush. Most camps in South Luangwa offer walks of two-four hours, and some have bush camps.

For example, guests of *Kapani Safari Camp* may go on walks lasting from two-four hours or spend one or two nights at Luwi Camp, a bush camp for only six guests, and take morning and afternoon walks from there. Tena Tena Camp and Chinzombo also offer walks.

Duplexes at Kapani Safari Camp make a visit to South Luangwa a comfortable adventure in the bush.

Bush camps are also excellent for guests who do not want to walk, but wish to simply experience the isolation in the bush.

Mfuwe Airport is about an hour flight from Lusaka. South Luangwa's main gate is 433 miles from Lusaka; driving takes about ten hours and is not recommended. Some international visitors fly into Lilongwe, Malawi, and are transferred by road to Mfuwe via Chipata.

ACCOMMODATION IN CENTRAL AND SOUTHERN SOUTH LUANGWA (Open Year-Round) — CLASS A: * *Kapani Safari Camp* is operated by Norman Carr who introduced walking safaris to Zambia. This exclusive camp has four large double chalets (16 beds) with ensuite facilities, private veranda and refrigerator. There is also a large swimming pool, and a library/video room where you can watch wildlife videos or even plug in your video recorder and view the footage shot during your safari. The cuisine is superb. Kapani offers day and night game drives, as well as walks, and has excellent guides.

Guests may also spend one or two nights at Luwi Camp, Kapani's bush camp, and take morning and afternoon walks from the camp. Luwi Camp is a two-hour game drive from Kapani in an isolated area of the park and is open June-

Dining room at Nsefu Camp, South Luangwa National Park.

October. Accommodation is in basic grass and bamboo huts catering to a maximum of six guests with a shared hot shower and flush toilet. A large hippo pool filled with crocs (many over ten feet in length) and over 40 hippo is a short walk from camp.

A five-day stay at Kapani, including one or two nights in the Luwi Camp, is recommended. Guests staying at Luwi Camp still keep their room at Kapani, so one person sharing a chalet may visit Luwi Camp while the other stays and enjoys the comforts of Kapani. Visits to a crocodile farm and a traditional African village can be arranged. Kapani is less than a 30-minute drive from the airport at Mfuwe.

CLASS B * *Chinzombo Safari Lodge* is located on the eastern bank of the Luangwa River across from the park. The camp has nine rondavels (18 beds) with ensuite facilities, swimming pool, and offers day and night game drives and short walks.

CLASS C: * *Mfuwe Lodge*, on a picturesque lagoon, has rooms with private facilities, swimming pool, and offers day and night game drives. * *Chichele Lodge* is set high on a hill in the park overlooking the Luangwa River. Rooms have ensuite facilities, most with air-conditioning. Day and night game drives and short walks are offered.

ACCOMMODATION IN NORTHERN SOUTH LUANGWA (Usually open June-October/November) — CLASS B: * *Nsefu Camp* has six attractive brick and thatch rondavels (doubles) with private facilities, across the river from the Nsefu sector of the park, one- to one-and-a-half-hours drive from the airport at Mfuwe. Day and night game drives and short walking excursions are offered. * *Tena Tena* is a tented camp with six tents (doubles), each set under a thatched canopy and private facilities situated on the banks of the Luangwa River within the park. Day and night game drives and walks are offered. * *Chibembe Lodge*, located on the banks of the Luangwa River just across from the park, has rustic chalets with private facilities (40 beds) and swimming pool. Chibembe is about a two-and-one-half-hour drive from Mfuwe Airport through several small friendly villages. Three-day walking safaris (see description above), day and night game drives and village trips are offered.

CAMPING: Camping is not allowed in the park except with a licensed tour operator.

NORTH LUANGWA NATIONAL PARK

As the name implies, this largely undeveloped 1790-square-mile park lies north of South Luangwa National Park in the upper Luangwa Valley.

Mark and Delia Owens, coauthors of *Cry of the Kalahari*, are conducting wildlife research here, and are working to reduce poaching and create an infrastructure to attract tourists.

The park lies between the 4600-foot-high Muchinga Escarpment on the west and the Luangwa River on the east, with altitudes ranging from 1640-3610 feet. Vegetation includes miombo woodland, scrubland and riverine forest.

Wildlife includes lion, leopard, black rhino, elephant, buffalo, zebra, eland, kudu, Cookson's wildebeest, impala, bushbuck, hippo and crocodile. Nearly 400 species of birds have been recorded, including bee-eaters, ibises, storks and waterfowl.

Walking is allowed in this seldom-visited park. You will virtually have the park to yourself. In fact, it is doubtful you will encounter any other groups on your visit.

The rainy season is November-April. The best time to visit is July-October.

For an hour, this baby hippo nudged and bit this croc and finally succeeded (with mama behind him) in chasing the croc off his sand bank.

ACCOMMODATION: None. Mobile tented safaris are available.
CAMPING: Campsites are available.

LUAMBE NATIONAL PARK

This undeveloped, 98-square-mile savannah and woodlands park is located just northeast of South Luangwa National Park. Luambe has many of the same species and features of South Luangwa National Park, but lacks first class tourist facilities to accommodate visitors.
ACCOMMODATION — CLASS F: Self-service bandas.
CAMPING: Camping sites are available.

NYIKA PLATEAU NATIONAL PARK

Located in northeast Zambia on the border with Malawi, this 31-square-mile park includes the small Zambian portion of the Nyika Plateau. This is a good park to visit for a keen naturalist or anyone wishing to escape the summer heat of the valleys below. Due to the high altitude, night temperatures sometimes drop below freezing May-September. Montane grassland and relic montane forest dominate the scene. A great variety of orchid and butterfly species are present, along with Moloney's monkey, blue monkey, civet and a number of other small mammals. Leopard, serval, bushbuck, reedbuck, blue duiker and klipspringer are present but rarely seen. Several species of birds not found elsewhere in Zambia may be seen. The best time for bird watching is November-June. ACCOMMODATION — CLASS D/F: A self-service lodge is available.

SUMBU NATIONAL PARK

Sumbu National Park borders the huge inland sea of Lake Tanganyika in the extreme north of Zambia. Visitors come to this 780-square-mile park mainly for fishing and water sports. This part of Lake Tanganyika is reputedly bilharzia-free, but be sure to check for its current status.

Forest and wetland wildlife species are plentiful. In fact, visitors are often accompanied to the sandy beaches by wildlife guards. Elephant, lion, buffalo, eland, puku, roan, blue duiker and Sharpe's grysbok may be seen. The shoreline is inhabited by hippo, crocodiles and water birds. Savannah dominates the park inland.

Day and night game drives in open vehicles, guided walks, and day and night game viewing by boat for crocodiles are available.

Fishing for goliath tiger fish, vundu (giant catfish), lake salmon and Nile Perch in Lake Tanganyika is excellent, especially November-March. The Zambia National Fishing Competition at Kasaba Bay is held every March or April, depending on the water level. Boats are available for hire. Quickest access is by air from Lusaka via Ndola.

ACCOMMODATION — CLASS C: * *Kasaba Bay Lodge* has 18 chalets (doubles) with private facilities a few hundred yards from the beach. The lodge offers fishing, game viewing and boating. * *Ndole Bay Lodge* has chalets (18 beds) with facilities ensuite; game viewing, fishing and boating are available. * *Nkamba Bay Lodge*, 15 miles from Kasaba Bay in the park on a hill overlooking the beach, has ten chalets (doubles) with ensuite facilities. Activities include fishing, boating and game viewing.

THE SOUTH AND WEST

LUSAKA

Lusaka, the capital of Zambia, has little to offer the international tourist. I suggest you spend as little time here as possible.

Sights include the Luburma Market, and the Munda Wanga Botanical Gardens and Zoological Park with over 400 different species of plants and a small zoo, and Chief Mungule's Village. Wood carvings made by local craftsmen can be seen at Kabwata Cultural Center.

There is a duty-free shop in town that only takes foreign currency; this shop has liquor and other items you may be unable to find in other stores, since shopping is limited. The airport is 16 miles from the city.

ACCOMMODATION — DELUXE: * *Lusaka Inter-Continental Hotel* is an air-conditioned hotel with 402 rooms with facilities ensuite, 24-hour room service, three restaurants, casino, and swimming pool. * *Pamodzi Hotel*, a 480-bed, air-conditioned hotel with facilities ensuite, has a restaurant, coffee shop, four bars, swimming pool, nightly entertainment, and 24-hour room service.

FIRST CLASS: * *Ridgeway Hotel*, an air-conditioned, 215-bed hotel, with facilities ensuite, restaurant and swimming pool.

TOURIST CLASS: * The *Andrews Motel* is a 180-bed, air-conditioned motel with swimming pool.

LOCHINVAR NATIONAL PARK

Lochinvar is a bird watcher's paradise with over 400 species recorded. In addition, the park is host to about 30,000 Kafue lechwe (their stronghold), 2000 blue wildebeest and 700 zebra. Greater kudu, bushbuck, oribi, hippo, side-striped jackal, reedbuck and common waterbuck are also present.

Kafue lechwe are unique to the Kafue Flats and are related to the red lechwe of the Busanga Swamps of Kafue National Park.

Bird watching is good year-round and is best November to May. Water birds such as the wattled crane are especially abundant. Other bird species include fish eagles. The park also encompasses part of Chunga Lake, which is fished by villagers

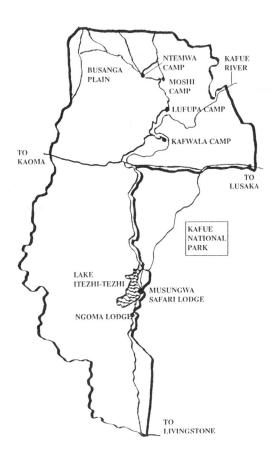

living outside the park boundaries.

The park is open year-round and is located 145 miles southwest of Lusaka, 30 miles northwest of Monze off the Lusaka-Livingstone road. A four-wheel-drive vehicle may be necessary in the rainy season.

ACCOMMODATION — CLASS C: * *Lochinvar Lodge* has rooms with ensuite facilities.

KAFUE NATIONAL PARK

Kafue National Park is one of the largest in Africa, covering 8650 square miles, making it two and one-half times the size of South Luangwa National Park and half the size of Switzerland.

Kafue has the largest number of different antelope species

Burchell's zebra.

of any park in Africa. However, game is more difficult to see here than in South Luangwa, since much of Kafue, especially the southern area, is clothed with a double-canopy forest. The southern and central parts are open all year while the northern area is only open during the dry season, June-October/November. Game is especially difficult to spot in the rainy season.

Game drives in this park are sometimes a combination of riding in a vehicle and walking, according to the wishes of the group.

On daylight game drives in the south of the park, we found elephant, impala, warthog, hippo, sable antelope, Burchell's zebra, wildebeest and buffalo. By air we spotted several illegal fishermen's huts on an island in the lake. Lion are also seen.

Night game drives produced sightings of impala, oribi, hundreds of spring hares, greater kudu, buffalo, serval, bushbuck, duiker, spotted hyena, Burchell's zebra, elephant, Defassa waterbuck and bushbabies.

Lake Itezhi-Tezhi, formed as the result of a hydroelectric dam constructed at the southern end of the Kafue Flats, provides fishing, bird watching and boating opportunities for visitors.

On a motorboat ride along the Kafue River, we passed numerous fishermen, several small villages, crocodiles, hippo,

Elephants have right-of-way in the bush!

many magnificent fish eagles, spur-winged geese, pied kingfishers herons, sacred ibis, Egyptian geese, egrets, and water
monitors.

We traveled farther along the river than most visitors and
found men transporting hippo meat in several canoes. Upon
our return to Musungwa Lodge, we reported the incident to
the manager. The manager immediately took two park rangers
in the lodge's boat (the park had no vehicles or boats of its
own) to where we had seen them. The poachers were arrested.
Such cooperation of private enterprise with government conservation efforts is highly commendable.

On a drive from Musungwa to Nanzhila Camp in the southern part of the park, we saw hundreds of elephant with one
herd numbering over 40, scattered Burchell's zebra, sable,
Lichtenstein's hartebeest, wildebeest, plentiful reedbuck and
oribi, and huge herds of buffalo numbering in the thousands.
On our return to Musungwa Lodge, we were stuck in the mud
for one-and-a-half hours, which delayed us sufficiently to allow
another opportunity for a night game drive.

The Busanga Plains and marshes in the north have a
greater number and variety of wildlife species. Wildlife is easier
to spot here than in the dense woodland savanna in the south.
This region is characterized by mopane and miombo forests,

rock hills, open plains, marshes and riverine forests. The Kafue River runs through the northern part of the park and along its east central border.

Large herds of rare red lechwe are often seen on the Busanga Plains. Sitatunga may be found in the Busanga Swamps on the northern border of the park. Buffalo, elephant, puku, wildebeest, impala, roan, sable, kudu, waterbuck, leopard, lion, hyena and cheetah are also present. The Kafue Flats are an excellent location to spot many of the park's more than 400 recorded species of birds.

There is little to be seen on the four-hour, 170-mile drive from Lusaka, so those with limited time may wish to charter a plane.

ACCOMMODATION IN SOUTHERN KAFUE (Open Year-Round) — CLASS B: * *Hippo Camp* is a small camp (eight beds) with a two-story pontoon boat used for day trips. * *Musungwa Safari Lodge* (46 beds) is located just outside the eastern boundary of the park. Most rooms have private facilities. An attractive pool and veranda is available for your enjoyment. The lodge offers sunset cruises, river trips, and game drives.

CLASS C: * *Ngoma Lodge* has a swimming pool and airstrip; each two rooms share bathroom facilities.

ACCOMMODATION IN NORTHERN KAFUE (Open June-October/November) — CLASS C: The following four camps specialize in walk-ride safaris and offer night game drives. Most chalets have private showers and toilets. * *Moshi Camp* is situated on a hill. * *Ntemwa Camp* is the most northern river side camp on the Lufupa River and is also the most comfortable (6 beds). * *Kafwala Camp* overlooks the Kafwala Rapids. * *Lufupa*, situated in the center of the northern region near the confluence of the Kafue and Lufupa Rivers, also offers good fishing and game viewing by boat.

MOSI-OA-TUNYA (VICTORIA FALLS) NATIONAL PARK

Called Mosi-oa-Tunya (the smoke that thunders), Victoria Falls should not be missed. Visitors may walk along the Knife Edge Bridge for a good view of the Eastern Cataract and Boiling Pot.

The "Sunset Cruise" departs from the Rainbow National Lodge and is very pleasant; hippo and crocodiles are often

White-water rafting on the Zambezi River.
Photo: Brian Clark/SOBEK.

seen. Fishing for tigerfish on the Zambezi River is best from June-October (September is best) before the rains muddy the water.

The falls are located about three miles from Livingstone. See the chapter on Zimbabwe for a detailed description of the falls.

White-Water Rafting

The Zambezi River below Victoria Falls is one of the most exciting white-water rafting experiences in the world. Numerous fifth-class rapids (the highest class runable) make this one of the most challenging rivers on earth. One-, two-, three- and seven-day trips are operated on the Zambezi River below Victoria Falls from the Zambia and/or Zimbabwe side of the Zambezi River. No experience is required; just hang on and enjoy the ride!

The one-day trip is rated as the wildest commercially run one-day trip in the world. Rafts with up to eight riders and one oarsperson disappear from sight as they drop into deep holes and crash into waves over 12 feet high, being further dwarfed by sheer cliffs which often rise hundreds of feet on both sides of the canyon.

White-water rafting on the Zambezi River.

Hippo and crocs are more frequently seen further downstream on multi-day trips. Klipspringer and other wildlife can be seen on the banks, especially during the dry season.

Camp is made on sandy river banks, and all meals are prepared by the staff. These trips are not for those who wish to be pampered. There are no facilities en route. One-day trips are operated March, April, and mid-June through December, and the longer trips from mid-July through December only.

For the one-day trip, I would suggest you wear a swimsuit and take a hat and sunglasses with something to tie them onto yourself, short-sleeved shirt, sunscreen, tennis shoes (tackies) or Tevas (a type of sandal), polypropylene undershirt and fast-drying nylon shorts. During Winter (June-August) also bring wetsuit booties, heavy polypropylene underwear, a wool sweater and rainsuit. For the longer trips, get a checklist from your travel agent.

Plans are underway to build a dam to relieve some pressure off the Kariba Dam downstream. Such a dam would flood the gorge and make these river trips a thing of the past. Go now while there are still rapids to run!

ACCOMMODATION — FIRST CLASS: * *Mosi-Oa-Tunya Inter-Continental Hotel*, a 200-bed hotel with air-conditioning, swimming pool and three restaurants, is a five-minute walk from Victoria Falls.

TOURIST CLASS: * *Rainbow Lodge*, in Mosi-oa-Tunya National Park, has traditionally styled rondavels and rooms with air-conditioning (104 beds) and ensuite facilities. * The *New Fairmount Hotel* is a small hotel with air-conditioned rooms with private facilities, swimming pool and casino.

LIVINGSTONE

Livingstone is a small town of about 80,000 inhabitants, three miles from Victoria Falls. Driving from Lusaka takes five to six hours (295 miles) and flying takes a little over an hour.

The Livingstone Museum is the National Museum of Zambia, and is renowned for its collection of Dr. Livingstone's memoirs. Other exhibits cover the art and culture of Zambia. The Maramba Cultural Center exhibits bandas from various districts in Zambia and presents colorful costumed performances by Zambian dancers.

Livingstone Zoological Park is a small fenced park near Livingstone, covering 25 square miles. It is stocked with greater kudu, white rhino, impala, and other wildlife. The best time to visit is from June to October.

Victoria Falls on the Zambezi River.
Photo: Michael K. Nichols/SOBEK.

ZIMBABWE

ZIMBABWE

FACTS AT A GLANCE

AREA:	151,000 SQUARE MILES
APPROXIMATE SIZE:	CALIFORNIA OR ONE AND A HALF TIMES THE SIZE OF GREAT BRITAIN
POPULATION:	9 MILLION (1990 EST.)
CAPITAL:	HARARE (POP. EST. 800,000)
LANGUAGES:	OFFICIAL: ENGLISH
	OTHER: SHONA AND SINDEBELE

Victoria Falls.

ZIMBABWE

Thought by some to be the land of King Solomon's mines, Zimbabwe (previously called Rhodesia) is a country blessed with good farmland, mineral wealth, beautiful and varied landscapes, and excellent game parks.

Most of Zimbabwe consists of a central plateau 3000-4000 feet above sea level. The highveld, or high plateau, stretches from southwest to northeast from 4000-5000 feet with a mountainous region along the eastern border from 6,000-8,000 feet in altitude.

The Zambezi River runs along the northeastern border, and the Limpopo River along the southern border. The Zambezi Valley is an extension of the Great Rift Valley. The southern edge of the Zambezi Valley is formed by the Zimbabwean escarpment. The Zambian escarpment, situated north of the Zambezi River, forms the northern edge of the Zambezi valley.

The climate is moderate and seasons are reversed from the northern hemisphere. Winter days (May-August) are generally dry and sunny with day temperatures averaging 59-68° F. Summer daytime temperatures average 77 - 86° F. with October being the hottest month. The rainy season is November-March.

The major ethnic groups are the Mashona and Ndebele. About 50% of the population is syncretic (part Christian and part traditional beliefs), 25% Christian, 24% traditional, and 1% Hindu and Muslim. English is understood by about half of the population.

In the first century, the region was inhabited by hunters related to the Bushmen. Cecil Rhodes and the British South

Africa Company took control in 1890, and the area was named Southern Rhodesia, which became a British Colony in 1923. Unilateral Declaration of Independence (UDI) from Britain was declared by Prime Minister Ian Smith and the white minority on November 11, 1965. Officially Zimbabwe became independent on April 18, 1980.

Zimbabwe has one of the most widely diversified economies in Africa, consisting of industry, mining and agriculture (in which they are self-sufficient). Main foreign exchange earners are tobacco, minerals, agriculture and tourism.

WILDLIFE AND WILDLIFE AREAS

Zimbabwe has excellent and well-maintained parks and reserves. The country's three premier reserves, which also rate as three of the best reserves in Africa, are Hwange, Mana Pools and Matusadona National Parks.

Hwange National Park is famous for its huge elephant population (over 25,000) and numerous large pans. Matusadona National Park, located along the southern shores of beautiful Lake Kariba, has an enormous buffalo population and the country's largest concentration of black rhino. Mana Pools on the Zambezi River has one of the highest concentrations of wildlife of any park on the continent during the dry season.

Adventurers wishing to do more than view wildlife from a vehicle should seriously consider a safari in this country. Zimbabwe offers the greatest variety of methods of wildlife viewing in Africa, including day and night game drives in open vehicles, boat game drives, walking, canoeing, kayaking, white-water rafting and travel by houseboat.

Many of the safari camps are able to offer very personalized service because they cater to only eight to sixteen guests. Accommodations and food are excellent.

Instead of driving to the reserves, many people fly to the parks, taking advantage of Air Zimbabwe's daily flights connecting Kariba, Victoria Falls, Hwange, Bulawayo, Masvingo and Buffalo Range. There are also a number of overland safaris available.

Game viewing is by open landrover, and walking is allowed with a licensed guide. Night game drives are conducted in some areas adjacent to the reserves.

Victoria Falls.

Reservations for all national park accommodations, camping and caravan sites can be made with the National Parks Central Booking Office, P.O. Box 8151, Causeway; tel: Harare 706077. Information concerning the national parks can be obtained from the Zimbabwe Tourist Development Corporation (ZTDC) or from the Department of National Parks, P.O. Box 8365, Harare; tel: 707624.

THE WEST

VICTORIA FALLS NATIONAL PARK

Dr. David Livingstone became the first white man to see Victoria Falls on November 16, 1855, and named them after his queen. In his journal he wrote, "On sights as beautiful as this, Angels in their flight must have gazed."

Victoria Falls is approximately 5600 feet wide, twice the height of Niagara Falls, and one and one half times as wide. It is divided into five separate waterfalls: Devil's Cataract, Main Falls, Horseshoe Falls, Rainbow Falls and Eastern Cataract,

Victoria Falls, Zimbabwe side. Photo: Kamau Amen-Ra.

ranging in height from 200-355 feet.

Peak flood waters usually occur around mid-April when 150 million gallons per minute crash onto the rocks below spraying water up to 1650 feet in the air. At this time (March-April) so much water is falling that the spray makes it difficult to see the falls. December-February is actually a better time to see them, keeping in mind that they are spectacular any time of the year.

Victoria Falls and the Zambezi River form the border between Zambia and Zimbabwe. The banks of the 1675-mile-long Zambezi River, the only major river in Africa to flow into the Indian Ocean, are lined with thick riverine forest. Daytime and sundowner cruises operate above the falls where hippo and crocs may be spotted and elephant and other wildlife may be seen coming to the shore to drink.

Fortunately the area around the falls has not been commercialized, and there are unobstructed views from many vantage points connected by paved paths. Be prepared to get wet as you walk through a luxuriant rain forest surrounding the falls, a result of the continuous spray. A path called the Chain Walk descends from near Livingstone's statue into the gorge of the Devil's Cataract, providing an excellent vantage point.

Spencer's Creek Crocodile Ranch has specimens up to 14 1/2 feet in length and weighing up to 980 pounds. The **Craft Village** in the middle of town is very interesting with living quarters and other structures representing traditional Zimbabwean life of the country's major tribes. **Big Tree** is a giant baobab over 50 feet in circumference, 65 feet high and 1,000-1,500 years old. The **African Spectacular**, presented every night at the Victoria Falls Hotel, features tribal dancing at its finest.

The **"Flight of Angels,"** a flight over the falls in a small plane, is highly recommended to acquire a feeling for the true majesty of the falls. Game-viewing flights upstream from the falls along the Zambezi River and over Victoria Falls National Park are also available. It is best to reserve seats in advance.

The falls can also be viewed from Zambia. Zambian visas are available at the border but in case of change it is better to obtain a visa in advance.

Generally speaking, the falls are more impressive and the accommodations and tourism infrastructure is better on the Zimbabwean side.

The Zambezi River offers one of the most exciting (if not the most exciting) **white-water rafting** trips in the world. Rafting trips are available July-January (depending on the water level of the river) in the gorges below Victoria Falls from both the Zimbabwean and Zambian sides of the river. The Zambezi River is rated fifth class (the highest class runable). Rafters meet around 8:00 a.m. at the Victoria Falls Hotel and take a short walk down to the river's edge where the rafting safari begins. For many travelers, it is a highlight of their safari (see chapter on Zambia for details). Rafters must be 16 years of age or older to participate.

Kayaking Safaris (white-water canoeing) are a great way to explore the upper Zambezi from near Kazungula to just above Victoria Falls; these safaris are offered June-October. Adventurers pass numerous hippo, crocs and other wildlife as they paddle two-man expedition kayaks on a three-day/two-night safari.

No previous kayaking experience is necessary. However, the tricky part is that two of the most difficult rapids are the second and third rapids encountered, which doesn't allow much time for training! Most kayaks (including ours) flip once — an experience in itself!

Two-man expedition kayaks used on kayaking safaris.

Bush camping on the kayak safari.

Victoria Falls Hotel.

A crew traveling in a landrover sets up camp ahead of the group. Participants sleep under the stars (beware of lions). There are no shower or toilet facilities at the camps. Under special arrangement, safari companies can arrange a more deluxe tented program with shower and toilet tents.

ACCOMMODATION — DELUXE * *Victoria Falls Hotel* has maintained much of its colonial elegance with its colonial architecture, spacious terraces and colorful gardens. The hotel has 139 air-conditioned rooms with private facilities, swimming pool and tennis courts and is only a ten-minute walk from the falls.

FIRST CLASS: * *Makasa Sun Hotel* is a modern hotel situated adjacent to the Victoria Falls Hotel with 95 air-conditioned rooms with ensuite facilities, casino, swimming pool and tennis courts.

TOURIST CLASS: * *Rainbow Hotel* is located next to Victoria Falls Village and has air-conditioned rooms with private facilities and swimming pool. * The *A'Zambezi River Lodge*, one of the largest buildings under traditional thatch on the continent, is located one and one half miles from town. The lodge has a swimming pool and 83 air-conditioned rooms with private facilities.

CLASS F & CAMPING: * *Victoria Falls Rest And Caravan Park* has small hostel, camping and caravan sites.

ACCOMMODATION NEAR VICTORIA FALLS — CLASS A: * *Westwood Camp* is a 45-minute drive from Victoria Falls and is situated on a 120,000-acre private concession bordering the

Zambezi National Park. Westwood caters to a maximum of eight guests in thatch and stone chalets (doubles) with private facilities situated on the banks of the Zambezi. Day and night game drives, walking, kayaking, boating and fishing are offered. * *Imbabala Camp*, located on private land only a mile from the Botswana border, has nine chalets (doubles) with private facilities and swimming pool. Day and night game drives by vehicle, boat game drives and fishing are offered. CLASS D: See "Zambezi National Park."

ZAMBEZI NATIONAL PARK

Victoria Falls National Park includes Victoria Falls as well as 215-square-mile Zambezi National Park. The park is located west of the falls and extends for 25 miles along the Zambezi River.

Zambezi National Park is well known for its abundance of sable antelope. Among other species are white rhino, black rhino, elephant, zebra, eland, buffalo, giraffe, lion, kudu and waterbuck.

Day safaris are offered from Victoria Falls. Fishing is very good for tiger fish, tilapia, and giant vundu (giant catfish). There are 30 sites along the river for picnicking and fishing (beware of crocodiles). Since the game reserve does not have all-weather roads, parts of it are usually closed during the rains from November 1-May 1.

ACCOMMODATION — CLASS D: * *Zambezi National Park Lodges*, scenically situated on the banks of the Zambezi, consist of 15 self-service lodges, each catering to a maximum of six people.

KAZUMA PAN NATIONAL PARK

Located north of Hwange National Park in the Matetsi Safari Area, Kazuma Pan National Park is a small park that has a series of pans that flood in the rainy season. The eastern part of the park is wooded with more water and a greater variety and concentration of wildlife than the western side of the park, which is predominantly grasslands. Lion, cheetah and rhino are often seen. The park is open to campers who are self-contained. Walking is allowed with a licensed guide. There are no facilities.

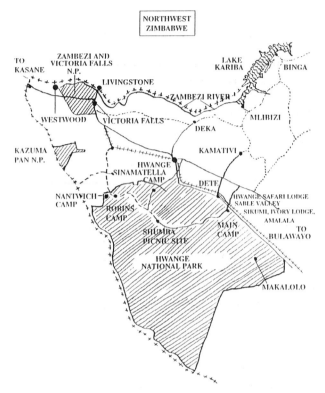

NORTHWEST ZIMBABWE

HWANGE NATIONAL PARK

Hwange (previously called Wankie) is Zimbabwe's largest national park and famous for its large herds of elephant. Other predominant species include buffalo, giraffe, zebra, wildebeest, sable, white and black rhino, cheetah, wild dog and bat-eared fox. This is also one of the best parks on the continent to see sable antelope.

Hwange is slightly larger than the state of Connecticut, covering 5600 square miles. The park is located in the northwest corner of the country just south of the main road between Bulawayo and Victoria Falls. Hwange boasts over 100 species of mammals and 400 species of birds.

The park ranges from semidesert in the south to a plateau in the north. The northern part of Hwange is mudstone and basalt, and the southern part is Kalahari sand veld. The park has an average altitude of 3300 feet. Winter nights can drop to below freezing, and summer days can be over 100° F., while average temperatures range from 65-83° F.

There are no rivers and only a few streams in the north of the park, but boreholes (wells) provide sources of water year-round for wildlife. During the dry season these permanent water holes (pans) provide an excellent stage for guests to view wildlife performing day-to-day scenes of survival.

Generally, there are no seasonal animal migrations. The best time to see wildlife is during the dry season from August-October when the game concentrate near permanent water. Game viewing is good June-July, fair in April, May and November, and poor during the rainy season from December-March when the game is widely dispersed.

Game viewing is usually very good within ten miles of Main Camp and Park Headquarters. Wildlife commonly seen nearby include elephant, giraffe, zebra, greater kudu, impala, buffalo, sable, wildebeest, tsessebe, black-backed jackal, lion, hyena, and cheetah. Rhino may also be seen. We saw a very large male lion with a full mane guarding a buffalo kill while a jackal darted in and out, snatching morsels as dozens of vultures waited their turn.

Moonlight game viewing occurs from one or two nights before and after a full moon when park staff escort guests to the Nyamandhlovu (meaning "meat of the elephant") Platform near main camp. Morning walks with a national park game scout are also available.

The area around Sinamatella Camp in the northern part of the park is good for spotting kudu, elephant, giraffe, impala, hippo, klipspringer, warthog, lion, hyena, and leopard. The Bumbusi Ruins, the third largest ancient stone buildings in Zimbabwe, are located behind Bumbusi Camp, 15 miles north-west of Sinamatella Camp.

The northwestern part of the park near Robins Camp is known for its large lion population. Other species often seen include impala (which attract the lion), buffalo, kudu, sable, roan, waterbuck, elephant, giraffe, reedbuck, tsessebe, lion, side-striped jackal, cheetah, and hyena.

Hwange has 300 miles of roads, some of which are closed during the rainy season. All-weather roads run through most of the park. Some roads are tarmac, which detracts a bit from the feeling of being in the bush.

Vehicles must keep to the roads and visitors are not allowed

Black rhino in Hwange National Park. Photo: Alison Wright.

to leave their vehicles except at the hides, game-viewing platforms and at fenced-in picnic sites. Open vehicles are allowed.

An airstrip is available for small aircraft at Main Camp. The closest rail station is Dete Station, 15 miles from Main Camp.

ACCOMMODATIONS — Sable Valley Lodge, Sikumi Tree Lodge, Ivory Lodge and Hwange Safari Lodge are all located in 60,000-acre Dete Vlei (private reserve) bordering Hwange National Park, a 15-30 minute drive from Hwange Airport; *Makalolo Tented Camp* is located deep within the park, about a three-hour drive from the airport.

CLASS A: * *Sable Valley Camp* accommodates 16 guests in luxury thatched lodges with ensuite facilities overlooking a water hole.

CLASS A/B: * *Amalala* is a refurbished farmhouse (1920's) accommodating a maximum of 14 guests in thatched chalets with ensuite facilities. * *Ivory Lodge* is a small camp (20 beds) of tree houses with facilities ensuite; game drives are offered. Horseback safaris and game drives are available. * *Sikumi Tree Lodge* has nine thatched chalets (doubles) set in mangwe trees and two family chalets set closer to the ground. The lodge has excellent food, a swimming pool, and caters to up to 24 guests. All chalets have private facilities.

CLASS B: * *Makalolo Tented Camp* is situated in the Makalolo

Wilderness Area, a remote region of the park teeming with game. Only guests of Makalolo are allowed in this part of the park, guaranteeing exclusivity. Tents with private facilities accommodate a maximum of 14 guests. The camp offers day and night game drives and walks. * *Hwange Safari Lodge* has 100 double rooms with private facilities, swimming pool and an elevated game-viewing platform with bar. Game drives are offered in large trucks and open vehicles.

CLASS D, F & CAMPING: There are six *National Park Camps*, all of which have lodge accommodation. Some rooms have private facilities. Ablution blocks are available for campers and for people in rooms without private facilities.

The following three camps are open year-round and have lodge as well as caravan and camping sites. Walks may be available from these camps with a park game scout. * *Main Camp* is located in the northeastern part of the park. It is the site of Park Headquarters and Hwange's largest camp (118 beds) and has a restaurant, bar and small grocery store. * *Sinamatella Camp* is situated in the northern part of the park on a small plateau affording unobstructed views and overlooks a water hole frequented by elephant in the afternoon. There is a restaurant, bar and small store. * *Robins Exclusive Camp* is located in the northwestern part of the park, only 75 miles from Victoria Falls. Robins has lodges available year-round and two- and four-bedded chalets with a communal ablution block available May-October.

Each of the following camps may be booked by only one group at a time: * *Bumbusi Exclusive Camp* is open year-round and is located 15 miles northwest of Sinamatella Camp on a scenic road which passes through rocky outcrops. The camp is situated near the Deka River and is shaded by a grove of enormous ebony trees. A-frame thatched lodges accommodate a single group of up to 12 persons. The camp is self-catering; bring your own food and drink. Escorted by an armed wildlife guard, guests may walk to hides situated near water holes. * *Lukosi Camp* is located in the Sinamatella area and caters to a single group of up to twelve persons. The camp is open year-round. * *Deka Exclusive Camp*, located 16 miles from Robins Camp, accommodates up to 12 guests in A-frame thatched lodges and is open May-October. * *Nantwich Exclusive Camp* has lodges with private facilities and is seven miles from Robins Camp. The lodge is usually open year-round.

Meikles Hotel is a Five-Star hotel in Harare. Photo: Zimbabwe National Tourist Board.

THE NORTH

HARARE

Formerly called Salisbury, Harare is the capital and largest city. It is one of the cleanest and most modern cities on the continent. Points of interest include the National Museum, National Art Gallery, Botanical Garden, Houses of Parliament and the Tobacco Auction Floors. Mbare Msiki Market is good for shopping for curios.

A beautiful park adjacent to the Monomotapa Hotel features a large variety of brilliant flora. Harare Botanical Gardens has indigenous trees and herbs.

Harare's best restaurants include Tiffany's, L'Escargot, La Chandelle, La Fontaine, and The Bamboo Inn. Pino's Restaurant is famous for its fresh prawns from Mozambique. Jackets for men and dresses for women areappropriate attire for the top restaurants.

A short drive from Harare are the Larvon Bird Gardens, Ewanrigg Botanical Gardens and Lake McIlwaine Game Park. Imire Game Park has an animal orphanage.

ACCOMMODATION — DELUXE: * *Meikles Hotel* has 277

rooms with ensuite facilities, swimming pool, sauna, and traditional old-world atmosphere. * *Sheraton Hotel* has 325 air-conditioned rooms with ensuite facilities, swimming pool, tennis courts, sauna and gym. * *Monomotapa Hotel* has 214 air-conditioned rooms with ensuite facilities, swimming pool and convention facilities. * *Cresta Jameson Hotel* has 128 air-conditioned rooms with facilities ensuite and swimming pool.

FIRST CLASS: * *Holiday Inn* has 205 air-conditioned rooms with ensuite facilities, swimming pool and the popular Harper's Night Club.

TOURIST CLASS: * *Bronte Hotel* has 108 rooms with private facilities and swimming pool.

ACCOMMODATION — NEAR HARARE — CLASS A: * *Pamuzinda Safari Lodge*, located 53 miles from Harare, is a private game ranch with 12 bungalows (doubles) overlooking the water hole and has a swimming pool.

LAKE KARIBA

Sunsets over the deep blue waters of Lake Kariba dotted with islands are rated among the most spectacular in the world. This is one of the largest man-made lakes on earth covering over 2,000 square miles and formed by damming the Zambezi River in 1958. The lake is 180 miles long and up to 20 miles in width and is surrounded for the most part by untouched wilderness.

When the dam was completed and the waters in the valley began to rise, animals were forced to higher ground, which quickly became islands soon to be submerged under the new lake. To save these helpless animals, Operation Noah was organized by Rupert Fothergill. Over 5000 animals, including 35 different mammal species, numerous elephant and 44 black rhino, were rescued and released in what are now Matusadona National Park and the Chete Safari Area.

Lights from commercial kapenta fishing boats are often seen on the lake at night. Fishing is excellent for tiger fish, giant vundu, bream, cheesa, and nkupi. October is the optimum month for tiger fishing and November-April for bream. Birdlife is prolific, especially waterfowl.

The Lake Kariba Ferry usually takes 22 hours to cruise from Mlibizi to Kariba Town. If you are thinking of taking a vehicle

EASTERN LAKE KARIBA AND MATUSADONA N.P.

ZAMBIA

KARIBA

LAKE KARIBA

FOTHERGILL ISL.

SPURWING ISL.

BUMI HILLS

MATUSADONA N.P.

SANYATI LODGE

SANYATI GORGE

ZIMBABWE

through Zimbabwe from Victoria Falls to Kariba, this ferry will save you over 775 miles of driving.

KARIBA (TOWN)

Kariba is the major gateway to both Matusadona and Mana Pools National Parks. Many people fly here from Harare, Victoria Falls or Hwange and are then transferred by aircraft, boat or vehicle to their respective camps.

Kariba Dam, one of the largest in Africa, is a short distance from town. Water sports (beware of crocodiles and hippo) and cruises on the lake are available.

ACCOMMODATION — TOURIST CLASS: *Caribbea Bay Resort*, located on the shores of Lake Kariba, is a Sardinian-style resort with 43 rooms (some air-conditioned) with ensuite facilities, two swimming pools, popular poolside bar and casino.
* *Lakeview Inn* has 52 air-conditioned rooms and swimming pool overlooking Lake Kariba.

CAMPING: * *M.O.T.H. Campsite* is located just below the Lakeview Inn.

MATUSADONA NATIONAL PARK

Situated on the southern shore of Lake Kariba and bounded on the east by the dramatic Sanyati Gorge and the

A morning walk with an armed guide in Matsudona National Park.

west by the Umi River, this scenic 600-square-mile park has an abundance of elephant, kudu, impala and buffalo — especially along the shoreline in the dry season (May-September). Other game includes lion, sable, roan and waterbuck. This is one of the best parks in Africa to see black rhino while on escorted walks. Leopard are occasionally spotted in the Sanyati Gorge.

Game viewing by boat near shore and walking safaris are popular. Fishing is excellent but beware of crocodiles. Four-day walking safaris with professional guides using the exclusive camps listed below or private tenting is another great way to experience the bush. Houseboats complete with captain and staff may be rented, providing private parties great freedom and comfort for exploration.

ACCOMMODATION — CLASS A: * *Sanyati Lodge* is an exquisite 12-bed camp with chalets made of stone and thatch. Each chalet is very private, located along its own path out of view of the rest of camp. Sanyati, situated on the side of a hill at the mouth of the Sanyati Gorge, is famous for great fishing — especially tiger fish. Boat safaris are offered, and guests wishing to go on game drives and walks are taken by boat across the gorge to the park. Black rhino are often sighted. The lodge is located up the side of a hill and is not recommended for people who have walking problems. * *Bumi Hills Safari*

Guests of Water Wilderness on Lake Kariba visit each other and the dining houseboat by canoe.

Lodge, located on the western outskirts of the park on a hill overlooking the lake, has 20 rooms with ensuite facilities and swimming pool. Game drives by vehicle (day and night), by boat, and walks are offered.

CLASS B * *Water Wilderness,* situated in an isolated area of the lake, consists of four houseboats (doubles) with private facilities surrounding a dining houseboat. Guests of each houseboat are given a canoe for transport among the houseboats. Game drives by boat and morning walks are conducted. Black rhino are prolific in this area and are often seen on walks. Guests first fly to Bumi Hills Safari Lodge and are then transferred by boat to Water Wilderness. * *Fothergill Island Safari Camp* has 25 comfortable Batonka lodges (doubles) with private facilities and swimming pool. Game viewing on foot, by boat and by vehicle is offered. Access is from Kariba by boat (most common) or charter aircraft. Due to the fluctuating water level of Lake Kariba, Fothergill may be connected to the mainland by a peninsula. * *Spurwing Island* has a swimming pool and accommodates up to 40 guests in comfortable cabins and tents.

CLASS D: The National Park has three exclusive self-service

Elephant on the shore of Lake Kariba in Matusadona National Park.

camps with two family lodges with private facilities. Each camp may be booked by one party only; they are usually booked by safari operators. * *Ume* is located near the Tashinga airstrip on the east bank of the Ume River. * *Mbalabala* is located on the Bumi River 500 feet upstream from Ume Camp. * *Muuyu* is located on Elephant Point.

CAMPING: The two National Park Campsites have ablution blocks. * *Tashinga* is located on the lake shore. A small airstrip is located nearby. * *Sanyati* is a small campsite located in the eastern part of the park a short hike from the shoreline.

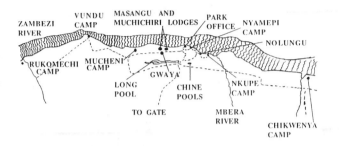

MANA POOLS
NATIONAL PARK
(NORTHERN PART)

MANA POOLS NATIONAL PARK

During the dry season, Mana Pools National Park has one of the highest concentrations of wildlife on the continent. The park is situated on the southern side of the Zambezi River downstream (northeast) of Lake Kariba.

This 965-square-mile park is uniquely characterized by fertile river terraces reaching from the slow-moving Zambezi River inland for several miles. Small ponds and pools such as Chine Pool and Long Pool were formed as the river's course slowly drifted northward. Reeds, sandbanks, and huge mahogany and acacia trees near the river give way to dense mopane woodland to the park's southern boundary along the steep Zambezi Escarpment.

Mana Pools National Park covers part of the Middle Zambezi Valley, which is home for 12,000 elephant and 16,000 buffalo (with herds of over 500 each).

Species commonly seen in the park include kudu, zebra, eland, impala, bushbuck, lion, leopard, jackal, hyena, and crocodile. Large schools of hippo are sometimes seen lying on the sandbanks soaking up the morning sun. Occasionally spotted are wild dog, cheetah, black rhino and the rare nyala. Large varieties of both woodland and water birds are present.

Canoe Safaris

Canoe safaris lasting from three to nine days are operated from below Kariba Dam and drift downstream for up to

Elephant "greeting" our canoe safari on the Zambezi River.

159 miles past Mana Pools to Kanyemba near the Mozambique border and provide excellent game-viewing opportunities.

For the adventurous traveler, this is one of the best ways to experience the African bush and is one of my favorite safaris on the entire continent.

During my recent seven-day canoe safari from Chirundu to Kanyemba, we spotted several hundred hippo along with hundreds of crocodile, waterbuck and impala, dozens of elephant, several lion and leopard, among many other species. Birders in our party spotted 135 species.

Traveling silently by canoe, one can approach closely to wildlife which has come to drink along the shore. Most importantly, you actively participate in the adventure.

On one occasion a huge elephant walked out into the river in front of us and completely submerged underwater with the exception of its trunk waving in the air. When it came up we were almost on top of it, and we paddled madly to get out of the way. When the elephant finally noticed us, it trumpeted

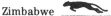

A few seconds after this photo was taken, this elephant completely submerged under water except for his trunk.

loudly and began running in the water after us. Fortunately, it stopped after a few steps, and the mighty Zambezi moved us quickly downstream out of danger. What fun!

From below Kariba Dam canoeists pass through the Kariba Gorge on the way to Chirundu. The portion of the river along Mana Pools National Park is best for wildlife viewing. However, game viewing below (east)of Mana Pools is also very good.

Downstream (east) of Mana Pools National Park lies the rugged and remote Mupata Gorge. Passing through the gorge, we spotted a leopard stalking two Egyptian geese. My partner and I paddled as hard as we could to get a close view of the action. The leopard's leaping attempt failed — fortunately for the geese! Further downstream three lion came down to drink and wandered off as if we were not even there.

The less expensive canoe safaris do not have a support vehicle on land. Camping is often done on islands in the Zambezi where there are no facilities. Participants sleep in tents or under mosquito nets. Everyone pitches in with the chores.

Midrange canoe safaris provide four-wheel-drive vehicle backup to the canoe safari. Camp is prepared in advance of your arrival. Guests are accommodated in comfortable tents; shower and toilet tents are set up for the group. Game drives may also be conducted from camp. For those who do not wish to camp, some national park exclusive camps have lodge accommodation (see below).

The best of all worlds (and the most expensive option) is to have a professional guide licensed for walks as your escort; this will allow you to canoe, go on game drives by vehicle and walk. Unless your guide is licensed to take guests on walks, walking inland is limited to 50 meters (yards) from the riverbank.

Your guide will instruct you on safety precautions to use on your canoe safari. However, here are a few tips. When getting out of a canoe onto shore, always place the canoe between you and the open water (and possible crocodiles). Keep away from the river's edge whenever possible. Walk along the upper riverbank where crocodiles cannot reach you. Be very careful when drawing water from the river, especially at night. Again, keep the canoes between you and the open water. Better yet, let your guide do it for you.

Crocodiles will not try to turn over a canoe. However, there is a slight chance that hippos may attack your canoe if you don't give them enough distance or if you cut them off from their line of escape to deep water. When threatened, hippos run or swim to safety, heading for the deepest part of the river, and you don't want to be in their way!

Previous canoe experience for these trips is not necessary. However, spending at least a few hours in a canoe before your African safari would allow you to feel more comfortable canoeing in a foreign environment.

Walking Safaris ranging from a few hours from your camp to four days may be arranged. On the three-night/four-day walking safaris, porters transport all luggage and equipment by canoe while guests take the most interesting route on land.

The best time to visit the park for one of the finest exhibitions of wildlife on the continent is at the end of the dry season (September-October) when elephant, buffalo, waterbuck and

Elephant along the Zambezi River.

impala come to the river by the thousands to drink and graze on the lush grasses along its banks. Game viewing is also excellent in August and very good in June-July. During the rainy season, most large land mammals move away from the river toward the escarpment.

Many roads within the park are closed during the rainy season from November 1-April 30. However, Chikwenya and Ruckomechi camps may still be visited (provided they are open) by canoe or by road. National Park campsites may also be booked. Charter flights also operate to the park. Petrol is not available in the park. Power boats are not allowed.

All visitors driving to Mana Pools and the Zambezi Valley must present their booking confirmation and obtain an entry permit at the National Parks Office at Marongora, which is located on the Harare-Lusaka (Zambia) road between Kariba Town and the turnoff to Mana Pools. Four-wheel-drive vehicles are recommended in the dry season and necessary in the rainy season.

Canoes are available for hire. Inquire at the Mana Pools Reception Office.

ACCOMMODATION — CLASS B: * *Ruckomechi Camp*, just outside the western boundary of the park, has eight comfortable chalets (doubles) and one chalet with two double rooms; all chalets have ensuite facilities. Day and night game drives, walks and canoeing are offered. * *Chikwenya Camp* is situated on the Zambezi River just outside the eastern border of the park. Chikwenya has eight thatched lodges (doubles) with private facilities and offers walking and game viewing by vehicle and by boat.

CLASS D: * *Masangu Lodge* and * *Muchichiri Lodge*, upstream from Nyamepi Camp, are fully equipped and cater to up to eight persons each. Bring your own food and drink.

CLASS F: * *Vundu Camp*, eight miles west of Nyamepi, has two sleeping huts, a living hut, kitchen and ablution block with hot and cold water.

CAMPING: A limited supply of firewood is available at Nyamepi Camp. Bring a gas stove for cooking. * *Nyamepi Camp* has 29 caravan/camping sites and ablution blocks with hot and cold water. There are several exclusive camps within the park that are often used by tour operators on overland safaris. These camps are limited to a maximum of two vehicles and 12 persons: * *Mucheni* is five miles west of Nyamepi and has four campsites. * *Nkupe* is a half mile east of Nyamepi and has one campsite. * *Ndungu* is just east of the car park area and has two campsites. * *Gwaya (Old Tree Lodge)*, located just upstream from Masangu and Muchichiri Lodges, has one campsite with cold shower and flush toilet.

CHIZARIRA NATIONAL PARK

This relatively undeveloped park is situated on the Zambezi Escarpment overlooking the Zambezi Valley and the southern part of Lake Kariba. Chizarira covers 740 square miles of wild, untouched bush with plateaus, deep gorges, thick woodlands and flood plains.

Chizarira is a park for the adventurer more interested in experiencing the bush than in seeing huge herds of animals or enjoying the creature comforts offered by deluxe lodges. Much of the park is heavily wooded, making game viewing difficult. However, walking is allowed if accompanied by a fully licensed

guide or armed National Park game scout; this is the best way to explore this seldom visited park. Black rhino are seen often. The best view of Lake Kariba and the Zambezi Valley is from Mucheni View Point. Roads are rough; a four-wheel-drive vehicle is recommended year-round and is necessary in the rainy season. Petrol is not available in the park. All visitors are required to report at the warden's office upon arrival. The park is a day's drive from Matusadona National Park. Easiest access is by charter aircraft.

ACCOMMODATION — CLASS F & CAMPING: There are three exclusive national park campsites, each limited to one party (maximum 12 persons), which are often booked by tour companies. All campers must bring their own food and equipment. * Kasiswi Bush Camp, located four miles from Park Headquarters on the Lusilukuli River, has two sleeping shelters, dining shelter, and ablution block. * Mobola Bush Camp, situated on the Mucheni River four miles from Park Headquarters, has only a long-drop toilet and bush shower. * Busi Bush Camp, is 22 miles from Park Headquarters on the Busi River and has two sleeping shelters, one dining shelter and long-drop toilet.

ACCOMMODATION NEAR CHIZARIRA — CLASS A/B: * Sijarira Camp is located on the shores of Lake Kariba in the Sijarira Forest Reserve below Chizarira National Park. Accommodation is in Batonka-style chalets (with private facilities) built on stilts. Activities include game cruises on the lake, game drives, walks and lazing around the swimming pool. Access is by boat from Binga, which is a five-hour drive from Victoria Falls.

THE EAST

NYANGA NATIONAL PARK

Most of this beautifully forested and mountainous park lies above 6560 feet (2000 m.), rising to 8504 feet (2592 m.). Mt. Inyangani is the highest mountain in Zimbabwe. Trout fishing, horseback riding, hiking and golf are just a few of the many sports enjoyed in this refreshing environment.

The park covers 127 square miles and is located near the Mozambique border north of Mutare.

ACCOMMODATION — FIRST CLASS: * Pine Tree Inn is a

The White Horse Inn near Vumba Botanical Garden and Reserve.
Photo: Alan Allen, Zimbabwe Ministry of Information.

small country inn; rooms have facilities ensuite. * *Troutbeck Inn* has 74 rooms with ensuite facilities and offers horseback riding, trout fishing, bowls, squash, tennis and golf. * *Montclair Hotel* has rooms with private facilities.
CAMPING: Numerous camping and caravan sites are available.

VUMBA BOTANICAL GARDEN AND RESERVE

Located just south of Mutare, Vumba Botanical Garden is beautifully landscaped around a number of small streams. The garden also affords extensive views of Mozambique to the east.

This 33-foot-high conical tower is part of the Great Zimbabwe Ruins. Photo: Zimbabwe National Tourist Board.

The **Bunga Forest Botanical Reserve**, located adjacent to the botanical garden, has footpaths through unspoiled indigenous forests.

ACCOMMODATION — FIRST CLASS: * *White Horse Inn* is a small hotel (20 beds); rooms have private facilities.

CAMPING: Camp and caravan sites are available.

CHIMANIMANI NATIONAL PARK

This rugged, mountainous park with deep gorges and numerous streams includes most of the Chimanimani Mountain Range, which rises to 7995 feet (2437 m.). This is an excellent park for hiking and backpacking. Eland, sable and bushbuck are often seen.
ACCOMMODATION — CLASS F: A mountain hut is available for refuge.
CAMPING: Camping is allowed in the park.

THE SOUTHEAST

GREAT ZIMBABWE RUINS

These impressive stone ruins, located 11 miles from Masvingo, look distinctly out of place in sub-Saharan Africa where almost all traditional structures have been built of mud, cow dung, straw and reeds. The origin of these ruins is still not understood.

In 1890, Masvingo became the first settlement of whites in what is now Zimbabwe. The settlers first discovered the Great Zimbabwe Ruins in 1898.

The city which these ruins represent was at its prime from the thirteenth to the fifteenth centuries. The Acropolis or Hill Complex, traditionally the king's residence, is situated high on a granite hill overlooking the Temple (a walled enclosure) and the less complete restoration of the Valley complex.
ACCOMMODATION — TOURIST CLASS: * *Great Zimbabwe Hotel* is a country hotel, located a few minute's walk from the ruins, with swimming pool and 45 rooms with private facilities.

KYLE RECREATIONAL PARK

Located twenty miles southwest of Masvingo, this 85-square-mile park is a great place to go horseback riding among white rhino and a variety of other game. Pony trails are lead by a park ranger into the fenced wildlife section of the park.
ACCOMMODATION — CLASS C: See "Zimbabwe Ruins."
CLASSES D & F: * *National Park Lodges*, some with private facilities and others without, are available.

CAMPING: Camping and caravan sites with ablution blocks are located near the National Park office and at Sikato Bay Camp on the west bank of Lake Kyle.

GONAREZHOU NATIONAL PARK

The second largest park in Zimbabwe, Gonarezhou, borders the country of Mozambique in southeastern Zimbabwe and covers over 1930 square miles of bush.

Gonarezhou means "the place of many elephants" and is definitely elephant country. Other species commonly seen are lion, buffalo, zebra, giraffe, and a variety of antelope species. Nyala are regularly seen in riverine areas. Rarely seen are roan antelope, Lichtenstein's hartebeest and black rhino.

Elephant, rhino and buffalo have been heavily hunted and poached in this area. Visitors should approach these and other large mammals with extreme caution; these animals (especially elephant) have a justifiable grudge against man and are more likely to charge than in most other parks.

This park is off the beaten path and is seldom visited by international tourists. In spite of concentrated efforts, poaching is still a problem; check the current status before venturing there.

The park is divided into two regions, the Chipinda Pools section, which includes the Lundi and Sabi subregions, and the Mabalauta section. Game viewing is best in the Lundi subregion.

Gonarezhou is usually only open in the dry season, May 1-October 31. Winter temperatures are mild; however, summer temperatures can exceed 104° F. (40° C.).

From Masvingo drive southwest to Chiredzi, then continue either 36 miles to Chipinda Pools or 105 miles to Mabalauta Camp. Four-wheel-drive vehicles are highly recommended. No food or fuel is available at the park.

ACCOMMODATION — CLASS F: * *Swimuwini*, meaning "the place of baobabs," is located five miles from the Warden's Office and has three self-service chalets and an ablution block.

CAMPING: * *Chipinda Pools Camping and Caravan Site* and * *Chinguli* have ablution blocks. Seven remote campsites with basic facilities are also available. * *Mabalauta* has five camping/caravan sites.

The "Chura Bull," Matusdona National Park. Photo: Alison Wright.

BULAWAYO

Bulawayo is the second largest city in Zimbabwe and holds the National Museum and Railway Museum — both well worth a visit.

Special **Steam Train Safaris** from Bulawayo to Victoria Falls lasting three days are available for the railroad enthusiast. The train stops at Hwange National Park for a day of game viewing; guests have the option of spending that night on the train or at Hwange Safari Lodge.

Chipangali Wildlife Orphanage, 15 miles southwest of Bulawayo on the Esigodini/Beit Bridge road, cares for a variety of young animals, often including lion, leopard, genet, civit, elephant and chimpanzee.

ACCOMMODATION — FIRST CLASS: * *Churchill Arms Hotel* is a modern Tudor-style hotel with 50 rooms with ensuite facilities, located four miles from the city center. * *Bulawayo Sun Hotel* is located in the center of town and has 172 air-conditioned rooms with private facilities.

MOTOPOS (MATOBO) NATIONAL PARK

Hundreds of kopjes supporting thousands of precariously balanced rocks give the 167-square-mile Motopos National Park one of the most unusual landscapes in Africa. The highly underrated park is divided into two sections — a general recreational area, where pony trails are very popular, and a game reserve.

Motopos National Park has the highest concentration of black eagles in the world. Leopard and jackal are the only predators.

Accompanied by a national park ranger in the game reserve, we walked near two white rhino and a baby which were eventually scared off when a herd of wildebeest stampeded nearby.

Cecil Rhodes was buried on a huge rock kopje called "View of the World" from which one has sensational panoramas of the rocky, barren countryside.

Nswatugi Cave **rock paintings** include images of giraffe and antelope. For Bambata Cave rock paintings, allow one and a half hours for the hike. White Rhino Shelter rock paintings are also worth a visit.

ACCOMMODATION — FIRST CLASS: see Bulawayo.

CLASSES D & F: * *National Park* bungalows with and without ensuite facilities are available.

CAMPING: Camping and caravan sites with ablution blocks are available at *Maleme Dam* and *Toghwana Dam.*

Victoria Falls from the Zimbabwe side.

THE
SAFARI PAGES

THE
SAFARI PAGES

We have endeavored to make the information that follows as current as possible. However, Africa is undergoing constant change.

My reason for including the following information, much of which is likely to change, is to give you an idea of the right questions to ask — not to give you information that should be relied on as gospel. Wherever possible, a resource has been given to assist you in obtaining the most current information.

AGENCIES SPECIALIZING IN AFRICA

The Africa Adventure Company, P.O. Box 2567, Pompano Beach, FL 33072; tel (305) 781-3933 or (800) 882-9453. Mark Nolting, the author of this guidebook, personally plans and books tour packages and tailor-made itineraries for individuals, groups and incentive trips.

AIRLINES (See GETTING TO AFRICA below.)

AIRPORT DEPARTURE TAXES

Call an airline servicing your destination, the tourist office, embassy, or consulate of the country(ies) in question for current international and domestic airport taxes.

International airport departure taxes must be paid in U.S. dollars or other hard currency, such as British Pounds or German Marks. Be sure to have the exact amount required — they will not give change. Domestic airport departure taxes are usually payable in local currency.

At the time of this writing, international airport departure taxes for the countries in this guide do not exceed U.S. $20; domestic departure taxes are usually under U.S. $5.

AUTO ASSOCIATIONS

BURUNDI: Club Automobile Burundi   2749
B.P. 544 or 1069, Bujumbura, Burundi
KENYA: Automobile Association of Kenya

        720 882
Nyaku House, Hurlingham, P.O. Box 40087 or 40037,
Nairobi, Kenya
RWANDA: Auto Motor Club of Rwanda
P.O. Box 822, Kigali, Rwanda
SOUTH AFRICA: Automobile Association of South Africa
        281 400
Corbett Place, 66 de Korte Street, P.O. Box 596, Braamfontein,
Johannesburg 2001, South Africa
The Automobile Association of South Africa
#7 Martin Hammerschlag Way, P.O. Box 70,
Cape Town, South Africa
TANZANIA: The Automobile Association of Tanzania
        21965
P.O. Box 3004, Cargen House, Maktaba Street,
Dar es Salaam, Tanzania
ZAIRE: Zaire Automobile Federation
Bldg. Forescom 118, Avenue du Port, B.P. 2491,
Kinshasa, Zaire
ZIMBABWE: Automobile Association of Zimbabwe
        70 70 21
57 Samora Machel Avenue, P.O. Box 585,
Harare C1, Zimbabwe

AUTO/VEHICLE RENTAL COMPANIES (International)

AVIS: Offices in Botswana, Kenya, Lesotho, Mauritius, South Africa, Zaire, and Zimbabwe.
BUDGET: Offices in Mauritius, Namibia, South Africa, and Zaire.
HERTZ: Offices in Kenya, Mauritius, Namibia, South Africa, Swaziland, Tanzania, Uganda, Zaire, and Zimbabwe.

NATIONAL: Offices in Kenya, Mauritius, Rwanda, South Africa, Zaire, and Zimbabwe.

Hire vehicles in Burundi through the Burundi Tourist Office (see **TOURIST OFFICES** listed below). In Tanzania, vehicles are only rented with chauffeur.

BANKS

Barclays and Standard Chartered Banks are located in most of these countries.

BANKING HOURS

Banks are usually open Monday-Friday mornings and early afternoons, sometimes on Saturday mornings, and closed on Sundays and holidays. Most hotels, lodges and camps are licensed to exchange foreign currency.

CLUBS & ASSOCIATIONS

Utilizing memberships in certain international associations and clubs (i.e., Lions Club, Rotary) can lead to personal contact in Africa with people that share similar interests. This is an excellent and seldom used method of gaining insight into a country.

Bring proof of certification for all sports or activities (i.e., SCUBA diving) in which there is any chance you may want to participate. This will facilitate rental of equipment or guest memberships in various clubs and associations.

Botswana: Botswana Bird Club, P.O. Box 71, Gaborone; tel: 351500

Kenya: Cave Exploration Group of East Africa, P.O. Box 47583, Nairobi.

East African Wildlife Society, Hilton Hotel, P.O. Box 20110, Nairobi.

Flying Doctors Society of Africa, P.O. Box 30125, Nairobi; tel: 501301. Medical evacuation insurance.

Kenya Divers Association, P.O. Box 9575, Mombassa; tel: 471347.

Mountain Club of Kenya, Wilson Airport, P.O. Box 45741, Nairobi; tel: 501747. Weekly meetings Tuesdays at 7:30 p.m. at the clubhouse.

United Kingdom: Globetrotters Club, BCM/Roving, London WC1N 3XX. *Globe* magazine is excellent for ideas on out-of-the-way places to visit. Most members are well-traveled and will assist fellow members with information and in some cases accommodation.

CREDIT CARDS

Major international credit cards are accepted by most top hotels, restaurants, and shops. Visa and MasterCard are most widely accepted. American Express and Diner's Club are also accepted by most first class hotels and many businesses.

CURRENCIES

The currencies used by the countries included in this guide are as follows:

Botswana (1 pula = 100 thebe)
Burundi (1 Burundi franc = 100 centimes)
Kenya (1 Kenya shilling = 100 cents)
Lesotho (1 malote = 100 licente)
Mauritius (1 rupee = 100 cents)
Namibia (1 South African rand = 100 cents)
Rwanda (1 Rwanda franc = 100 centimes)
South Africa (1 rand = 100 cents)
Swaziland (1 lilangeni = 100 cents)
Tanzania (1 Tanzania shilling = 100 cents)
Uganda (1 Uganda shilling = 100 cents)
Zaire (1 Zaire = 100 makutas)
Zambia (1 kwacha = 100 ngwee)
Zimbabwe (1 Zimbabwe dollar = 100 cents).

The currencies of Lesotho and Swaziland are on par with the South African rand. The South African rand is widely accepted in Lesotho and Swaziland; however, the currencies of Lesotho and Swaziland are not accepted in South Africa.

Current rates for many African countries can usually be found in the financial section of a large newspaper and in periodicals such as *Newsweek*. Call an airline that travels to the country you wish to visit and ask for the current rate of exchange (see **GETTING TO AFRICA BY AIR** below).

CURRENCY RESTRICTIONS

Most African countries require visitors to complete currency declaration forms upon arrival; all foreign currency, travelers checks and other negotiable instruments must be recorded. These forms must be surrendered on departure.

When you leave the country, the amount of currency you have with you must equal the amount with which you entered the country less the amount exchanged and recorded on your currency declaration form.

For most countries in Africa, the maximum amount of local currency that may be imported or exported is strictly enforced. Kenya, for instance, does not allow visitors to take any Kenyan currency into or out of the country. Check for current restrictions by contacting the tourist offices, embassies or consulates of the countries you wish to visit.

In some countries, it is difficult (if not impossible) to exchange unused local currency back to foreign exchange (i.e., U.S. dollars). Therefore, it is best not to exchange more than you feel you will need.

CUSTOMS

Australian Customs:
Contact the offices below for current information:
The Collector of Customs, Sydney, NSW 2000;
tel: (02) 20521
The Collector of Customs, Melbourne, Victoria 3000;
tel: (03) 630461
Canadian Customs
For a brochure on current Canadian customs requirements, ask for the brochure "*I Declare*" from your local customs office, which will be listed in the telephone book under "Government of Canada, Customs and Excise."
New Zealand Customs:
Two of the several customs offices are listed below. Contact them for current information:
Box 29, Auckland; tel: 773 520
Box 2098, Christchurch; tel: 799 251
United Kingdom:
Contact the office below for current information:

HM Customs and Excise, Kent House, Upper Ground, London SE1 9PS

U.S. Customs:

Travelers to the countries included in this guide may qualify for additional allowances through the Generalized System of Preferences (GSP). Contact your nearest custom office and ask for the leaflet "GSP & The Traveler" and for the usual duty-free allowances currently allowed. This information is available from the U.S. Customs Service, P.O. Box 7407, Washington, D.C. 20044; tel: (202) 566-8195.

For current information on products made from endangered species of wildlife that are not allowed to be imported, contact *Traffic* (U.S.A.), World Wildlife Fund, 1250 24th Street N.W., Washington, D.C. 20037; tel: (202) 293-4800 and ask for their leaflet "Buyer Beware" for current restrictions.

DIPLOMATIC REPRESENTATIVES OF AFRICAN COUNTRIES

IN AUSTRALIA:

Kenya: 474788/474722/474688 or 474311
Sixth Floor, QBE Building, 33-35 Ainslie Ave., P.O. Box 1990, Canberra ACT 2601, Australia

Mauritius: 811 086 or 811 203
43 Hampton Circuit, Yarralumla, Canberra ACT 2600, Australia

South Africa: 732424
Rhodes Place, Yarralumla, Canberra, ACT 2600, Australia
4-6 Vligh St., Vligh House, 17th Fl. 2338188
Sydney, NSW 2001, Australia

IN CANADA:

Burundi: (613) 236-8483
151 Slater St., No. 800, Ottawa, Ontario, K1P 5H3, Canada

Kenya: (613) 563-1773/4/5/6
Suite 600, 415 Laurier Ave. East, West Ottawa, Ontario, K1N 6R4, Canada

Lesotho: (613) 236-9449
202 Clemow Ave., Ottawa, Ontario, K1S 2B4, Canada

Rwanda: (613) 722-5835
1221 Sherwood Dr., Ottawa, Ontario, K1Y 3V1, Canada

South Africa: (613) 744-0330
15 Sussex Drive, Ottawa, Ontario, K1M 1M8, Canada
Consulate in Toronto.
Tanzania: (613) 232-1509
50 Range Rd., Ottawa, Ontario, K1N 8J4, Canada
Uganda: (613) 233-7797
170 Laurier Ave. West, Suite 601, Ottawa, Ontario, K1P 5V5, Canada
Zaire: (613) 232-3983
18 Range Rd., Ottawa, Ontario, K1M 8J3, Canada
Zambia: (613) 563-0712
130 Albert St., Suite 1610, Ottawa, Ontario, K1P 5G4, Canada
Zimbabwe: (613) 237-4388
112 Kent St., Place de Ville, Tower B, Ottawa, Ontario, K1P 5P2, Canada

HIGH COMMISSIONS IN THE UNITED KINGDOM:
Botswana: (01) 499-0031
6 Stratford Place, London W1N 9AE, England
Kenya: (01) 6362371/5
45 Courtland Place, London W1N 4AS, England
Lesotho: (01) 373-8581
10 Collingham Road, London SW5 0NR, England
Mauritius: (01) 5810294/5
32/33 Elvaston Place, London SW 7, England
South African Consulate: (01) 9304488
South Africa House, Trafalgar Square, London WC2N 5DP, England
Swaziland: (01) 581-4976/7
58 Pont St., London SW1, England
Tanzania: (01) 499-8951-6
43 Hertford St., London W1 8DB, England
Uganda: (01) 839-5783/0
Uganda House, 58/59 Trafalgar Square, London WC 2N 5DX, England
Zaire: (01) 23-57122
Swix 8, HH, 26 Chesham, London 2, England
Zambia: (01) 589-6655
2 Palace Gage, Kensington, London W8 5NG, England
Zimbabwe: (01) 8367755
429 Strand, London WC 2R OSA, England

IN THE UNITED STATES:
Botswana: (202) 244-4990/1
Suite 404, 4301 Connecticut Ave. N.W., Washington, D.C. 20008
Burundi: (202) 343-2574
Suite 212, 2233 Wisconsin Ave. N.W., Washington, D.C. 20007
Kenya: (202) 387-6101
2249 R Street N.W., Washington, D.C. 20008
Consulates in:
9100 Wilshire Blvd., (213) 274-6635
#111, Beverly Hills, CA 90212
424 Madison Ave., (212) 486-1300/3
New York, NY 10017
Lesotho: (202) 797-5533
251 Massachusetts Ave. N.W., Washington, D.C. 20008
1601 Connecticut Ave. N.W., Washington, D.C. 20009
Mauritius: (202) 244-1491/2
Suite 134, 4310 Connecticut Ave. N.W., Washington, D.C. 20008
Rwanda: (202) 232-2882/3/4
1714 New Hampshire Ave. N.W., Washington, D.C. 20009
Rwanda Consulate: (708) 439-9090
10 Gould Center, Suite 707, Rolling Meadows, IL 60008
South Africa: (202) 232-4400
3051 Massachusetts Ave. N.W., Washington, D.C. 20008
Consulates in Chicago, Houston, New York and Los Angeles.
Swaziland: (202) 362-6683
3400 International Dr. N.W., Suite 3M, Washington, D.C. 20008
Tanzania: (202) 939-6125
2139 R Street N.W., Washington, D.C. 20008
Uganda: (202) 726-7100/3
5909 16th Street N.W., Washington, D.C. 20011-2896
Zaire: (202) 234-7690
1800 New Hampshire N.W., Washington, D.C. 20009
Zambia: (202) 265-9717
2419 Massachusetts Ave. N.W., Washington, D.C. 20008
Zimbabwe: (202) 332-7100
2852 Mc Gill Terrace N.W., Washington, D.C. 20008

Missions to the United Nations or Consulates in New York:
Botswana: (212) 889-2277
103 East 37th St., New York, NY 10016
Burundi: (212) 687-1180
201 East 42nd St., New York, NY 10017

Kenya:	(212) 421-4740

424 Madison Ave., New York, NY 10017

Lesotho:	(212) 661-1690

204 East 39th St., New York, NY 10016

Mauritius:	(212) 949-0190/1

211 East 43rd St., New York, NY 10017

Rwanda:	(212) 696-0644

124 East 39th St., New York, NY 10016

South Africa:	(212) 371-7997

326 East 48th St., New York, NY 10017

Swaziland:	(212) 371-8910

866 United Nations Plaza, Suite 420, New York, NY 10017

Tanzania:	(212) 972-9160

205 East 42nd St., New York, NY 10017

Uganda:	(212) 949-0110

Uganda House, 336 East 45th St., New York, NY 10017

Zaire:	(212) 754-1966

77 Third Ave., 25th Floor, New York, NY 10017

Zambia:	(212) 758-1110

237 East 52nd St., New York, NY 10022

Zimbabwe:	(212) 980-9511

19 East 47th St., New York, NY 10017

DIPLOMATIC REPRESENTATIVES IN AFRICA

Australian High Commissions:

Kenya: tel: 334666/7
Development House, Moi Ave., P.O. Box 30360, Nairobi, Kenya

South Africa: tel: 3254315
Fourth Floor, Mutual and Federal Center, 220 Vermuelen St., Pretoria 0002, South Africa, or

Tenth Floor, 1001 Colonial Mutual Building   tel: 232160
101 Adderby St., 8001 Cape Town, South Africa

Tanzania:
Seventh and Eighth Floors, NLC Investment Bldg., Independence Ave., P.O. Box 2969, Dar es Salaam, Tanzania

Zambia: tel: 219001/3
Third Floor, Memaco House, Sapele Road, P.O. Box 35395, Lusaka, Zambia

Zimbabwe: tel: 794591/4
Third Floor, Throgmorton House, Samora Machel Ave. & Julius Nyerere Way, P.O. Box 907 (45341), Harare, Zimbabwe

Canadian High Commissions:

Kenya: tel: 334033
Comcraft House, Haile Selassie Ave., P.O. Box 30481, Nairobi, Kenya

Mauritius: tel: 20821
c/o Blanche Birger Co., Ltd., Port Louis, Mauritius

South Africa: tel: 287062
Nedbank Plaza, 856 Kingsleys Center, Deatrix St., Arcadia, Pretoria 0007, South Africa

Tanzania: tel: 20651
Pan African Insurance Bldg., P.O. Box 1022
Dar es Salaam, Tanzania

Zaire: tel: 22706
Édifice Shell, P.O. Box 8341, Kinshasa, Zaire

Zambia: tel: 216161
Barclays Bank, North End Branch, Cairo Road, P.O. Box 31313, Lusaka, Zambia

Zimbabwe: tel: 793801
45 Baines Ave., P.O. Box 1430, Harare, Zimbabwe

United Kingdom High Commissions:

Botswana: tel: 52841/2/3
Private Bag 0023, Gaborone, Botswana

Burundi: tel: 23711
British Liaison Office, 43 Ave. Bubanza, B.P. 1344,
Bujumbura,Botswana
Permanent staff in Kinshasa, Zaire

Kenya: tel: 335944
Bruce House, Standard St., P.O. Box 30465, Nairobi, Kenya

Lesotho: tel: 313961
P.O. Box MS 521, Maseru 100

Mauritius: tel: 865795/6/7/8
King George V Ave., Floreal, P.O. Box 186, Curepipe, Mauritius

Namibia: tel: (61) 223022
British Liaison Office, 116A Lentwein St., Windhoek, Namibia

Rwanda: tel: 75219
Honorary Consul, Ave. Paul VI, B.P. 351, Kigali, Rwanda
Permanent staff in Kinshasa, Zaire

South Africa: tel: 3319011/4
Consulate: Fifth Floor, Nedbank Mall, 145 Commissioner St., Johannesburg 2001, P.O. Box 10101
Tenth Floor, Fedlife House, tel: 3052929/20
320 Smith St., P.O. Box 1404, Durban 4001, South Africa

Swaziland: tel: 42581
Alister Miller St., Mbabane, Private Bag, Mbabane, Swaziland
Tanzania: tel: 29601
Hifadhi House, Samora Ave., P.O. Box 9200, Dar es Salaam, Tanzania
Uganda: tel: 257054/9 and 257301/4
10-12 Parliament Ave., P.O. Box 7070, Kampala, Uganda
Zaire: tel: 21327
191 Ave. de l'Équateur, Fifth Floor, Boîte Poste 8049, Kinshasa, Zaire
Zambia: tel: 228955
Independence Ave., P.O. Box 50050, Lusaka, Zambia
Zimbabwe: tel: 793781 or 728716
Stanley House, Stanley Ave., P.O. Box 4490, Harare, Zimbabwe

United States Embassies:
Botswana: tel: 267 353982/3/4
P.O. Box 90, Gaborone
Burundi: tel: 23454
B.P. 1720, Ave. du Zaire (no direct dialing)
Bujumbura, Burundi
Kenya: tel: 254 2 334141
Embassy Building, Haile Selassie & Moi Avenues, P.O. Box 30137, Nairobi, Kenya
Lesotho: tel: 266 312666
P.O. Box MS 333, Maseru 100, Lesotho
Mauritius: tel: 230 082347
Rogers Bldg., Fourth Floor, John Kennedy St., Port Louis, Mauritius
Namibia: tel: 254 61 229791
Ausplan Bldg., 14 Lossen St., P.O. Box 9890, Windhoek 9000, Namibia
Rwanda: tel: 205 755601/2/3
Blvd. de la Révolution, B.P. 28, Kigali, Rwanda
South Africa: tel: 27 12 284266
Phibault House, 225 Pretorius St., Pretoria, South Africa
Consulate: tel: 27 11 3311681
11th Floor, Kine Center, Commissioner & Kruis Sts., P.O. Box 2155, Johannesburg, South Africa
Swaziland: tel: 268 46441/2/3/4/5
Central Bank Bldg., Warner St., P.O. Box 199, Mbabane, Swaziland

Tanzania: tel: 255 51 375012/3/4
36 Laibon Road (off Bagamoyo Rd.), P.O. Box 9123, Dar es Salaam, Tanzania
Uganda: tel: 256 41 259791/2/3/4/5
British High Commission bldg., 10/12 Parliment Ave., P. O. Box 7007, Kampala, Uganda
Zaire: tel: 243 12 258812/3/4/5/6
310 Ave. des Aviateurs, Kinshasa, Zaire
Zambia: tel: 260 1 228595
Independence & United National Aves., P.O. Box 31617, Lusaka, Zambia
Zimbabwe: tel: 263 14 794521
172 Rhodes Ave., P.O. Box 3340, Harare, Zimbabwe

DUTY-FREE ALLOWANCES

Contact the nearest tourist office or embassy for current duty-free import allowances for the country(ies) which you intend to visit. The duty-free allowances vary; however, the following may be used as a *general* guideline: One litre of wine and one litre alcoholic beverage, two cartons of cigarettes or 50 cigars or 8 3/4 oz. of tobacco, and a small quantity of perfume.

ELECTRICITY

Electric current is 220-240 volt AC 50Hz.

GETTING TO AFRICA
BY AIR:

Most all travelers from North America flying to the countries listed in this guide must pass through Europe. The exception is Zambia Airways flight from New York to Lusaka via Monrovia.

Many airlines from around the world fly to and within Africa. For the best advice and rates on air tickets and air/land packages, contact a travel company specializing in Africa.

At the time of this writing, the international airlines servicing the countries included in this guide are as follows:
Botswana: British Airways.

Burundi: Air France, Sabena.

Kenya: Air Afrique, Air France, Alitalia, British Airways, Iberia, Kenya Airways, KLM, Lufthansa, Pan Am, Sabena, Swissair, and Zambia Airways.

Lesotho: Connect through Johannesburg with Air Lesotho.

Mauritius: Air France, Air India, Air Madagascar, Air Mauritius, Air Zimbabwe, British Airways, Lufthansa, Singapore Airlines, South African Airways, and Zambia Airways.

Namibia: South African Airways.

Rwanda: Air France and Sabena.

South Africa: Alitalia, British Airways, Iberia, KLM, Lufthansa, Luxavia, Olympic, Sabena, South African Airways, Swissair, TAP, UTA, and Zambia Airways.

Swaziland: Connect through Johannesburg with Royal Swazi.

Tanzania: Killimanjaro Airport: KLM and Sabena; and Dar es Salaam: Air France, British Airways, Lufthansa, Sabena and Swiss Air.

Uganda: Air Rwanda, Ethiopian Airlines, Kenya Airways, Sabena, Tanzania Airways, and Uganda Airlines.

Zaire: Air Zaire, Iberia, Lufthansa, Sabena, Swiss Air, TAP, and UTA. Fly to Kigali, Rwanda, to visit most of Zaire's attractions included in this guide (see **RWANDA** above).

Zambia: Air Tanzania, Air Zimbabwe, Alitalia, Kenya Airways, Lufthansa, UTA, and Zambia Airways.

Zimbabwe: Air Zimbabwe, British Airways, Qantas, and TAP.

BY ROAD:

From Egypt to Sudan and Ethiopia to Kenya and southward; trans-Sahara through Algeria, Niger, Nigeria or Chad, Cameroon, Central African Republic, Zaire, Rwanda and eastern and southern Africa. Allow several months. Roads are very bad.

BY SHIP:

Round-the-world cruise ships such as the QE II (Cunard), Sagafjord, RM St. Helena Line, and Lykes Line (freighter) occasionally stop at Kenyan and South African ports.

GETTING AROUND AFRICA

See each country's map for details on major roads, railroad lines and waterways.

BY AIR:

Capitals and major tourist centers are serviced by air.

Botswana: Air Botswana services Maun, Francistown and Selebi Phikwe.

Burundi: Air Burundi. Domestic charter service only.

Kenya: Kenya Airways services Kisumu, Malindi, Mombasa, Lamu and Nairobi. Charter services are available to Amboseli, Masai Mara, Nyeri, Nanyuki, Samburu, Lake Turkana and Lamu.

Lesotho: Air Lesotho services major centers.

Mauritius: Air Mauritius services Rodrigues Island.

Namibia: Namib Air services major cities and Etosha National Park.

Rwanda: Air Rwanda services Gisenyi and Ruhengeri.

South Africa: South African Airways services the cities of Bloemfontein, Cape Town, Durban, East London, George, Johannesburg, Kimberley, Port Elizabeth, Upington and Windhoek. The "Visit South Africa Pass" is a real bargain, valid for all South African cities SAA services as long as the visitor travels in a clockwise or counterclockwise direction within a three-week period. Comair flies from Johannesburg to Skuzuza and Phalaborwa (Kruger Park).

Tanzania: Air Tanzania services Kilimanjaro International, Dar es Salaam, Kigoma, and Zanzibar.

Uganda: Uganda Airways flies to Arua, Kasese, Gulu, and Mbarara.

Zaire: Air Zaire services Goma, Bukavu, Kisangani, and Lubumbashi from Kinshasa. Goma and Bukavu are also serviced by Scribe. Virunga Air Charters services the region covered in this guide.

Zambia: Zambia Airways services to Chipata, Lusaka, Livingstone (Victoria Falls), Mfuwe (South Luangwa National Park), and Ndole.

Zimbabwe: Air Zimbabwe services Buffalo Springs, Bulawayo, Harare, Hwange, Kariba, Masvingo, and Victoria Falls.

BY ROAD:

Major roads are tarmac (paved) and are excellent in Namibia, South Africa and Zimbabwe. Most major roads are tarmac in fair condition in Botswana, Kenya, Rwanda, Swaziland, and Zambia, and poor in Tanzania and Uganda. Burundi, Lesotho, and Zaire have very few tarmac roads. Many dirt roads (except in Namibia) are difficult and many are impassable in the rainy season (especially Zaire), often requiring four-wheel-drive vehicles.

Petrol and diesel are readily available in Botswana, Kenya, Lesotho, Mauritius, Namibia, South Africa, Swaziland, and Zimbabwe; may be difficult to obtain in Burundi, Rwanda, Tanzania, and Zambia; and very difficult to obtain in Zaire.

Taxis are available in the larger cities and at international airports. **Service Taxis** travel when all seats are taken and are an inexpensive but uncomfortable means of long-distance travel. Deluxe **Express buses** are available between major cities in South Africa, Zambia and Zimbabwe; less comfortable express buses operate in Kenya. **Local Buses** are very crowded, uncomfortable, and are recommended only for the hardiest of travelers. Pick-up trucks (matatus in East Africa) often crammed with 20 passengers, luggage, produce, chickens, etc., are used throughout the continent. Be sure to agree on the price before setting off.

BY RAIL:

Trains in South Africa are excellent (especially the Blue Train). The "Lunatic Express" from Nairobi to Mombasa in Kenya is also very good. See the chapters on Kenya and South Africa for details.

Otherwise, train travel is slow and not advised for deluxe travelers. Train travel is possible from Arusha (Tanzania) through Zambia, Zimbabwe, Botswana to Cape Town, South Africa. Railway lines are depicted on the maps of each country in this guide.

SAVE (South Africa Visitors Exclusive Pass) gives a 40% discount off all first- and second-class fares to Senior Citizens (60 years or older).

BY BOAT:

Steamer service on Lake Tanganyika services Bujumbura (Burundi), Kigoma (Tanzania), Mpulungu (Zambia), and Kalemie (Zaire) about once a week; steamers on Lake Victoria service Kisumu (Kenya) and Musoma and Mwanza (Tanzania) and Kampala-Port Bell (Uganda).

HEALTH

Malarial Risk exists in all countries covered except Lesotho, so be sure to take your malaria pills as described before, during and after your trip. Contact your doctor, an immunologist, and the Center for Disease Control in Atlanta for the best prophylaxis for your itinerary. Use an insect repellent. Wear long-sleeved shirts and slacks for further protection.

Bilharzia is a disease that infests most lakes and rivers on the continent. Do not walk barefooted along the shore, wade or swim in a stream, river or lake unless you know for certain it is free of Bilharzia. Bilharzia does not exist in salt water.

If you must get in the water, as with canoe or kayak safaris, do not get out of the canoe where there are reeds in the water. A species of snail is involved in the reproductive cycle of bilharzia; these snails are more often found near reeds and in slow-moving water. Follow your guide's instructions and your risk of contacting the disease will be minimized. If you feel you may have contacted the disease, go to your doctor for a blood test. If diagnosed in its early stages, it is easily cured.

Tap water is safe in many of the larger cities; but to be safe, it should not be drunk. Wear a hat and bring sunblock to protect yourself from the tropical sun. Drink plenty of fluids and limit alcohol consumption at high altitudes.

For further information, obtain a copy of "Health Information for International Travel" from the U.S. Government Printing Office, Washington, D.C. 20402.

HEALTH SERVICES

The Flying Doctors Society of Africa
(01) 874 0098
London House (AMREF)

68 Upper Richmond Road
London SW15 2PR, Great Britain
International Association for Medical Assistance to Travelers,
736 Center Street, Lewiston, NY 14092
International Association for Medical Assistance to Travelers,
123 Edward Street, Suite 725
Toronto, Ontario M5G 1E2, Canada
Medic Alert Foundation
(209) 668-3333
Turlock, California 95380
Medical Passport Foundation, Inc.
(904) 734-0639
P.O. Box 820
Deland, FL 32720.
Zambia Flying Doctor Service
Box 71856
Ndola, Zambia

INSURANCE

Be sure your medical insurance covers you for the countries you plan to visit. Acquire additional insurance for emergency evacuation should your present policies not include it.

Travel insurance packages often include a combination of medical, baggage, and trip cancellation — all of which are highly recommended. The peace of mind afforded by such insurance far outweighs the cost. Ask your travel agent for assistance.

METRIC SYSTEM OF WEIGHTS & MEASURES

The metric system is used in Africa. The U.S. equivalents are:

1 inch — 2.54 centimeters (cm.)	1 cm. — 0.39 inch
1 foot — 0.305 meters (m.)	1 m. — 3.28 feet
1 mile — 1.6 kilometers (km.)	1 km. — 0.62 miles
1 square mile — 2.59 sq. km.	1 sq. km. — 0.3861 sq. mile
1 quart liquid — 0.946 liter (l.)	1 l. — 1.057 quarts
1 ounce — 28 grams (g.)	1 g. — 0.035 ounce
1 pound — 0.454 kilograms (kg.)	1 kg. — 2.2 pounds

Temperature

−20° C. = −4° F.	15° C. = 59° F.
−15° C. = 5° F.	20° C. = 68° F.
−10° C. = 14° F.	25° C. = 77° F.
−5° C. = 23° F.	30° C. = 86° F.
0° C. = 32° F.	35° C. = 95° F.
5° C. = 41° F.	40° C. = 104° F.
10° C. = 50° F.	

Converting Centigrade into degrees Fahrenheit: Multiply Centigrade by 1.8 and add 32.

Converting Fahrenheit into degrees Centigrade: Subtract 32 from Fahrenheit and divide by 1.8.

MAPS

Michelin Map #955 (1:4,000,000) is excellent and covers all the countries included in this guide. It is best to purchase maps before arriving in Africa as they are not readily available except in Kenya and South Africa. Maps may be obtained by contacting the Departments of Lands and Surveys of the country in question.

MONEY

Have money sent by telegraph international money order (Western Union), telexed through a bank or international courier (i.e., DHL).

PASSPORT OFFICES

To obtain a passport, contact your local post office for the passport office nearest you. Then call the passport office to be sure you will have everything on hand which they will require.

SECURITY

For an update on security for the countries you wish to visit, contact the Department of State, Washington, D.C. (tel: 202-647-5225) for their advisories on international travel.

SEMINARS ON AFRICA

The Africa Adventure Company
(305) 781-3933
P.O. Box 2567
Pompano Beach, FL 33072
Seminars by Mark Nolting, author of this guide.

SHOPPING/SHOPPING HOURS

If you like bartering, bring old clothing to trade for souvenirs. This works particularly well at roadside stands and in small villages, although the villagers are becoming more discerning in their tastes.

Shops are usually open Monday-Friday from 8:00/9:00 a.m. - 5:00/6:00 p.m. and 9:00 a.m. - 1:00 p.m. on Saturdays. Shops in the coastal cities of Kenya and Tanzania often close mid-day for siesta. Use the shopping hours given below as a general guideline; exact times can vary within the respective country.

Botswana: Baskets and carvings are sold in Maun, Kasane and the Mall in Gaborone. Also consider products made from karakul fleece, pottery, tapestries, and rugs. There are curio shops in many safari camps, hotels and lodges.

Burundi: Crafts available in numerous shops.

Kenya: Makonde and Akomba ebony wood carvings, soapstone carvings, colorful kangas and kikois (cloth wraps). In Mombasa, Zanzibar chests, gold and silverwork, brasswork, Arab jewelry, and antiques.

Lesotho: Basotho woven carpets are known worldwide, tapestry-weaving and conical straw hats.

Mauritius: Intricately detailed handmade model sailing ships of camphor or teak from Camajora or Jose Ramar in Curepipe, pareos (colorful light cotton wraps), macrame wall hangings, and Mauritian dolls.

Namibia: Semiprecious stones and jewelry (SWA Gemstones in Outjo, south of Etosha N. P. is excellent), karakul wool products, wood carvings, and beadwork. Bring your passport and return air ticket and you will not have to pay the 13% sales tax.

Swaziland: Beautiful handwoven tapestries, baskets, earthenware and stoneware, and mouthblown handcrafted glass animals and tableware.

Tanzania: Makonde carvings and Meerschaum pipes.
Uganda: Few shops for tourists.
Zaire: Wood carvings, malachite, copper goods, semiprecious stones, and baskets.
Zambia: Wood carvings, statuettes, semiprecious stones and copper souvenirs.
Zimbabwe: Carvings of wood, stone and Zimbabwe's unique verdite, intricate baskets, ceramicware and crocheted garments.

THEFT

The number one rule in preventing theft on vacation is to leave all unnecessary valuables at home. What you must bring, lock in safety deposit boxes when not in use. Theft in Africa is generally no worse than in Europe or the U.S.A. One difference is that Africans are poorer and will steal things that most American or European thieves would consider worthless.

TIME ZONES

EST+7/GMT+2
Botswana
Burundi
Lesotho
Namibia
Rwanda
South Africa
Swaziland
Zaire (Eastern)
Zambia
Zimbabwe

EST+8/GMT+3
Kenya
Tanzania
Uganda

EST+9/GMT+4
Mauritius

TIPPING

A ten percent tip is recommended at restaurants for good service where a service charge is not included in the bill except in Zambia where tipping is against the law.

TOURIST INFORMATION

In addition to the addresses below, information may also be available through embassies or consulates of the countries in question. See **DIPLOMATIC REPRESENTATIVES** above.

Offices in Africa:
Botswana:
Division of Tourism   (267) 53024/3314
Private Bag 0047, Gaborone, Botswana
Burundi:
National Office of Tourism   22023, 22202
Liberty Ave., P.O. Box 902,   (no direct dialing)
Bujumbura, Burundi
Kenya:
Ministry of Tourism and Wildlife   (254 2) 331030
Utalii House, P.O. Box 30027, Nairobi, Kenya
Lesotho:
National Tourist Board   (266) 32-3760
P.O. Box 1378, Maseru 100, Lesotho
Mauritius:
Government Tourist Office   (230) 011703
Emmanuel Anquetil Bldg., Jules Koenig St., Port Louis,
Mauritius
Namibia:
SWA Directorate of Trade and Tourism   (254 61) 26571
Private Bag 13297, Windhoek 9000, Namibia
Rwanda:
Office Rwandais du Tourisme et des   (250) 76514/15
Parcs Nationaux (ORTPN) B.P. 905, Kigali, Rwanda
South Africa:
Tourism Board   (271 2) 471131
Mellyn Park Office Block, Private Bag X164, Pretoria 0001,
South Africa
Swaziland:
Government Tourist Office   (268) 42531
Swazi Plaza, P.O. Box 451, Mbabane, Swaziland
Tanzania:
Tourist Corporation   (255 51) 27671
Maktaba St., P.O. Box 2485, Dar es Salaam, Tanzania
Zanzibar: Tanzania Friendship Tourist Bureau   32344
P.O. Box 216, Zanzibar, Tanzania
Uganda:
Ministry of Tourism and Wildlife   (256 41) 32971/4
P.O. Box 4241, Kampala, Uganda

Zaire:
Office National du Tourisme   (243 12) 30070 or 30022
Avenue des Orangers 2A/2B, B.P. 9502, Kinshasa/Gombe, Zaire
Office National du Tourisme, Blvd. Mobutu, B.P. 242, Goma, Zaire
Also contact Sabena Airlines for information.
Zambia:
National Tourist Board   (260 1) 217761
Century House, Cairo Road, P.O. Box 30017, Lusaka, Zambia
Tourist Centre   3534/5
Mosi-oa-tunya Road, P.O. Box 60342, Livingstone, Zambia
Zimbabwe:
Tourist Development Corporation   (260 1) 793666/7/8/9
P.O. Box 8052, Harare, Zimbabwe

Offices in Austraila:
South Africa: 231 6166
AMEV-UDC House, 115 Pitt St., Sydney, NSW 2001

Offices in Canada:
South Africa:
Suite 1001, 20 Eglington Ave. West, Toronto, Ontario, M4R 1K8

Offices in the United Kingdom:
Kenya: (01) 3553144
25 Brooks Mews, Davis St., London W1Y 1LG
Lesotho: 242 3131
433 High Holborn House, 52 High Holborn, London WC1V 6RB
Mauritius: (01) 4377508/9
49 Conduit St., London W1R 9FB
South Africa: 439 9661
Regency House, I-4 Warwick St., London W1R 5WB
Swaziland:
58 Pont St., London W1X 1HA
Tanzania: 499 7727
77 South Audley St., London W1Y 5TA
Zambia: (01) 5896343/4
2 Palace Gate, Kensington, London W8 5NF
Zimbabwe: 629 3955
Collette House, 52-55 Piccadilly, London W1V 9AA

Offices in the United States:
Kenya:
Office of Tourism   (212) 486-1300/3
424 Madison Ave., New York, NY 10017
Doheny Plaza, Suite 111,   (213) 274-6635
9100 Wilshire Blvd., Beverly Hills, CA 90212
Mauritius:
Government Tourist Information Service   (212) 239-8367
15 Penn Plaza, 401 Seventh Ave., New York, NY 10001
Namibia:
See **South Africa** below.
South Africa:
Office of Tourism (SATOUR)   (213) 275-4111
9465 Wilshire Blvd., Beverly Hills, CA 90212
307 N. Michigan Ave.,   (312) 726-0517
Chicago, IL 60601
747 Third Ave., 20th Floor,   (212) 838-8841
New York, NY 10018
Zambia:
National Tourist Board   (212) 308-2155/2162/2171
237 East 52nd St., New York, NY 10022
Zimbabwe:
Tourist Office   (800) 621-2381, (212) 307-6565
1270 Avenue of the Americas, Suite 1905, New York, NY 10020

TRAVELERS CHECKS

American Express, Thomas Cook's, MasterCard and Visa Traveler's Checks are widely accepted. Stay away from lesser-known companies; you may have difficulty cashing them.

VACCINATIONS

Check with the tourist offices or embassies of the countries you wish to visit for current requirements. If you plan to visit one or more countries in endemic zones, (i.e., in Africa, South America, Central America, or Asia), be sure to mention this when requesting vaccination requirements. Many countries do not require any vaccinations if you are only visiting their country directly from the U.S.A., Canada or Western Europe; but if you are also visiting countries in endemic zones, there may very well be additional requirements.

Then check with your doctor and preferably an immunologist, or call your local health department or the Center for Disease Control, Atlanta, GA 30333, tel: (404) 639-3311, for information. They may very well recommend some vaccinations in addition to those required by the country you will be visiting.

Make sure you are given an International Certificate of Vaccination showing the vaccinations you have received.

Malarial prophylaxis (pills) are highly recommended for all the countries included in this guide except for Lesotho. However, international travelers must at least pass through South Africa in route to Lesotho.

VISA REQUIREMENTS

Travelers from most countries must obtain visas to enter many of the countries included in this guide. Apply for visas with the closest diplomatic representative well in advance and check for all current requirements (see **DIPLOMATIC REPRE-SENTATIVES** above). You may also contact the Department of State, Washington, D.C. (tel: 202-647-5225).

VISA REQUIREMENTS CHART

Traveling to	AUS	CAN	NZ	UK	USA	Requirements / Restrictions
Botswana	No	No	No	No	No*	*Maximum visit of 90 days.
Burundi	Yes	Yes	Yes	Yes	Yes	Onward ticket; sponsorship for business visa.
Kenya	Yes	No	No	No*	Yes	*UK citizens of Asian origin need visa. Visitor's pass issued upon arrival.
Lesotho	No	No	No	No	No	
Mauritius	No	No	No	No	No	Maximum 3-month stay.
Namibia	See South Africa					
Rwanda	Yes	Yes	Yes	Yes	Yes	
South Africa	Yes	Yes	Yes	No	Yes	Letter from employer for business visa.
Swaziland	No	No	No	No	No	
Tanzania	No*	No*	No*	No*	Yes	*Visitor's pass required. For business visa, letter of invitation.
Uganda	No	No	No	No	Yes	Letter from company for business visa.
Zaire	Yes	Yes	Yes	Yes	Yes	Certified sponsorship letter from government for business visa.
Zambia	No	No	No	No	Yes	
Zimbabwe	No	No	No	No	No	Require a return ticket.

WARNING:

Visitors with South African visas stamped in their passports may be refused entry into some African countries. Call the embassies of the countries you wish to visit (do not give your name) for current information. The U.S. Passport Office often will issue you a second passport in these circumstances.

If you need a visa for South Africa, you may be able to avoid future problems by asking the South African Embassy/Consulate to issue you a loose-leaf visa.

WILDLIFE ASSOCIATIONS

African Wildlife Foundation, 1717 Massachusetts Ave. N.W., Washington, D.C.; (202) 265-8394.

David Shepherd Conservation Foundation, Winkworth Farm, Hascombe, Godamling, Surry GU8 4JW, England; tel: Hascombe 220.

Digit Fund/Morris Animal Foundation, 45 Inverness Dr. East, Englewood, CO 80112, U.S.A. Following Dian Fossey's murder at Christmas 1985, this organization has continued her work of protecting, studying and providing veterinary care for the gorillas.

East Africa Wildlife Society, P.O. Box 82002, San Diego, CA 92138; tel: (619) 225-1233. U.S.A. office.

Fauna and Flora Preservation Society, c/o Zoological Society of London, Regents Park, London NW1 4RY.

World Wildlife Fund, 1250 24th Street N.W., Washington, D.C. 20037; tel: (202) 293-4800.

SAFARI GLOSSARY

ablution block — a building containing showers, toilets and basins, similar to those found at campsites in national parks in the U.S.A.

banda — a basic shelter or hut, often constructed of reeds, bamboo, grass, etc.

bilharzia (schistosomiasis) — a disease caused by a parasite which is present in most rivers and lakes in Africa. For further details, see "Health" in the Safari Pages.

boma — a place of shelter, a fortified place, enclosure, community (East Africa).

bungalow — an African-style structure for accommodation, usually made of grass, reeds, or other local materials.

camp — camping sites; also refers to lodging in chalets, bungalows or tents in a remote location.

calving season — period when births of a particular species occur. Not all species have calving seasons. Most calving seasons occur shortly after the rainy season commences. Calving seasons can also differ for the same species from one park or reserve to another.

caravan — a trailer.

carrion — remains of dead animals.

carnivore — an animal that lives by consuming the flesh of other animals.

diurnal — animals active during the day.

endemic — refers to species that are found only in a particular region or locale.

grazer — an animal that eats grass.

habitat — an animal or plant's surroundings that has everything it needs in order to live.

herbivore — an animal that consumes plant matter for food.

hide — a camouflaged structure from which one can view wildlife without being seen.

indigenous — refers to species that are natural to a country or region but are found in other regions or countries as well.

kopje — (pronounced kopee) piles of boulders sitting above the surrounding countryside, usually caused by wind erosion. (East Africa).

koppie — same as kopje (Southern Africa).

kraal — same as "boma" (Southern Africa).

mammals — warm-blooded animals that produce milk for their young, which are usually born alive.

nocturnal — animals active by night.

pan — hard-surfaced flatlands that collect water in the rainy season.

predator — an animal that hunts and kills other animals for food.

prey — animals hunted by predators for food.

pride — a group or family of lions.

rondavel — an African-style structure for accommodation.

scavenger — an animal living from carrion or remains of animals killed by predators or that have died from other causes.

species — a group of plants or animals with specific characteristics in common, including the ability to reproduce among themselves.

spoor — a track (i.e., foot print) or trail made by animals.

tarmac — asphalt-paved roads.

territory — the home range or domain which an animal may defend against intruders of the same or other species.

tribe — a group of people united by traditional ties.

veld — open land (Southern Africa).

LATIN/SCIENTIFIC NAMES OF WILDLIFE

MAMMALS

Aardvark (Antbear)	*Orycteropus afer*
Antelope, Roan	*Hippotragus equinus*
Antelope, Sable	*Hippotragus niger*
Baboon	*Papio anubis*
Baboon, Chachma	*Papio ursinus*
Bongo	*Boocercus eurycerus*
Buffalo	*Syncerus caffer*
Bushbaby, Greater	*Galago crassicaudatus*
Bushbuck	*Tragelaphus scriptus*
Bushpig	*Potamochoerus porcus*
Caracal	*Caracal caracal*
Cheetah	*Acinonyx jubatus*
Chimpanzee	*Pan troglodytes*
Civet	*Civettictis civetta*
Colobus, Black and White or Guereza	*Colobus guereza*
Dikdik, Kirks	*Rhynchotragus kirki*
Dog, African Wild	*Lycaon pictus*
Duiker, Grey Bush	*Sylvicapra gimmia*
Eland, Patterson's	*Taurotragus oryx*
Elephant, African	*Loxodonta africana*
Fox, Bat-eared	*Otocyon megalotis*
Gazelle, Grant's	*Gazella granti*
Gazelle, Thompson's	*Gazella thomsoni*
Gemsbok or Oryx	*Oryx gazella*
Genet	*Genetta tigrina*
Giraffe, Masai	*Giraffa camelopardalis tippelskirchi*
Giraffe, Reticulated	*Giraffa camelopardalis reticulata*
Giraffe, Rothschild's	*Giraffa camelopardalis rothschildi*
Gorilla	*Gorilla gorilla*
Hare, African	*Lepus capensis*
Hare, Spring	*Pedetes capensis*
Hartebeest	*Alcelaphus buslaphus*
Hippopotamus	*Hippopotamus amphibius*
Hog, Giant Forest	*Hylochoerus meinertzhageni*
Hyena, Brown	*Hyaena brunnea*
Hyena, Spotted	*Crocuta crocuta*
Hyena, Striped	*Hyaena hyaena*
Hyrax, Bush	*Dendrohyrax brucei*
Hyrax, Rock	*Procavia johnstoni*
Hyrax, Tree	*Dendrohyrax arboreus*

Impala	*Aepyceros melampus*
Jackal:	
Black-backed	*Canis mesomelas*
Golden	*Canis aureus*
Side-striped	*Canis adustus*
Klipspringer	*Oreotragus oreotragus*
Kongoni	*Alcelaphus buselaphus*
Kudu, Greater	*Tragelaphus strepsiceros*
Lechwe	*Kobus lechwe*
Leopard	*Panthera pardus*
Lion	*Panthera leo*
Mongoose:	
Banded	*Mungos mungo*
Dwarf	*Helogale parvula*
Slender	*Herpestes sanguineus*
White-tailed	*Ichneumia albicauda*
Monkey, Patas	*Erythrocebus patas*
Monkey, Vervet	*Cercopithecus aethiops*
Nyala	*Tragelaphus angasi*
Oribi	*Ourebia ourebi*
Oryx, Fringe-eared	*Oryx beisa*
Pangolin,	
Temmnick's Ground	*Manis temmincki*
Porcupine, Crested	*Hystrix africaeaustralis*
Ratel	*Mellivora capensis*
Reedbuck, Mountain	*Redunca fulvorufula*
Rhinoceros, Black	*Diceros biconis*
Rhinoceros, White	*Ceratotherium simum*
Roan	*Hippotragus equinus*
Serval	*Leptailurus serval*
Sitatunga	*Tragelaphus spekei*
Steenbok	*Raphicerus campestris*
Topi	*Damaliscus korrigum*
Tsessebe	*Damaliscus lunatus*
Waterbuck, Common	*Kobus ellipsiprymnus*
Waterbuck, Defassa	*Kobus defassa*
Wildebeest	*Connochaetes taurinus*
Zebra, Burchell's	*Equus burchelli*
Zebra, Grant's	*Equus granti*
Zebra, Grevy's	*Equus grevyi*
Zorilla	*Ictonyx striatus*

FRENCH WORDS AND PHRASES

antelope	l'antilope
baboon	le babouin
bird	l'oiseau
buffalo	le buffle
cheetah	le guépard
crocodile	le crocodile
elephant	l'éléphant
gazelle	la gazelle
giraffe	la girafe
gorilla	le gorille
hippo	l'hippopotame
hyena	l'hyène
jackal	le chacal
leopard	le léopard
lion	le lion
monkey	le singe
ostrich	l'autruche
rhino	le rhinocéros
snake	la palette
wildebeest	le gnou
zebra	le zèbre
good morning	bonjour
good day	bonjour
good night	bonne nuit
How are you?	Comment allez-vous?
very well	très bien
goodbye	au revoir
mister	monsieur
madam	madame
yes/no	oui/non
please	s'il vous plait
thank you	merci
very much	beaucoup
today	aujourdi'hui
tomorrow	demain
yesterday	hier
toilet	toilette
left	gauche
right	droite
I want	Je désire . . .

How much?	Combien?
How many?	Combien?
Where is?	Où est . . .?
When?	Quand?
to eat	manager
one	un
two	deux
three	trois
four	quatre
five	cinq
six	six
seven	sept
eight	huit
nine	neuf
ten	dix
eleven	onze
twenty	vingt
thirty	trente
forty	quarante
fifty	cinquante
sixty	soixante
seventy	soixante-dix
eighty	quatre-vingt
ninety	quatre-vingt-dix
hundred	cent
thousand	mille
food	nourriture
water	eau
coffee	café
tea	thé
milk	lait
beer	bière
bread	pain
butter	beurre
sugar	sucre
salt	sel
pepper	poivre
hot, fire	chaud/feu
cold	froid
ice	glace

SWAHILI WORDS AND PHRASES

antelope	swara
baboon	nyani
bird	ndege
buffalo	nyati
cheetah	duma
crocodile	mamba
elephant	tembo
gazelle	swalla
giraffe	twiga
hippo	kiboko
hyena	fisi
jackal	mbweha
leopard	chui
lion	simba
monkey	tumbili
ostrich	mbuni
rhino	kifaru
snake	nyoka
wildebeest	nyumbu
zebra	punda milia
hello	jambo
How are you?	Habari?
fine, good	nzuri
goodbye	kwaheri
mister	bwana
madam	bibi
yes/no	ndio/hapana
please	tafadhali
thank you	asante
very much	sana
today/tomorrow	leo/kesho
yesterday	jana
toilet	choo
left	kushoto
right	kulia
I want	nakata
I would like	napenda
How much?	Pesa ngapi?
How many?	ngapi?
Where is?	. . . iko wapi?

When?	Lini?
to eat	kula
food	chakula
water	maji
coffee	kahawa
tea	chai
milk	maziwa
beer	pombe
bread	mkate
butter	siagi
sugar	sukari
salt	chumvi
hot, fire	moto
cold	baridi
ice	baraf
one	moja
two	mbili
three	tatu
four	nne
five	tano
six	sita
seven	saba
eight	nane
nine	tisa
ten	kumi
eleven	kumi na moja
twenty	ishirini
thirty	thelathini
fourty	arobaini
fifty	hamsini
sixty	sitini
seventy	sabini
eighty	themanini
ninety	tisini
hundred	mia
thousand	elfu

SUGGESTED READINGS

Wildlife:

A Field Guide to the Birds of East and Central Africa by J. G. Williams, 1967, (Collins, London).

A Field Guide to the Mammals of Africa by T. Haltemorth and H. Diller, 1977, (Collins, London).

Among the Elephants by Iain and Ona Douglas-Hamilton, 1975, (Viking). Elephant research at Lake Manyara National Park, Tanzania.

Antelopes: Global Survey and Regional Action Plans Part 1 — East and Northeast Africa, compiled by R. East, 1989, (International Union for Conservation of Nature and Natural Resources/ICUN, Cambridge, U.K.). Wildlife research.

Antelopes: Global Survey and Regional Action Plans Part 2 — Southern and Southcentral Africa, compiled by R. East, 1989, (ICUN, Cambridge, U.K.). Wildlife research.

Birds of Eastern and Northern Africa by C. W. Mackworth-Praed and C. H. B. Grant, 1981, (Longman, London).

Collins' Guide to the Wildflowers of East Africa by Michael Blundell, 1987, Collins, London).

Conservation and Wildlife Management in Africa, edited by R. H. V. Bell and E. McShane Caluzi, 1984, (World Wildlife Fund, Washington, D.C.). Research.

Elephant Memories by Cynthia Moss, 1988, (Fawcett Columbine, New York).

Golden Shadows, Flying Hooves by George Schaller, 1973, (Knopf).

Gorilla: Struggle for Survival in the Virungas by Michael Nichols, 1989, (Aperture Press). Color photo book.

ICUN Directory of Afrotropical Protected Areas, 1987, (ICUN, Cambridge, U.K.). Research.

In the Shadow of Man by Jane Goddall, 1983, (Houghton Mifflin Co., Boston, MA).

Newman's Birds of Southern Africa by Kenneth Newman, 1983.

Portraits in the Wild: Animal Behavior in East Africa by Cynthia Moss, (Hamish Hamilton, London).

Run Rhino Run by Esmond Martin and Chrissee Bradley, 1982, (Chatto & Windus, London).

Safari: The East African Diaries of a Wildlife Photographer by Gunter Ziesler and Angelika Hofer, 1984 (Facts on File, New York).

The Chimpanzees of Gombe, Patterns of Behavior, 1986, (Harvard University Press, Cambridge, MA). Chimpanzee research.

The Marsh Lions, The Story of an African Lion Pride by Brian Jackson and Johnathan Scott, 1982, (Elm Tree Books).

Africa:

Africa: A Continent Revealed by R. Gordon, 1981, (St. Martins Press, New York).

African Expedition Gazette, One Penn Plaza, Suite 100, New York, NY 10019. Quarterly newspaper devoted exclusively to safari adventure travel. One-year subscription: $20.00 in U.S.A.; $35.00 internationally.

Backpacker's Africa — East and Southern by Hilary Bradt, 1989, Bradt Publications (Chalfont St. Peter, Bucks, England). Great for backpackers and overlanders traveling on very tight budgets.

Cultural Atlas of Africa edited by J. Murray, 1981, (Facts on File, New York). Large photo book.

International Travel Health Guide by Stuart R. Rose, M.D., 1989, (Travel Medicine Inc., Northhampton, MA).

North of South by Shiva Naipaul, 1979, (Penguin).

The African Safari by P. Jay Fetner, 1987, (St. Martins Press, New York). Lots of photos and information on wildlife.

The Blue Nile by Alan Moorehead, 1962, (Harper & Row).

The Making of Mankind by Richard Leakey, 1981, (Michael Joseph).

The Tropical Traveller by John Hatt, 1985, (Pan Books, London). Tips on travel in hot countries.

The White Nile by Alan Moorehead, 1960, (Harper & Row).

Trees of Southern Africa by Keith Coates Palgrave, 1977, (Struik, Cape Town, South Africa).

East Africa:

East Africa International Mountain Guide by Andrew Wielochowski, 1986, (West Col Productions, Reading, Berks, U.K.) Rock and ice routes.

Guide to Mt. Kenya and Kilimanjaro edited by Iain Allen, 1981, (Mountain Club of Kenya, Nairobi, Kenya). Rock and ice routes.

Safari: The East African Diaries of a Photographer by Gunter Ziesler, 1984, (Facts on File).

Southern Africa:

Doing Business With Southern Africa by Les de Villiers, 1989, (Business Books International, New Canaan, CT).

Mountains of Southern Africa by D. Bristow and C. Ward, 1985, (Struik, Cape Town, South Africa). Large photo books.

Botswana:

Cry of the Kalahari by Mark and Delia Owens, (Houghton Mifflin Co., Boston).

Kalahari by Michael Main, 1987, (Southern Book Publishers, Johannesburg, South Africa).

Okavango: Jewel of the Kalahari by Karen Ross (Macmillan Publishing Co., New York).

Okavango, Sea of Land, Land of Water by P. Johnson and A. Bannister, 1977, (Struik Publishers, Cape Town, South Africa). Large photo book.

The Bushmen by P. Johnson, A. Bannister and A. Wallenburgh, 1979, (Struik, Cape Town, South Africa). Large photo book.

Kenya:

Born Free by Joy Adamson, 1960, (Harcourt, Brace and World, New York).

Eating Out Guide to Kenya by Kathy Eldon. Available in Kenya.

Journey to the Jade Sea by John Hillaby, 1964, (Simon & Schuster).

Out of Africa by Isak Dinesen, 1937, (Vintage Books).

Specialities of the House by Kathy Eldon. Features Kenya's tastiest recipes. Available in Kenya.

The Flame Trees of Thika by Elspeth Huxley, 1959, (Morrow).

The Lunatic Express by Charles Miller, 1971, (Macmillan).

West With the Night by Beryl Markham, 1983, (North Point Press, Berkeley, CA).

Namibia:

Namibia: Africa's Harsh Paradise by A. Bannister and P. Johnson, 1978, (Struik Publishers, Cape Town, South Africa). Large photo book.

Skeleton Coast by Amy Schoeman, 1984, (Macmillan South Africa). Pictorial and informative.

Rwanda:

Gorillas in the Mist by Dian Fossey, 1989, (Penguin Books).

Tanzania:

Kilimanjaro by John Reader, 1982, (Universe Books).

Kilimanjaro: The White Roof of Africa by Harald Lange, 1985, (The Mountaineers Books, Seattle, WA). Large photo book.

Serengeti Shall Not Die by Bernard and Michael Grzimek, 1960, (Hamish Hamilton, London).

Uganda:

Mountains of the Moon by Patric Synge, 1986, (Hippocrene Books). Travel in Uganda in 1934.

Zaire:

Guide to the Ruwenzori by H.A. Osmaston and D. Pasteur, 1972, (West Col Productions, Reading, Berks, U.K.). Rock and ice routes.

The Forest People by Colin Turnbull, 1962, (Doubleday). On pygmies of the Ituri Forest.

The River Congo by Peter Fobath, 1977, (Harper & Row). History.

Zambia and Zimbabwe:

Zambezi by L. Watermeyer, J. Dabbs and Y. Christian, 1988, (Albida Samara Pvt. Ltd., Harare, Zimbabwe). Large photo book.

INDEX

INDEX — ANIMALS

INDEX — BIRDS

ABOUT MARK NOLTING
AUTHOR & AFRICA EXPERT

Mark Nolting wanted adventure. He found it as Olympic sportscaster, international businessman, oil engineer, Hollywood actor, author and Africa travel expert.

Nolting operates The Africa Adventure Company, Pompano Beach, Florida. He is the author of two award-winning books, *Africa's Top Wildlife Countries* and *Travel Jouranl Africa.*

Known as the "Travel Expert of Africa Travel" in the industry, Nolting arranges tours and advises travelers who want to go on an African safari.

It all began in 1975.

Nolting had graduated from Florida State University with a degree in business administration and minors in chemistry, physics, math and biology. For a year and a half, he had worked for a South Florida marketing firm. But the call of the wild beckoned.

"One morning," says Nolting, "I just woke up and realized I wanted to travel around the world. And I decided, 'If I don't go, I'll always regret it, and if I don't go now, I never will."

Two weeks later, he departed for Luxembourg with only $840. Never mind. With Nolting's background, daring, and just plain good luck, he soon landed a series of jobs others would kill for.

Take the 1976 Winter Olympics in Innsbruck, Austria, for instance. Nolting wound up working for ABC.

"I just hitchhiked into town because I knew the Olympics were coming on and that I could probably find a job," says Nolting. "They snapped me up in a second."

Next he found a job with the third-largest mail order catalog house in Germany. "At the time, the Germans really respected American business degrees," Nolting points out, "so I literally came off the street and said, 'Hi, I'm here,' and the next thing I know I'm in middle management of a billion-dollar corporation."

But Nolting wasn't trying to become a European business-man. He was out to see the world.

Although his itinerary called for him to head for India, Nepal and the Far East, he took a six-month detour through Africa — and hitchhiked across the Sahara Desert.

"What you have to do is get a ride that is going at least to the next oasis," Nolting says with a grin, "then you look for another ride just like the last one."

Mostly, Nolting caught empty produce trucks being ferried across the desert. Once he rode with some accidental tourists.

"I had a ride with a middle-aged couple from Australia who thought there was a paved road all the way across the Sahara Desert and they were getting ready to cross it," says Nolting. "So, I got out my Michelin maps and said, 'I'm sorry. But the road stops here.' They knew absolutely nothing about what they were doing and I wondered how they had managed to make it this far!"

He toured Central and East Africa, staying with natives in mud huts with thatched roofs, learning the culture. Then, he found his way to the Mideast and was fast-tracked through a program for oil drilling engineers — though he had no experience.

Eventually, Nolting left the oil business behind and toured Thailand, Malaysia, Singapore and exited via Hong Kong, Taiwan, Korea, and Japan on his way to Los Angeles. Upon arrival in Los Angeles, he had worked his way through more than 50 countries. And, by the way, he still had his original $840 plus $20,000 more he had banked during this adventure of a lifetime.

In Los Angeles, it occurred to Nolting that he'd never tried acting. So, he decided to give it a shot and wound up working for four years. "Actually, I did fairly well," says Nolting. "I did a lot of soaps — *The Young and the Restless*, *General Hospital*, that sort of thing. I did a film called, *Elvis*. And I worked on programs like *Today's FBI*."

Yet, the yearning to travel was still with him. Especially Africa. He couldn't shake the memory of the wildlife and the spectacular terrain he had seen there. And so, once again, he was off, heading for Africa, a purpose in mind.

During the next two years, he gathered material for his books and established contacts with safari and tour guides. Since then, he has returned to Africa many times to repeat the process. Hard-to-find information on Africa is always at his fingertips — and it is always accurate and precise.

Today, Nolting has traveled to more than 60 countries. He talks to people about the kinds of trips they want, then arranges them.

"The main allure of Africa is that you can find adventure there still," says Nolting. "When you go on safari, you never know what you're going to see or what's going to happen. Every safari is exciting. It doesn't matter if you go on photo safari, a hot-air balloon ride across the Masai Mara National Game Reserve in Kenya, fish for marlin off Tanzania, climb Mount Kilimanjaro or go white-water rafting. With the right assistance and guidance from an expert in Africa travel, there's no finer adventure."

Prices range from under $4,000 per person (land and air from New York) for a 14-day lodge safari to over $500 per person per day for a deluxe mobile tented camp safari. But whatever your cup of tea may be, Mark is *the* expert on adventure in Africa!

The Publishers

THE AFRICA ADVENTURE COMPANY

Dear Adventurer:

We at The Africa Adventure Company are dedicated to planning and booking African safaris for individuals, special groups, businesses and incentive trips.

Heading up The Africa Adventure Company is Mark Nolting, the definitive authority on travel to Africa. Mark has explored the African continent for more than three years, researching the many diverse and exciting features Africa has to offer. His research culminated in two highly acclaimed guides to game viewing and photographic safaris to Africa . . .

AFRICA'S TOP WILDLIFE COUNTRIES
and
TRAVEL JOURNAL AFRICA

In fact, Mark is a consummate authority on travel worldwide. Over the past 20 years, he has journeyed through more than sixty countries around the globe. During his first extensive trip to Africa, Mark traveled alone for six months by landrover, river boat, banana truck, canoe and foot, across the Sahara Desert and through Central and Eastern Africa. This placed Mark in close contact with the tribes of the African continent, where he experienced first-hand the enormously adventurous and colorful environment. In the doing, he grew to love the panorama of beauty which Africa has to offer.

While you may want to be "adventure bound," planning a vacation to Africa is not an easy matter. "It's tremendously important," Mark says, "that anyone considering a visit to Africa should book their trip with someone who knows the destinations and complexities of Africa well." So . . . it's vitally important to have someone of Mark's calibre and experience to plan your trip to Africa for you.

Most travel agents have little or no experience booking clients on safaris to Africa. In fact, very few have ever set foot on the continent. This is understandable, for less than 1% of most travel agencies' business comes from booking clients on African safaris. Travel agents cannot be expected to know much about a part of the world which brings in so little revenue.

Most travel agents (retailers) must rely on the "expertise" of African tour operators (wholesalers) to advise them on the best tours for their clients. The problem here is that the majority of the staff working for most tour operators specializing in Africa have little or no first-hand experience in Africa either. Many lack extensive on-site experience that is so important in booking Africa. There are, of course, exceptions. But few, if any, can match the experience Mark Nolting has in this field.

Many tour companies send you a brochure and ask you to pick a tour you like. At The Africa Adventure Company, we do things differently.

"The key," says Mark, "is to understand the personal experience an individual wants to have in Africa and to match that experience with the optiumum itinerary specifically designed to the client's needs, wants and desires." This can best be accomplished *only* if the person advising the client has *extensive on-site experience* in *all* the top safari countries. No amount of office training can substitute for actually having been there.

"Once I have a good feeling for what my client wants," continues Mark, "I then recommend the African countries which can best provide that experience, along with the best parks and reserves, specific hotels, lodges, camps, and safari activities that I feel would be of greatest interest to them. Only then do I pick a few tour options or create a special itinerary for my clients to consider. Doing anything less would be compromising the best interests of my clients."

Dispense with the uncertainties of traveling to Africa. Save yourself and your energies for the adventure of your Africa trip . . . Let Mark Nolting and The Africa Adventure Company roll up their sleeves and go to work for you, just as they have done for other happy, satisfied clients.

Remember, The Africa Adventure Company's services are provided to you at no cost!

To begin planning your safari to Africa today, pick up the telephone and call 305/781-3933 or toll free 1-800-882-9453 (1-800-822-WILD). It's just that easy to be "adventure bound."

WHAT OTHERS SAY ABOUT
THE AFRICA ADVENTURE COMPANY

"We were amazed at the thoroughness and detail of the arrangements on our safari to Botswana and Zimbabwe. Everything went perfectly. We were met on time at airports, hotels, camps and lodges — and expected on proper dates and times at all places. This was no easy task with five airlines, three charters, involving eleven flights in two weeks.

"The game viewing was excellent and varied from camp to camp. We got eighteen rolls of excellent pictures and memories for a lifetime — thanks to Mark Nolting."

John E. Sowers
Atlanta

"Thank you so much for the *great* itinerary that you put together for us, allowing us to visit Kenya, Tanzania, Botswana, Zimbabwe and South Africa in thirty days. We were able to stay in eight different safari camps, each unique and interesting. The flora and fauna were truly amazing . . . Your good planning and safari advice were keys to our success.

"The bush visits, which lasted about five days at a time, were interspersed with a day or so in the most famous hotels in the big cities. This allowed us a change of pace. We used the time to shop, relax in comfort, have our clothes cleaned, repack to smaller luggage for another trip to the bush, as well as temporarily storing at no charge the belongings we did not need.

"People we met throughout our travels were amazed and highly complimentary of our itinerary and travel arrangements made by our travel experts. Again, thank you for the superb job that you did to make our 'trip-of-a-lifetime' such a great success."

George W. Page
Bryans Road, MD

"Mark Nolting was able to do for me in three hours what four other travel agents could not do in three weeks!"

Cheryl Lynea Lewis
Chicago, IL

"I just want to thank you for the most wonderful experience of our lives. The wonderful itinerary you organized for us was precisely what we were looking for. Anyone who wants to get the real sensation of being out in the wilds with yourself, the animals and nature should plan a walking safari at any cost . . . It was by far the highlight of our trip.

"It's hard to imagine not seeing anyone else for days on end and not hearing an airplane, car or any mechanical noises the whole time. But we did!

"Your suggestion to also mix in the driving safaris was an equally good idea, because as your book mentions, it provided us the opportunity to see more animals and get a lot closer to them.

"In summary, all I can say is it was *the most*!!!"

Bill and Betty Campbell
Roswell, GA

"We had a great time on our safari! Our favorites in Tanzania were the Tarangire, Lake Manyara, and the Ngorongoro Crater. Kenya was magnificent. Meanwhile, the *rustic* camping was quite nice. In fact, I think we had some of our best food there.

"We finally have our slides put together. The pictures are great and we have done some slide shows.

"We loved the bartering and came away with some nice things. It wouldn't take much to talk us into going again. Thanks again for your help and your interest."

Margie Holland &
Becky Billings
Bradford, PA

"After completing a three-month series of safaris in East Africa, we found Mark Nolting's advice accurate and well balanced. It prepared us for some of the rough spots in our overland trucking expeditions. My wife and I have no hesitation in recommending him to anyone planning to travel to Africa."

Jay and Patricia Freeman
New York, NY

AVAILABLE FROM
THE AFRICA ADVENTURE COMPANY

TRAVEL JOURNAL
AFRICA
by Mark Nolting

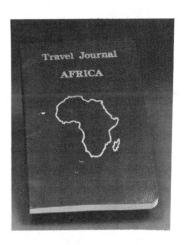

Travel Journal AFRICA is the perfect companion for an African safari. Before, during and after an African vacation, you will proudly show this book to your family, friends and travel companions. This handsome 160-page travel journal is printed in rich brown ink. Its durable yet flexible gold-stamped rich leatherette cover will stand up against the roughest of conditions. The 5 1/2" by 8 1/2" size fits easily, handily into a safari jacket pocket or tote bag.

Over 75 illustrations of wildlife and their spoor (footprints) allow for easy identification while on safari. Adjacent to each illustration is the animal's name in English, Latin, French and Swahili, weight range, shoulder height range, and general description to help the African traveler become an instant authority!

VALUABLE JOURNAL FEATURES INCLUDE:
★ Wildlife Checklist for recording sightings in reserves
★ Safari Glossary
★ French and Swahili words and phrases
★ Map of Africa
★ African Facts at a glance
★ Time Zones
★ Packing Checklist and Luggage Inventory
★ Metric System of weights and measures

CONVENIENTLY ORGANIZED PAGES OF
RECORDING IMPORTANT INFORMATION
★ Journal Author Information
★ Travel and Medical Insurance
★ Personal Medical Information
★ Travel Companions names and addresses

★ Itinerary listing up to 28 days
★ Photographic Record (up to 28 rolls of film)
★ Shopping List
★ Travelers Check Record
★ Expenditures
★ Important Addresses
★ Newfound Friends
★ Journal Contents (of your trip)
★ Journal Entry Pages (over 70)
The perfect book to take on safari!
160 pages/75+ Illustrations
Table of Contents/Glossary
Gold Stamped Leatherette

LC No. 88-080812
ISBN: 0-939895-01-3
Price: $12.95

AFRICA'S TOP WILDLIFE COUNTRIES
by Mark Nolting

Africa's Top Wildlife Countries is the quintessential safari planner which no traveler considering a journey to Africa should be without! A concise, quick, ready reference providing the reader with a broader information base to work with when planning the travel experience of a lifetime. Surely this book is destined to become a classic of the how-to guides for African safari travel.

African Expedition Gazette
$14.95

AEROBICS WITH SOUL
AFRICAN RHYTHMS
Featuring Maria Bergh

This award-winning video won First Place in the Aerobic Combination Category by New York's "City Sports Magazine." This unique video tape features both low and high impact cultural workouts to the magic of African Rhythms. Includes basic moves illustrations. Original stereo soundtrack. Available in VHS or BETA.

$24.95

AFRICA ADVENTURE
COMPANY T-SHIRT

These eye-catching cream-colored T-shirts with black printing feature The Africa Adventure Company logo surrounded by zebra stripes. These high-quality T-shirts are 100% cotton and are available in medium, large or extra large.

$9.95

ORDER FORM

Please rush me . . .

_____ Copies of *TRAVEL JOURNAL AFRICA* @ $12.95 each.

_____ Copies of *AFRICA'S TOP WILDLIFE COUNTRIES*
@ $14.95 each.

_____ Copies of *AEROBICS WITH SOUL* @ $24.95 each.

_____ AFRICA ADVENTURE COMPANY T-SHIRTS @ $9.95 each.
(___ Medium   ___ Large   ___ Extra Large)

Make checks and money orders payable to Global Travel Publishers,
Inc. Mail to Global Travel Publishers, Inc., P.O. Box 2567, Dept. B,
Pompano Beach, FL 33072, USA, or call (305) 781-3933 or toll-free
1-800-882-9453 (1-800-882-WILD) and charge to Visa/MasterCard.

___ Check/M.O. Enclosed   ___ Visa   ___ MasterCard

Card No. _____ Exp. _____/_____

Telephone Day: (   )   Home: (   )

_____

Signature _____

Name _____

Company _____

Street Address _____

City _____ State_____ Zip _____

TRAVEL JOURNAL AFRICA @ $12.95 $ _____

AFRICA'S TOP WILDLIFE COUNTRIES @ $14.95 $ _____

AEROBICS WITH SOUL @ $24.95 $ _____

AFRICA ADVENTURE COMPANY T-SHIRT @ $9.95 $ _____

Purchase Total $ _____

Sales Tax* (See next page) $ _____

Shipping & Handling** (See next page) $ _____

                                        TOTAL $ _____

*Florida residents add 6% sales tax.
**For items shipped within the USA or Canada, add $3.00 for one item, $1.00 for each additional item for shipping and handling. Overseas orders add $3.00 for each item surface; for airmail add $8.00 for the first item, $5.00 for each additional item.

_____ We would like your Africa travel expert, Mark Nolting, to personally plan and book our vacation, expedition, business, group or incentive trip. We understand there's no charge for this service. We have enclosed a description of what we have in mind or will call (305) 781-3933 or toll-free 1-800-882-9453 (1-800-882-WILD) soon to discuss it.

_____ We would like Mark Nolting to speak to our club, organizaiton, business, etc. We have enclosed a brief description of our request.

Name: _____

Company: _____

Address: _____

_____

Telephone No.: _____